THE CHEEKY GUIDE TO BRIGHTON

The Cheeky Guide to Brighton

Written and researched by David Bramwell
Additional writing by Jeremy Plotnikoff, Richard Gilpinn and Marcus O'Dair

Comments or suggestions to: david@cheekyguides.com
Business enquiries: jeremy@cheekyguides.com

ISBN 0 95361106X
Published in 2004 by Cheekyguides Ltd
PO Box 243, Brighton, BN1 3XT
www.cheekyguides.com

Acknowledgements

Thanks to Alex, Justin and Jonathan from Hexagon Archive, Simon Hodson, Freddie at Scene 22, Anna Moulson, Peter Pavement, Annie and all the staff at Waterstones for their endless support and enthusiasm, councillor Simon Battle, Barrie MacFarlane, Richard Gilpinn, Marcus O'Dair, Ian Helliwell, Andrew Sloane, Jeremy Hardy, and Positive television. Jeremy wishes to thank Debs for paying the rent, cooking the food, buying his clothes, and lastly for putting up with his endless stress infused abuses during the course of this book.

Special thanks to the following contributors:

Dave Mounfield ('Things to do in Hove when you're not Dead')
Brian Mitchell ('Top Five Greasy Spoon Cafes' and 'Dean')
Michael Keane and Andrew Bird (for numerous restaurant reviews)
Jo Shardlow and Melinda Saunders ('Where to Swim')
(article originally appeared in The Insight magazine.)

Artwork

Thanks to Lisa Holdcroft for the cover, maps, games and the innumerable cartoons that appear in this book. She is Brighton's answer to Rolf Harris and, should you wish to employ her talents or send her a saucy email, contact:
lisa.holdcroft@ntlworld.com

Photography

Club photos on pages 161, 164 and 167 supplied by kind permission of Brighton Source Magazine.
Club photos on page 159, 168 supplied by kind permission of Margo's Parties
p27 naked Kemptown boys reproduced by kind permission of Alexis Maryon, photo page 221 used by kind permission of Hexagon Archive, photo p25 by kind permission of Barry MacFarlane

The making of this book

Back in the good old days, Cheeky Guides were cobbled together in an afternoon using whatever resources were at hand, which was often little more than an old photocopier, some flour, water and a sprig of basil. Nowadays, making a Cheeky Guide requires a crack team of experts labouring day and night to bring you the jocular reviews, aesthetically pleasing photographs and exotic spellings that our devoted fans have come to know and love.

We have toiled day and night to be accurate with prices, times of opening etc, but we're only human (except Jeremy, who's Canadian) and things change quickly in Brighton; an hospital today could be a café-bar tomorrow. If you spot any changes or mistakes, please do drop us a line. Gushing adoration in the form of gifts and money will also be warmly received. Alternatively, if you would like to contribute, have an area of expertise about Brighton that you think would benefit this book, or simply wish to hang out with stylish people who have made something of their lives, then also feel free to get in touch.

How do we attain such honesty in our reviews?

Well I'm glad you asked. While it appears to be standard practice (in this town anyway) for local outlets to be relentlessly bullied into paying for a review (i.e. advertorial), we at Cheeky hold lofty ideals about integrity, and wish it to be known that **nobody** paid to be reviewed in this book. And, with the exception of a cookie, half a Guinness and the odd meal, we still haven't had any freebies. May I also add that we **never** discuss the fact that all the Cheeky team sacrifice their valuable free time helping out in a local orphanage.

And finally, a quick word about adjective abuse

We would like to reassure our more erudite readers that the word 'funky' does not appear in this book and gratuitous uses of the words 'cool', 'sexy', 'groovy' and 'Peacehaven' have been kept to a minimum. Thank you.

Key to Café and Pub locations

OL – Old Lanes	K – Kemptown	SD – Seven Dials
C – City centre	H – Hove	SC – Scunthorpe
NL – North Laine	S – Seafront	Places marked with an
Ha – Hanover	PC – Preston Circus	'L' are licenced

Jeremy and David are currently available for village fetes, gala lunches and children's tea parties, though not to host them, just to join in.

CONTENTS

In the beginning there was only Herring

1500s Brighton starts life as a prosperous fishing village, paying the government 400 herring a year in taxes.

1783 The town becomes a fashionable health resort when a certain Doctor Russell declares that drinking the sea water here would get rid of your boils and put hair on your chest. Not advisable today unless you want to get rid of your hair and have boils on your chest instead.

1790s Brighton's first massage parlour is opened by 'Brighton Shampooing Surgeon' Sake Deen Mohammed. It is, in actual fact, a genuine massage parlour, unlike the ones advertised in the back of the Evening Argus.

1823 The Prince Regent has the Royal Pavilion built as somewhere he can bring back a few mates after the pubs have closed.

1930s Torsos start turning up in boxes around the town beginning the reign of the infamous 'trunk murderer'. The King's elephant was suspected but nothing was ever proved.

1939 Movie star Johnny Weismuller opens the brand-new lido at Saltdean with the immortal line – *"Me Tarzan, you Saltdean Lido."*

1940 The West Pier is chopped in half by the War Office to prevent a 'German invasion via the ice cream kiosk'.

1960s Brighton is host to the 1964 'It's a Knockout', featuring the Mods and Rockers battling it out on the seafront. The town remains a popular choice for 'deckchair rage' over the next few years.

1972 Sir Laurence Olivier campaigns fiercely for kippers to be returned to the menu on the Brighton Belle railway line. He succeeds (for a while).

1973 Singer David Lee Roth re-locates to Brighton after quitting his band 'The Red Ball Jets', and opens an unsuccessful sandwich shop called 'Roth and Rolls'. A year later he returns to LA and forms the legendary Van Halen.

1974 The Eurovision Song Contest is held at the Dome Theatre. Swedish supergroup Abba scoop this prestigious award with 'Waterloo', while neighbouring Norway again scored 'Nul points' with 'Yes, we have no roll-mop herring.'

1979 Quadrophenia is released and Sting has his equity card revoked. Scuffles start up again on the beaches for a while as all the Mods completely miss the point of the movie.

1984 Lady Thatcher visits the bathroom and survives the IRA bombing of The Grand Hotel. Others are not so lucky.

1989 Hundreds of packets of cocaine are found washed up on the beach at Peacehaven. Police cordon off the area when Julie Burchill arrives for a closer look.

1992 Local cult 'the Temple of Psychic Youth' join hands around the Pavilion and attempt to levitate it, but are stopped at the last minute by the police. Apparently their founder, Genesis P.Orridge, had dropped 20p and just wanted to check that it hadn't rolled under there.

1995 The West Pier is declared an independent state by a bunch of squatters, but after two weeks they run out of Rizlas and abandon their plans. Inspired by this, only a few months later, Chris Eubank announces in the press that he wants to buy the West Pier, and set up his home there, with a helicopter pad at the end.

1999 The city's first independent guidebook, 'the Cheeky Guide to Brighton' becomes the town's best-selling book, spawning a host of copycat rivals, including the Saucy, Scratchy, Funky, Groovy, Kooky, Licky and Cheery Guides to Brighton.

2001 Brighton achieves city status after 1,000 cyclists ride all the way to Downing Street to present Mr Blair with several compromising photographs, taken during the Labour Conference here in 1992. The photos are said to feature The Prime Minister, a horse, an egg whisk and three blond Swedish students at a well-known Waterloo Street bordello.

July '01 The citizens of Brighton awake one morning to discover an army of uniformed thugs patrolling the streets and victimising nurses, doctors, builders, OAPs, teachers and local residents alike. The council claim the group to be Traffic Wardens, put here to 'improve' parking conditions in the city, though many are unconvinced and there is much anger at the controversial decision to supply them with firearms.

July '02 A quarter of a million people turn up for a mass piss-up on the beach. The Fatboyslim gig isn't bad either.

Dec '02 The West Pier continues to fall into the sea. Many blame it on storms, but later the actual cause is discovered to have been the excess weight of over 2 tonnes of bird shit in the Concert Pavilion.

Jan '03 The Palace Pier catches fire. Nothing is damaged except the Ghost train, which needed repairing anyway. Convenient that.

Mar '03 The West Pier burns down and, overnight, 20,000 starlings are made homeless.

May '03 The West Pier burns down *again*.

Feb '05 The last remaining shop in Kemptown closes and is replaced with a much-needed restaurant-café-bar.

Sept '09 The Pavilion, Free Butt, Dome Theatre, Sussex Square and newly refurbished West Pier all burn down and everyone finally buggers off back to London.

Revellers at the Fatboyslim Beach Party

BRIGHTON MYTHS

Hippy Stuff

New Age legend has it that a stone circle once stood in the Old Steine, but was smashed up by the Victorians and used to form the base of the big fountain there. This feature is actually claimed by some as being the source of all Brighton's energy and weirdness. It is interesting to note that Old Steine means 'old stone'. Give Julian Cope a ring; he'll put you straight.

Grave Tales

Brighton seems particularly rich in tales of underground tunnels and burial chambers. One particular story tells of a house in Orange Row, underneath which is said to be the original entrance to the old Brighton catacombs. Although blocked off with railway girders now, the room is still said to be littered with the dead bodies from an ancient flu epidemic.

Also, keep your eyes peeled for the pyramid-shaped grave of a guy called Mad Jack, who insisted on being buried sat upright at an iron table, wearing top hat and tails, a bottle of claret at arms length, and with his dinner in front of him*.

And where else would the world's most infamous occultist, Aleister Crowley, be cremated, other than our very own Woodvale Cemetery?

Phoebe Hessel

Phoebe Hessel, a local trader of fish, pincushions, gingerbread and apples, was a local celebrity in Brighton during the late eighteenth and early 19th century, and actually lived through six different monarchies to the glorious old age of 107. She was a celebrity, however, not for her longevity and comestibles but for her heroism and love. The story goes that when her lover, Samuel Golding, prepared to leave Brighton and join the army, Phoebe was unwilling to leave his side and so accompanied him disguised as a man. The two continued to serve in the army for 17 years and even fought and were wounded at the Battle of Fontenoy!

OK, so the fact that Phoebe lived until a ripe old age certainly gave her plenty of time to embellish her tale, and I am inclined to wonder how she hid her boobs for all those years, but the story does have a happy ending, as the two did finally return and get married.

Her grave can still be found in the churchyard of St Nicholas half way up Dyke Road where it is surrounded by a small metal fence.

*Since last year I discovered this to be true. The pyramid is in Brightling (well it's nearly Brighton) and his real name was John Fuller.

Murder Mystery

Take one of the tours during the festival and you will learn about some of the gruesome murders that happened in the 20s and 30s here. There are many accounts of body parts being left around town in trunks, and a severed head is said to have once been left in a bag by the Horse and Groom bar in Hanover (which, if you've visited the place, isn't all that surprising).

One year, Jason, a friend of mine, decided to do the murder tour, and left his house to walk down to Bartholomew Square where it was starting. The guide introduced the tour by saying-

"We'll commence by visiting the location of probably the most gruesome murder Brighton has ever known," and proceeded to walk the group back to Margaret Street, where Jason lived.

'Hey this is the street where I live!' he thought, with growing alarm.

"And it was in this house that the body was dismembered and stored in a cupboard for two weeks..." said the guide pointing at Jason's bedroom window.

Jason now lives in America.

The Ubiquitous Eubank Tale

This short and simple tale comes in many forms but the basis of it goes that Chris (*wherever* he is) is making a big public display of the fact that he's got a mobile telephone and is making a real show of taking important calls from important people, when, to his utter embarrassment, the phone starts ringing in his hand.

Now several people I've met lay claim to this one and seem to get a bit annoyed when I suggest it's an urban myth, even though I've heard countless versions, ranging from Chris shopping in the Old Lanes and Chris jogging along the seafront, to Chris sitting in a bath of Baked Beans in the Condom Store. For visitors to Brighton, this story that can be adapted and applied to any C-list celebrity from your hometown. Take it away, play with it and make it your own.

The Hand of Glory

A charm believed to cure lumps on the throat once carried the name of the 'Hand of Glory'. The recipe for this involved a number of gruesome things including the severed hand of a recently hung man, which was rubbed on the offending article or made into a candle(!). The last hanging to take place in Brighton was at the Steine in 1834, where a woman with a gammy neck is said to have run from the crowd, taken the dangling hand of the dead man and joyously rubbed it all over her affliction.

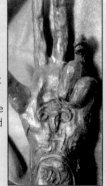

For anyone with an unsightly blemish on their neck, the recipe for the Hand of Glory is still available from local occult archivists 'Hexagon'.

How to get Here

BY RAIL

Trains from London leave Victoria and Kings Cross Thames Link about twice an hour. The Victoria link is usually quicker – about 50 minutes for the fast train. Be careful when returning to London late at night however, the last train usually leaves before 12am, even at weekends. There are also direct train services along the coast if you are not coming via London. Rumours abound about a 30-minute service to London starting sometime in the very near future, but I'm beginning to believe this is an urban myth.

National Rail Enquiries
08457 484950

www.thetrainline.co.uk
www.ticketmaster.co.uk

At the Station
You'll find cash machines, bureau de change, hotel reservation kiosk and buses and taxis waiting outside. If all that seems too formal just head straight out, keep walking, and you'll be at the beach in less than 10 minutes.

SUNDAY TRAINS

Irritatingly, there are often repairs to the tracks between Brighton and London on a Sunday, which means your journey may involve three coach journeys via Littlehampton, Eastbourne and Barnsley, so check before you travel. I kid you not, I have spent some miserable Sunday evenings dreaming of being at home by the fire sipping fine wines, when instead I'm standing in the rain in the middle of sodding nowhere, waiting for a BR bus driven by some fuckwit who doesn't know where he's taking you. And when he does eventually turn up an hour later and sets off, the bloody bus breaks down. And to top it all off, you don't have a seat. And yes this has happened more times than I care to mention. Now that's off my chest I feel much better. Ignore this at your peril.

13

BY PLANE

From Gatwick A train will get you to Brighton in 30 minutes. If there are four of you a taxi will probably cost less because the trains are so damned expensive here. The cheapest option is to get a coach.

From Heathrow What a drag, you must really enjoy doing things the hard way. Get a tube to Victoria then a train from there. It'll take two hours at the most.

BY COACH

National Express
(01273) 808080

Pool valley coach Station
(01273) 383744

Gobycoach.com
www.gobycoach.com

The trip to London takes about one and a half hours. Prices vary according to shoe size.

BY ROAD

Once you've packed your sandwiches, toothbrush, bucket and spade, make your way to the London orbital then take the M23/A23 all the way to Brighton. It shouldn't take more than forty-five minutes once you've left the M25. It's as simple as that. If you travel between 5pm and 7pm through the London rush hour, it's best to take a Travel Scrabble. If you're lucky enough not to be coming via London you'll probably be taking the coastal route along the A27.

BY SEA

Catch the two-hour hoverspeed from Dieppe to Newhaven and it's only a 25-minute drive from there.

BY HELICOPTER

You'll get as far as Shoreham airport and then it's a 2-hour walk to Brighton along the seafront. What do you mean you haven't got a helicopter?

Getting Around

TAXIS

202020 • 204060 • 747474 • 205205

There are plenty to choose from and all the services are pretty much the same. Typically though, taxi fares in Brighton are amongst the highest in the country and more expensive per mile than flying Concorde. Taxi-drivers in Brighton however, are required by law to carry inflatable rings under their seats, so check when you get in. If there isn't one you should be able to blag a free ride.

BUSES

Brighton & Hove Bus Company

(01273) 886200

For getting around the town centre there is a flat fare, which, at time of going to print, was £1.20. Buses are frequent and will take you practically anywhere (unless you're a cyclist, in which case they'll simply try and run you off the road and kill you).

Open-Topped Bus Tour

Palace Pier (01273) 540893

Runs April - Nov. Tours daily from 10am

www.city-sightseeing.com

Brighton for lazy-bones. Do the lot in one hour for £6.50.

Brighton Subway

BRIGHTON SUBWAY

Closed due to subsidence and waterlogging, Brighton's once-famous Metro-line used to stretch as far as Eastbourne, Worthing and London. Nowadays it is home to Brighton's expanding subterranean community and illegal bear-baiting societies.

BIKES

I'd love to say that cycling around Brighton is pleasant but it is actually quite hazardous, largely due to the laziness of the council and their half-arsed attempts to put proper cycle lanes around the city. You'll literally be taking your life in your hands cycling along Western Road and North Street as the constant cavalcade of buses squeeze you off the road onto the busy pavement. Elsewhere the council have placed lanes that enable cyclists to go the wrong way down one-way streets, which is great in theory but extremely dangerous in practise, as drivers do not seem to respect cyclists having the right of way when they need to turn right (and therefore into the oncoming cyclist). The cycle lane at the top of Church Street is one of the stupidest things the council have ever designed and I'm sure if I ever suffer an early death it'll be there, or on the Seven Dials roundabout.

On a more positive note, the seafront is great for cycling – it's long and flat and you can go all the way from Hove to the Marina and beyond, via the undercliff pass to Rottingdean. In summer, though, be prepared to spend most of your time dodging the dozy gits who walk in the seafront cycle lanes.

WALKING

Visitors from LA might be interested to learn that this mode of transport is still immensely popular in Brighton.

PARKING

Devilishly tricky **and** expensive. There are, however, several multi-storey car parks in the town, which are all signposted. Parking meters are also being phased in for the streets close to the city centre. One of the cheapest places to leave your car is the car park near the bottom of Trafalgar Street, just down from Brighton Station. If you want my advice though – park out of town and walk/ get a bus, it's never that far to anywhere in Brighton.

A SHORT RANT
ABOUT TRAFFIC WARDENS

The council's answer to the SS, Brighton traffic wardens – noted for their green Nazi style uniforms and hideously deformed faces – are the largest patrol working in the UK for a town this size, and are a constant source of irritation to many locals. While understanding the need for traffic calming schemes in Brighton, I know I'm not alone in finding that the system here not only dissuades visitors from parking willy-nilly all over the city centre, but also seems designed to victimise helpless residents as well.

A FEW HARD FACTS:

- Parking tickets are issued at a rate of one every two minutes in Brighton and generate more than £1 million profit for the council. (Ticket issuers are contracted to NCP, but both NCP and the council share the profits.)

- The days of voucher parking are numbered; the council have fitted solar powered pay and display meters throughout most of the town. It is interesting to note, however, that if a black piece of card is placed over the solar panel on the top of the meter, after three days, the meter ceases to function. Erm, allegedly.

- The council have repeatedly refused to grant parking permits for the teachers of Stanford School by the Seven Dials, despite the fact that it has no carpark, all the roads in the vicinity are permit only and many of its staff have to travel long distances to work every day.

- Brighton and Hove traffic wardens once issued a ticket to a hearse (the undertakers were moving a body), thus breaching the city's own parking laws.

- Drivers with severe medical conditions (such as colitis or Crohn's disease) face a fine if they park illegally while making a dash for a public toilet.

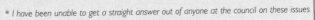

- Brighton has no 'Park and Ride' scheme.

- All traffic wardens are evil.

AREAS FOR DEBATE*:

- Can a driver be issued with a fine if double-parked?
- Does a traffic warden need to be wearing a cap to issue a fine?
- Is a driver exempt from a fine (for a couple of hours anyway) if they display a sign in the car saying – 'Broken down, AA called'?
- Is it better to use graffiti spray or a sledgehammer when attacking a parking sign?

* I have been unable to get a straight answer out of anyone at the council on these issues

17

Here, There & Everywhere

THE OLD LANES

A series of wonderfully confusing narrow passages and cobbled streets make up this part of Brighton, which is steeped in history and stories of smugglers, ghosts and randy nuns. The passages are known locally as Twittens, (an old smugglers' term for 'thin street with over-priced shops') and are enclosed by West Street, East Street and the seafront.

You should enjoy wandering around here and perusing the shops, but don't worry if you get lost, even long-term residents (such as myself) still do from time to time.

The Old Lanes is particularly renowned for its jewellers, antiques shops, its abundance of cafés, restaurants and clothes boutiques, and, though relatively conservative compared with the fashionable North Laine, at night the busy restaurants and pubs such as The Cricketers, Hop Poles and Victory give it a new lease of life.

At the centre of the maze lie the dolphin statues in the fountain at Brighton Square. It is an old Brighton custom to throw your shoes in here and make a wish, though a coin will suffice. If you head off past Rounder

Records, have a look at their back wall to see which album they have spray-painted on it. As a reference point, you'll be on your way to East Street.

If you haven't got long in Brighton, you should definitely make a stroll round here a priority. Choose from any number of enticing restaurants such as Food for Friends, Moshi Moshi, English's or Momma Cherries for lunch and make sure you poke your head in at Fabrica Gallery (opposite the post office on Ship St) to see what dazzling art installation they have in this beautiful building.

In summer this is a popular area for street entertainment. On East Street you'll find Jazz bands, performance artists and even Tarot readers. Once I even saw a girl busking with a rat here. She kept it on her shoulder whilst playing her guitar, and now and again she let it drink from her mouth. Eurrrgghh!

The best time to visit the Old Lanes is at dawn, when the noise of the seagulls and the light of early morning pierce through the empty alleyways. At times like this, eerie folklore tales about ghosts and ghoulish fishermen no longer seem like a load of old cobblers.

19

NORTH LAINE

Known as Brighton's bohemian quarter, North Laine has some of the best shops, pubs and cafés in town. Glamorous, young, posy, vibrant, and pretentious it may be, but Cleethorpes High Street it is not. In fact, this colourful area does its best to be Haight Ashbury, Carnaby Street and Greenwich Village, all rolled into just a handful of streets.

North Laine is, of course, posers' paradise, and from Sixties kitsch to Nu-Goth, every fashion gets a look in. Walk down Kensington Gardens in full 'KISS' make-up with cream crackers stuck to you, and still few heads will turn.

Many of the shops here are unique and shamelessly glitzy. Pussy, Borderline and Re-Vamp are just a few worth seeking out, where you will find everything from silver platforms and CDs by the Chocolate Watch Band to fetish kitchenware. This area has a

Three unique things about North Laine

1) Smoking is compulsory in most of the bars and cafés.
2) Everybody who works in a shop in the North Laine also plays in a band, DJs, acts, promotes gigs, paints, writes novels and has their own website.
3) If your parents turn up wearing Pringle jumpers, everyone will see it as an important fashion statement and rush out to buy their own.

fabulous collection of record shops and clothes shops too, not to mention kitsch and retro gear from the likes of Cissy-Mo and Rokit. And don't be afraid to stray off the beaten track at times; Acme Art with its surreal sculptures and eccentric owner is well worth seeking out, as are such shops as Blackout and Icon.

Priding itself too on its café culture, North Laine blossoms during the summer months when balconies heave with milkshakes and suntanned legs, and tables and chairs start to sprawl out onto the roads. It's a pleasure just to hang out on some of the café balconies here and watch the world and its dog go by. The Fringe Bar and Kensingtons are notably good haunts for this. On Saturdays, Gardner Street is pedestrianised, and becomes one heaving mass of cappuccinos and sunglasses.

The shops in the North Laine are a good starting point for checking out what's going on in the clubs and venues, as the streets visibly sag under the weight of posters and fliers in every window. In fact it can feel like you're in a ticker tape parade as they

are handed to you on street corners and even thrown from the tops of buildings. You'll even find them taped to the pavement at weekends. Stand around in the same spot for too long in Sydney Street and someone will bill poster you.

In the North Laine anything goes, the more flamboyant the better. Fashions and sub-cultures fight for space along these busy streets, so don't be surprised if you end up going home with an exotic tattoo and your genitals pierced, it will simply have been a Brighton experience.

For more information, go to *www.northlaine.org.uk*

Three things to look out for in North Laine

1) Big Ian standing outside Immediate Clothing on Sydney Street having a fag.
2) The UFO fairy lights at Christmas.
3) Simeon the cat lolling around in 'Brighton Books' on Kensington Gdns.

21

THE BEACH

'The beach washes away the ills of mankind.' Dr Richard Russell

Stretching from the nudist beach near the Marina across to Hove and beyond, this is one of the key inspirations behind all that is Brighton. In summer it's always swarming with life; you'll find families with kids, groups of foreign visitors, young couples indulging in a spot of heavy petting and the obligatory loony with a metal detector.

'Hey, I found another ring-pull.'

When the sun is out, you'll most likely want to join the crowds down here and brave the sea for a swim, hang around the cafés, or indulge in a spot of sunbathing. There's also a volleyball area if you like to do it Baywatch style, or the banana boat ride for the more adventurous.

In summer, between the two piers, the beach is always crowded with over-spill from The Fortune of War, Arc and other seafront bars, and there's usually a good buzz about the place. This is also a hot-spot for many

of Brighton's best-known clubs – the Zap, The Honey Club and The Beach are here – so in the evening expect the clubbing crowd to be out in force.

Sometimes though, when it's a warm night and you're in the mood, it's good to by-pass the busy bars and clubs. Just find a quiet spot, get some beers and food, and bring some friends to watch the sun going down.

If you're still around after all the clubs have cleared the beach does *eventually* get pretty empty, although there's always the odd clubber who's crashed out after too many pills, and a guy still looking for his contact lens. In fact, even in the cruellest winters you'll find little pockets of life here, like penguins on an iceberg.

And finally, it's time to come clean. Yes, it's true I'm afraid, there is no sand, only pebbles. Around 100 billion to be precise*, and not a decent one for skimming, but, as a small compensation, when you take your picnic down the beach and the wind whips up, you will not be crunching your way through a tuna and sand ciabatta…

*According to Dr Malcolm Cornwall at Brighton University. (He also reckons it'd take 2,500 years counting them all at the rate of one per second!)

THE WEST PIER

Let's face it; it wasn't a good year for the West Pier in 2003. In the space of four months, the sagging remnants of this mouldy old wedding cake were subject to storm damage and two fires, leaving little behind but its iron frame and a few barbequed pigeons. Despite this, there's *still* talk of restoration….

*For more information, go to **www.west-pier-trust.demon.co.uk***

BETWEEN THE PIERS

If you don't have a lot of time to spend in Brighton, make a priority of visiting the seafront between the Palace Pier and West Pier. Here you'll find café-bars, plenty of clubs, amusement arcades, the Fishing Museum, the Artists' Quarters, palmists, sculptures and an assortment of outdoor entertainment during summer. If you want a good walk, follow the seafront path all the way to the multi-coloured beach huts in Hove, and stop for some grub at the Meeting Place Café on your way back. Below are just some of the things to look out for in this area…

PALACE PIER

The epitome of cheesy seaside fun. This is Brighton's number one attraction and, in fact, the UK's top tourist attraction too. Experience 'life on the ocean waves' with the famous Dolphin Derby, ride the Go-Karts, see the Isle of Wight (on a clear day) from the top of the Helter Skelter, sing Elvis at Horatio's Karaoke Bar, eat some revolting food, lose your car-keys down the gaps in the floorboards, have your palm read by Australian backpacker 'Gypsy Kevin' or get soaking wet on the log flume. Brighton without the Palace Pier would be like Tommy Cooper without the fez.

VICTORIAN PENNY ARCADES

There are two to find between the piers, and for a £1 charge you get twelve old Victorian pennies to use on all the old games. There are 'What The Butler Saw' machines (look out for 'Two Lovely Ladies' and 'Easy Chair Frolics'), fortune-telling games, a 'Win a Fag' machine and more besides. Great for frittering away half an hour or so.

JACK AND LINDA'S

Located just to the left of the Fishing Museum, this is *the* place to stop for food on Brighton seafront. Ex-fisherman and fisherwoman, Jack and Linda, have been here for over five years now, dishing out their mouth-wateringly delicious take-way fish soup, smoked mackerel and potted crab, all at giveaway prices. The soup alone ranks amongst my top ten favourite things about Brighton! I cannot recommend this highly enough.

THE BIG GREEN BAGEL

This sculpture arrived about 8 years ago and was a gift from the Mayor of Naples (we donated his city a large bronze herring). Officially entitled 'Il Grande Bagel Verde' – but known locally as the 'Seasick Doughnut –it has survived four storms and several demolition attempts by local art puritans.

EAST OF THE PALACE PIER (MADEIRA DRIVE)

While this whole area of the seafront is in need of rejuvenation* it does come alive when there are car and motorbike rallies, or at events like the Dance Day when it fills with floats, and 1000's of hardcore clubbers get to see daylight for one day of the year.

Apart from two crazy golf courses and the Concorde 2, there isn't much in the way of entertainment, though the very lack of development does mean that in summer the stretches of beach here are mercifully quieter than between the two piers. And for kids, of course, there's the miniature Volks Railway, which runs along this stretch of the seafront all the way to the Marina – a reminder of how much smaller people were in the old days.

If you do take a wander down here, just beyond the Concorde 2 look out for the strange old house, set into the promenade. The story goes that before the promenade was built, all the houses along the front were sold and demolished, apart from one belonging to some stubborn old guy who refused to sell. The council couldn't move him, so in desperation they built the promenade over his house and it's still there today.

Beyond this point is the once controversial Nudist Beach, now mainly populated by the gay community and a character known as 'Windmill Man'. I'll leave you to figure out how he got his nickname.

*But please god, not **more** café-bars and concrete...

THE VOLKS RAILWAY

The Volks opened on 4th August 1883, making it the oldest electric railway in the world (you'll find it in the Guinness Book of Records, sandwiched between the world's biggest pair of shoes and a photo of a man with four metre long fingernails).

For its official opening day, the railway's creator, Magnus Volks, invited a number of civic dignitaries for the first ride but, owing to their combined weight (civic dignitaries were notoriously portly in those days), they managed to break one of the planked pedestrian crossings that ran across the track. The train's first ever journey came to an undignified halt and the dignitaries were unloaded, to the jeers of a group of cabbies, who were hostile to the railway – believing it would take away custom. They really needn't have worried.

A couple of happy poofs

KEMPTOWN

Cross over the Old Steine from the bottom of North Street and you'll find yourself in Kemptown, a haven of B&Bs, cafés, restaurants, some good shops, and home to much of Brighton's flourishing gay and lesbian community.

Bristling with life, day and night, this area's energy seems to come from a celebratory and ever-growing gay scene combined with the overspill of all that vitality emanating from the seafront.

Kemptown is also a place where many of Brighton's eccentrics seem to congregate and make up for lost time. Buy your strawberries next to a drag queen in Safeway, stumble across the guy who sports a sparkly top hat and decorates himself with posters of his guru, or witness (as I have) two guys rolling around on the floor half-naked at three in the morning singing 'the hills are alive with the sound of music'. Kemptown may not be a part of Brighton that has been dressed up for visitors, but it is precisely the rough edges that provide the appeal, and perhaps in truth this is the part of Brighton that **truly** deserves the label 'bohemian'.

To explore the area simply take a walk up St. James's Street. In recent years it seems to have filled up with restaurants and cafés, but is still home to health food shops, barbers, second-hand shops, a few good pubs, gay haunts, a beauty parlour for men (the Pink Pamper) and even a shop where you can buy T-shirts for your dog. Venture into the side streets that run down to the sea, however, and you'll soon be lost in endless strips of hotels and B&Bs.

Follow St James's St far enough and it eventually becomes St. George's Road. Here Kemptown begins to feel more like a village (and **is** actually known as Kemptown Village) and is quickly taking shape as a colourful new shopping area, with a great flea market painted in garish pink and unique shops like Cupcake, selling gifts and clothing for ankle-biters.

Continue far enough and – after stopping for a drink at such classic boozers as the Hand in Hand, Hanbury Ballroom, Barley Mow, and the Rock – you'll reach Sussex Square and Lewes Crescent. These stunning white flats are occupied by some of Brighton's most affluent bohemians, and have had their fair share of celebrities; Lewis Carroll, Gaz Coombs and Howard Marks being just a few. If you want to head back into Brighton now you can simply turn on your heels and go back the way you came. Alternatively you could take a stroll along the seafront, though you may want to turn a blind eye to hoards of grown men enjoying a bit of rough and tumble in the bushes at Duke's Mound.

WEST STREET

With its amusement arcades, clubs for the under-twelves, theme pubs and burger bars this is Brighton's answer to Las Vegas, but without the glamour and more violent. Hang around here all night and, chances are, you'll get into a fight with a 17 year old. Stick around too long and her boyfriend will have a go as well.

Kemptown Village
www.kemptown-village.co.uk

Nowhere in Brighton will you find a more pleasant, active community than in the stretch of shops, pubs and food outlets on St George's Road in Kemptown (which includes Wallis MacFarlane, Ghita Schuy, Charlie's Orbit, Pardon My French and cool pubs such as The Barley Mow and Hanbury Ballroom). Not only is there a convivial, supportive and easy-going spirit to these places but they even try and outdo each other every year with an over-the-top window display competition. Even the local charity shops join in the fun. In fact Marie Curie won one year with its Barbara Cartland theme, despite the kitchen utensil shop, 'Egg and Spoon', having an enticing display of nearly naked men in its window. Spend an afternoon here shopping and nattering with the friendly shopkeepers and those old days of trawling round the Churchill Shopping Centre will seem a distant nightmare.

PARKS AND GARDENS

Let's face it, Brighton is not renowned for its greenery. Down on the seafront the council seem to have done everything in their power to remove all traces of the stuff, while the town centre boasts little more than a bit of grass and a few flowers outside the Pavilion. But all is not lost. Head inland and Brighton has a modest selection of parks and open spaces to keep even the most ardent picnickers, tree-huggers and Ultimate Frisbee teams happy.

THE LEVEL
By St Peter's Church

Come and walk the dog whilst watching teenage boys imperil their gonads doing BMX tricks in the skateboarding park. There's a nice bit by the paddling pool area with its trellises, little kiosks and surreal bridges, but don't get too excited, this open area between London Road and Hanover officially belongs to the skateboarders, Frisbee throwers, jugglers and football teams. Don't miss the fair when it comes here for two weeks at the end of April and August.

DYKE ROAD CEMETERY
Dyke Road, opposite St. Nicholas' Church

From the Clock Tower go up Dyke Rd and you'll find this place on your left just after the traffic lights. Part cemetery, part park and relatively unknown, this is a perfect spot to flop about, read a book, bring a picnic or do some meditation. I love it here. It's never busy and it does the job if you want to feel like you've left the rat race behind. Look out for Gandhi's grave.

PRESTON PARK

Brighton's largest park is located a little way down Preston Road. For starters it's a great spot for cycling; you can use their professional track at the top of the park and then race back down over the bumpy road or simply cycle around the park's perimeter. There's also a café in the middle and loads of space for big sports games.

While it's a good place for a picnic, the ever-present noise of cars from the main road can sometimes spoil a tranquil afternoon.

Look out for the goatee beard brigade taking Ultimate Frisbee very seriously and try to find the Steve Ovett statue at the bottom of the park, facing the road. Remember the Alan Partridge sketch where he 'pops out' of his skimpy satin shorts? You're seconds away Steve…

QUEEN'S PARK

Between Kemptown and Hanover

Queen's Park may be a bit of a hike if approached from the town centre or seafront, but you'll soon forget those aching corns and bunions once you arrive at this beautifully sculpted park with its sloping hills, large green areas, lake and tennis courts.

Approach from the sea (up Egremont Place) and, once through the arch you'll find an excellent kids' play area, toilets and a café, all self-contained on the western side of the park. If you've come to escape kids/crowds etc, head around the lake (formerly a roller-skating rink in the Sixties) and up the hill to discover such curiosities as the tiny waterfall, the scented garden by the eastern entrance, and the 'Wildlife Area', full of butterflies, birds and wild fennel in the summer. Such features as this small overgrown wilderness demonstrate that Brighton council can be surprisingly inspired sometimes (though equally it could just be a ploy to save on pruning expenses). Other features to look out for in the park are its carved wooden benches and strange old monuments.

When you've had enough of the chaos and trendiness of the beach and city-centre, its good to know there's somewhere you can have a picnic, climb a tree, feed the ducks, play hide and seek in the bushes or simply curl up under an old oak for the afternoon with a good book and a treacle sandwich.

ST. ANN'S WELL GARDENS

This small park in Hove has a scent garden, a café run by a lovely old guy who plays Easy Listening music, a few picnic areas and tennis courts. It's also a popular spot for mums out with the young-uns, and has a resident old lady called Madge who'll engage you in conversations about boxing given half the chance. Tennis fans might like to know that if you want a free game, they don't charge here before 10am.

My favourite feature at St Ann's is the strange clock on a pole that overlooks the tennis courts and Bowling Green. It's straight out of the Sixties cult TV show the Prisoner and, in keeping with the spirit of the show, never, ever, ever tells the right time.

WOODVALE CREMATORIUM

Lewes Road/ Bear Road

Hidden away down the Lewes Road, Woodvale Cemetery is one of Brighton's best-kept secrets. The largest expense of greenery in the whole of the city centre, it is in turn mysterious, spooky and beautiful, particularly in spring when everything is in bloom.

Wander round its spacious and hilly terrain and you'll stumble across the columbarium, the memorial gardens, strange mausoleums (there's even one where you can peek through a crack in the door and see the dead bodies inside) and the little paths that disappear off into the undergrowth. If you want a quest you can look for the graves of Lance Schumacher (one of Custer's men) or the original Mr Hannington, though they might take a good couple of days to find.

Come on a cold overcast February (as I have) and it can feel a little sinister, particularly with the hospital high up on Elm Grove towering down like some dark satanic mill. In fact if Buffy the vampire Slayer lived in Brighton, she'd doubtless spend most of her evenings here, as in the gloom it can't help but inspire thoughts of the supernatural. Not surprising then that it's also the favoured haunt of local eccentric Adrian Shephard, who can occasionally be spotted wandering amongst the graves recording the disembodied voices of the dead.

When it's warm, however, the crematorium is the perfect place to clear the cobwebs, draw inspiration, picnic, meditate or simply enjoy a bit of nature and peace and quiet in a town that never stops.

THE PAVILION GARDENS AND CAFE

After a morning's shopping in the North Laine, these gardens behind the Pavilion make an ideal spot for a bit of lolling around in the sun. It can get quite busy here in summer, with groups of foreign students, picnickers, snogging couples, pigeons and the obligatory bloke strumming a guitar, but can be a pleasant alternative to the concreted seafront, as this is one of the rare spots in the town centre with a bit of decent greenery and is right in front of the Pavilion too. If you're in need of refreshments the café does drinks and is famous for its rock cakes. Look for the photos on the café history notice board on the side of the hut. They sure had big ears in those days.

Greetings from

HOVE

HOVE, AN APOLOGY

Over the years I have offended tens of people by not including Hove in the title of this book (as officially Brighton and Hove come as a package these days). But, as there's little in the way of entertainment in Hove, except for eating and drinking, it still doesn't seem to merit the inclusion. Hove begins at Boundary Passage (the longest alleyway in Brighton, opposite Little Western Street) and continues most of the way to Devon. Although it has partly succeeded in throwing off its old image of being a home for right-wing old ladies who spend their time making jam and writing angry letters to the Evening Argus, Hove is still primarily a residential area with a few good pubs and restaurants and a (rather incongruous) lap-dancing club.

What does need to be said though, is that some of the town's most beautiful buildings can be found here; Brunswick Square and Palmeira Square being particularly fine examples of Brighton (sorry, Hove) architecture at its best.

There is an age-old joke that Hove should be re-named 'Hove Actually', due to the countless times its residents, when asked if they live in Brighton, reply with snooty indignation –
'No, Hove actually.'

BRIGHTON EMBARRASSMENTs

THE MARINA

Mercifully hidden away in the outer reaches of Brighton seafront lies the Marina – a concrete jungle of factory shops, a casino, an Asda, a drive-through Macdonald's, the world's largest multi-storey carpark and the odd boat. The

antithesis of Brighton's saucy, seedy, devil-may-care spirit, it resembles some god-awful theme park crossed with Moss Side. The best solution for this place would be for the council to throw its hands in the air, say – 'Ooops' – and send in the bulldozers, but, like that sore tooth you can't resist poking, the buggers can't seem to leave the place alone. The latest £50 million investment being thrown at it includes two enormous Legoland tower blocks in day-glo colours, to be built right in the centre. Just what the place needs – more concrete.

THE LONDON ROAD

Dirty, smelly and unsightly, London Road is the home of the discount meat store, boarded up shops, Brighton's grimmest pubs and the occasional dead body. The visual equivalent of waking up after a heavy party to discover that someone's emptied an ashtray into your mouth.

THE AQUARIUM TERRACE

When the old Concorde and go-kart track opposite the Palace Pier were demolished a few years ago, did the council use this as an opportunity to add a bit of much-needed greenery to the seafront,

or something fun like an open-air pool? No, of course not! Instead they opted for the Aquarium Terrace – a monstrous, neon-lit white blob that remained empty for two years owing to a severe case of incontinence. Currently home to one restaurant, a Burger King, an amusement arcade and 300 for rent signs.

EMBASSY COURT

Also known as Bhaji Towers (because it's where new arrivals to this country get housed), this Art Deco building is a slight anomaly amongst this list of monstrosities as – in its prime – it was actually a beautiful piece of architecture (and even used to house such local luminaries as Keith Waterhouse). Now, however, with all the crumbling apparel and paint peeling off, it resembles Michael Jackson's face on a bad day, and it's only a matter of time before either chunks of it start dropping off or it falls victim to that ever-popular Brighton tragedy – the 'mysterious fire.'

GET A REAL TASTE OF THE ENGLISH
BRIGHTON

Lose loads of money at the American-style Casino.

Marvel at the American-style bowling alley.

See the stunning Asda car-park.

Enjoy an American-style in-car meal from the drive-through MacDonalds.

HARBOUR TOWN AT THE
MARINA

Brighton's architectural masterpiece

All the latest American movies at our Multiplex cinema. Over 300 screens and no subtitled foreign shit.

Factory outlet shopping offering overpriced tat, Dynasty style blouses for the modern lady and knitwear for rugged men.

Concrete galore!!!

Coming soon! The Brighton Marina American Football Stadium.

Wonderful Things To Do

MUSEUMS AND PALATIAL BROTHELS

The Pavilion

Old Steine (01273) 290900
Open 10am-5pm Oct-March
9.30am-5pm April-September
£5.35 adults, £3.30 children

If, like me, you have a pathological hatred for those dreary tours of stately homes, I guarantee you'll still enjoy a visit to the Pavilion. True, it's the familiar set-up with those awful little rope chains and hordes of American tourists giving 'oohs' and 'aaahs' in every room, but you can't escape the simple fact that the Pavilion is stunning and utterly unique. With the exception of the Pier, this is Brighton's most famous landmark. Could you really visit Paris and not go up the Eiffel Tower?

Built as a weekend retreat for the Prince Regent in 1823, this extravagant palace is home to some flamboyant architecture and even more flamboyant interior design. Despite the Indian look from the outside, the interior actually has a predominant Chinese theme. Inside it's a labyrinth of bamboo, dragon sculptures and some of the most astonishingly ornate rooms I've ever set eyes on, especially the Music room. It is well documented that the Prince was renowned for his love of women and food. In the bedroom look for the two secret doors for his midnight rendezvous with Mrs Fitzherbert and the bloke selling seafood in a basket. The door for food is in a corner, the other right next to the bed. Some nights Mrs F and the seafood guy would accidentally enter through the wrong doors, and if it was dark and the Prince was tipsy …well you can guess the rest, but this is Brighton after all.

Keep your eyes peeled for the most outrageous chandelier in the universe, bamboo trees in the kitchen, a fire-breathing dragon, and, if you watch the TV documentary they show upstairs, you won't have to waste money on a guidebook.

Dreamed-up and partly designed by the Prince Regent, this stately pleasure dome helped establish Brighton as a fashionable place to be seen. One

hundred and eighty years later, the Prince's devotion to art, music, extravagance and philandering have still left an indelible impression on the town. Holiday cottages do not come more exotic than this.

Brighton Museum and Art Gallery

Church Street/ Royal Pavilion Gardens
(01273) 290900
Open Tues-Sat 10am-5pm
Admission free
www.virtualmuseum.info

Re-opened in 2002, after a much-publicised refurbishment, Brighton museum is now modernised, more spacious, and packed with imaginative displays. And, after a local campaign, its beloved Gallet cat, Brummel (a giant model of one of the ornamental pair in the cabinet by Art and Design), is back by the entrance, awaiting a good stroke and your donations.

Much of the ground floor of the museum is now given over to the town itself, covering its social history, from sport, work and religion to pub and club culture. Whoever designed this section went overboard with inventive layout and interactive facilities, though in places it seems a little confused, with way too much emphasis on contemporary Brighton culture. Do you really need to go to a museum to see club fliers, posters,

BMX bikes and prostitute cards when you can walk down Sydney Street where this culture lives and breathes? But we'll say no more on the matter. Wander round and you can watch old videos of Brighton, listen to recorded voices, feel the mystery objects (a dead seagull and a 'Prince Albert'), peruse the paintings of Sake Deen Mohammed and Dr Russell, play on the old model seaside machines (if it weren't for the fact that they seem permanently out of order), and learn all about the Mods and Rockers. You're not meant to sit on the scooter in the far-left corner, but it makes a good holiday snap.

Elsewhere on the ground floor there's a Discovery Room for kids, which is an Alice in Wonderland style activity area with enormous wax crayons (sporting wigs!), 'House of Fun' mirrors and a giant Daliesque shirt. The World Art Gallery is also on this floor and has a curious selection of costumes, carvings of old favourites such as Ganesh and two very phallic totems over the doorway. Nearby

there's a room full of pottery and stuff for people who – unlike myself – get a kick out of perusing old plates in glass cabinets.

Upstairs are the gallery, café (unchanged since 1856), exhibition space, Human Body section (look for presidential candidate Barbie) and the History of Fashion. Even I have to concede that the fashion section isn't a patch on what it used to be, but at least it still contains the Prince Regent's enormous breeches, hand-made by High and Mighty.

Consistently excellent, however, is the museum's exhibition space. Previous highlights have included Fetishism, paintings by Captain Beefheart, some wonderfully bawdy images, stories and costumes for the Carnivalesque theme, and the History of Cinema in Brighton and Hove.

While local opinion remains divided about the new-look museum ('people seem about 70% happy', claimed one chatty curator), it can't be denied that its swanky new entrance and new lick of paint were much overdue.

The Prince Regent, shortly before his notorious goatée beard and corduroy phase.

The Booth Museum of Natural History

194 Dyke Road (01273) 292777
Admission free Open Mon-Sat 10am-5pm
Sun 2pm-5pm Closed Thurs

Originally opened as a private museum in 1874, by bird-stuffing enthusiast Mr Booth, this building has blossomed to become one of the main focal points and archives of natural history for the Brighton area. As well as being home to thousands of creatures, skeletons and strange things in specimen jars, it is a resource centre for local schools, while on special days they even do live taxidermy for the public. Should you stumble across any fresh road kill, just *'scoop it up and bring it in,'* as its Visitor Services Manager, John Cooper, cheerfully put it.

On entering the museum the first thing you'll notice is the smell of mothballs and the wonderfully gloomy atmosphere. Towers of stuffed birds line the walls, while in the centre lie two incongruous but beautiful stained-glass windows.

At this point, if you're in a group, I recommend splitting up and going it alone for maximum effect. Walk down the aisles at the side and enter Hitchcock's terrifying world of 'The Birds'. Down the centre you'll find the discovery lab – a hands on science area for kids – and, at the back, an impressive array of skeletons.
Look out for: the sheep that looks like Daisy in the Woody Allen movie, the charred remnants of a (half-eaten) dodo, the remains of a dog from Stanmer Park, the Harry Potter owls and the famous 'toad in the hole'. I bet you won't find the warthog's head though.

What you see in the museum is, however, only a small percentage of what's been collected over the years

as, owing to lack of space, they're unable to display everything. With special permission though, you can get a behind-the-scenes tour. I have been lucky enough to experience this and thoroughly enjoyed wandering through dusty old badger-lined corridors where they've got everything from the Reindeer that Hanningtons used to borrow every Christmas, to a scorpion found by a guest in the Grand Hotel. *'If you find odd things in your sandwiches they'll end up here,'* declared Keeper of Biology, Gerald Legg. Later he took me into a room with a large metal worktop and muttered: *'I've had a tiger on that table.'*

To find the museum, follow Dyke Road from the Clock Tower and you'll find it opposite the tennis courts after about a fifteen minutes walk.
Warning – check first for kids' visits, if you're childphobic they could spoil your experience.

Could you spend the night here on your own though? I swear they all come to life then.

Brighton Toy and Model Museum

52/55 Trafalgar Street (01273) 749494
Open Tues-Fri 10am-5pm, Sat 11am-5pm
Admission £3.50 adults, £2 children/ oldies

While not in the most glamorous of locations (housed under a damp railway bridge below Brighton Station), what this museum lacks in setting, it makes up with its pristine collection.

There are over 25,000 exhibits, beautifully displayed and all clearly the pride and joy of its enthusiastic manager Andrew Woodfield (they've even got his old model train-set in the far-right hand corner).

The model railways make up the bulk of the collection, and – unlike their full-scale counterparts upstairs – actually run. In fact, once a year in October they go mad and set off *everything* for the day – it's like a scene from Toy Story 2.

While internationally renowned for the extensive collection of 1930s model trains, there's plenty more to see here, including a toy theatre and puppet section, model cars and Smurfs galore.

Curios to look out for include the old Punch and Judy stand (with the baker hanging in the gallows), the pantomime horse underneath the model railway in the far right-hand corner; the Dribbler Train (also known as the Piddler), Edwina the wicked witch in the theatre and puppet section and – my favourite – the old 'Drunkards Dream' Machine (a drunk lies inebriated in a liquor basement, and if you stick in 10p you get to see his hallucinations, which range from scurrying rats to the devil, who pops out of a beer barrel!).

Children, trainspotter types and anyone with an interest in old toys and models will love this place. Weekend revellers will not. Watch out during schooldays, though; like the Booth Museum you may be surrounded by gangs of school-kids trying their best to knock over all the little figurines in the cabinets.

NB. The museum can be hired out for private parties. I came here once for a friend's wedding reception, and it made a refreshing change to the usual crap disco.

Hove Museum

19 New Church Road (01273) 290200
Open Tues-Sat 10am-5pm, Sun 2pm-5pm
Admission free
www.virtualmuseum.info

This beautiful old museum, situated way down Church Street in deepest, darkest Hove, has had a 'Zel' makeover in recent years. Gone are the psychedelic carpets and cardboard cutout of Ringo Starr, but the 1970's teashop, thankfully, still remains. They've done a great job with the refurbishment here though; the rooms are brighter and the displays are more interactive and imaginatively presented. And while the History of Hove section still does nothing to dissuade the opinion that Hove is 'quite dull', the 'Wizard's Attic' and 'History of Cinema' make the trek here very worth while.

The Wizard's Attic is a room that children (and adults) will thoroughly enjoy. The low-level lighting creates a wonderfully spooky atmosphere (to go with the attic theme); there are toys hanging from the ceiling, little cubbyholes with fairground mirrors, a tin bath full of soldiers, and even a painting where the eyes follow you around the room. And dare you put your hand in the hole below the box full of creepy-crawlies?

Elsewhere on the first floor, the History of Cinema section tells the fascinating history of Hove's role as the birthplace of the British film industry.

The exhibits in this section range from old zeotropes and magic lanterns to a six-seater cinema, which shows three short films every half-hour. I can thoroughly recommend waiting around to see 'Professor Heard's Magic Lantern Show', where a talking skull guides you through a magical journey in which ghosts and goblins rise from a witch's cauldron and the cautionary tale of the Miller and Sweep is learned. Look out also for the seven or eight old films that are constantly running in the room next door – the footage of people cycling off the pier into the sea is wonderfully silly.

And when you're all through with horsing around in the Attic, watching films, perusing the latest exhibition downstairs and spending your pennies in the gift shop, make sure to pay your respects to Hove's loveable grannies and Mrs Doyle types, by popping into the tea rooms for a big wedge of cake and a nice, hot cuppa.

GALLERIES, CHURCHES & OTHER INTERESTING PLACES

The Artists' Quarters

Kings RoadArches

Tucked away down on the seafront, between the two piers and below the kissing statue, this small area has been home for over nine years now to a colourful and flamboyant collection of local artists, whose workshops and galleries are permanently on display to the public. Originally owned by fishermen, these little rooms would once have been used for de-scaling fish (to be sold where the carousel now stands), which accounts for the occasional odd whiff.

Far more in keeping with Brighton's bohemian nature than the plethora of tacky café-bars found on the seafront, the Artists' Quarters perfectly capture the creative and communal spirit of the town. Open all year round, even in the most improbable gales, this is London gallery fodder at half the price, with work ranging from cards and paintings to exotic furniture and puppets.

Fabrica

40 Duke Street (01273) 778646
Open Wed-Sat 11.30am-5pm, Sun 2-5pm
Admission free
Closed Dec-April due to a lack of heating

Opposite the main post office on Ship Street, this converted church is now a gallery space for installations and contemporary art, and is an essential drop-in spot when visiting the Old Lanes in summer, even if it's only for a few minutes.

The Phoenix Gallery

10-14 Waterloo Place (01273) 603700
Open Mon-Sat 11am-6pm, Sun 12noon-4pm
Admission free *www.phoenixarts.org*

Over the last fifteen years this place has transformed from a grotty squat to a thriving art gallery. Exhibitions change on a monthly basis, and look out for more unusual events taking place here from time to time (I recall seeing maverick songwriter Daniel Johnson here a few years ago). They also organise a fair range of art-based workshops here, ranging from tapestry to ceramics.

The Sealife Centre

Marine Parade, opposite the Palace Pier
(01273) 604234 Open 10am-6pm Mon-Sun
Adults £7.25 Children £4.50

This place has improved dramatically since I first reviewed it five years ago. Housed inside a beautiful old Victorian building, it really is a fun place now to take children, as I discovered after visiting with my nephew Alex. Highlights for kids include the Captain Pugwash trail, a chance to see the fish being fed, a Jules Verne nautilus room (which is impressive, if a little pointless), and of course the underwater tunnels, where you get to see the sharks and other creatures swimming overhead. 'Look it's waving,' said Alex, as a stingray flapped by.

Keep a sharp lookout for the seahorses tank, which is also home to an utterly ridiculous creature with a long snout, the horse-shoe crab (resembling a genuinely scary Doctor Who monster); the plastic shark, and the camera right at the end of the tunnel, which you can control and have fun with if one of you goes back into the tunnel and stands around pulling faces.

They've even done a good job with the décor here (it's all shadowy corners and endless loops of the X-Files music). Don't you love a happy ending?

St. Bartholomew's Church

Ann Street (01273) 620491

Located behind Trafalgar Street and London Road, St Bartholomew's is definitely worth seeking out, as it's unique. It is, in fact, the biggest brick church in Europe and is impressively decorated with oil paintings, Italian mosaics and marble archways. It could well be the setting of a Peter Greenaway film.

They also put on a plenty of concerts here, particularly during the festival; the acoustics are ideal for Renaissance choral music.

You've seen the show at the Sealife Centre, now eat the stars

43

WHERE TO TAKE A GOOD STROLL

The Marina Breakwater

Down near the Marina is a breakwater that extends for about a quarter of a mile out to sea. Go when the sea's a bit rough and it can be a delightfully hairy experience. It'll take you about twenty minutes to walk there from the pier, and ideally you should try and time it well for sunset. Then you could stick around in the Marina for a drink (bad idea) or walk back into town and flop around at The Basketmakers (good idea).

The Undercliff walk to Rottingdean

From the Palace Pier head to the Marina, keep on the undercliff path once there and you'll reach Rottingdean in about one hour. Most of the path from the Marina onwards has been carved out of the imposing, chalky cliffs which, together with the magnificent views of the sea, makes this walk fairly spectacular. And it's good by bike too as it's completely flat. As you approach Rottingdean you'll start to chance upon rock-pools and little coves where people go winkle picking and crab fishing.

Rottingdean is, in contrast to Brighton, one of those classic seaside villages with old-fashioned shops and boutiques. In fact, I have it on good authority that one particular shop, 'the Cabin', is said to have been the inspiration behind the Local Shop in the League of Gentleman. One person emailed to tell me, *"I went in to buy a copy of the Guardian and the woman said defensively, 'Oh no. We only stock local papers in here…'"*

Once you've had a good nose around the village, you'll need to head back to Brighton, though, if you can't face doing the walk again, buses do run regularly back to town from here. This really is one of the best and most accessible local walks whatever the season. In summer there's a café halfway (usually serving coke and a

Glenda gets the willies

piece of shortbread wrapped up in cling-film), while in winter you may have your head blown off but if you wrap up warm you won't regret it. Finish off with mulled wine and a cigar in The White Horse at Rottingdean and you'll be in heaven. **NB** Due to erosion this walkway has been closed for some time now. If you do go down and it's still blocked, take the steps up to the top and, instead, take the coastal path by the main road until you reach Rottingdean. It's still a lovely walk, and you can always stop off for a game of pitch and putt, or for refreshments at Roedean Café.

Glynde to Lewes

Although I've never done this walk, friends have recommended it and one year I even even got a lovely email from a bloke called Adam urging me to include it. Directions are simple; take the train to Glynde and follow the 'stunning but straightforward walk back over Mount Caborn to Lewes'. You won't see a soul, the scenery is said to be spectacular and when you drop down the hill into Lewes, you are only a short walk from the Snow Drop pub.

GUIDED WALKS

Brighton Walks
(01273) 888596
www.brightonwalks.com
info@brightonwalks.com
Ghost Tour runs all year round, Quodrophenia tour runs all summer Private Walks available on request. All tours run for 90 minutes to two hours £5 adults, £3 children

The Bard of Brighton, Glenda Clarke has been running her guided walks for many years now, taking her wide-eyed posses around Brighton's famous landmarks and down secret alleyways to regale them with menacing tales and chilling stories and to point out where Phil Daniels shagged Leslie Ash in Quadrophenia.

While there are plenty of other tours to choose from during the Brighton Festival, it's the little touches that make Glenda's extra special. As well as having photos and newspaper articles to hand for the Ghost Tour, she dons a spooky pair of earrings and even hands round a bag of 'Monster Mix', leaving the group happily munching on jelly bats and toads as she weaves such hair-raising stories as 'the Grey Lady of Meeting House Lane'. For the Quadrophenia Walk she sports, of course, regulation 'Target earrings', and for each tour she isn't afraid to throw in a few comedy moments to spice things up.

Tours range from Ghost Walks and Murder Mysteries to Quadrophenia, Legends of the Lanes and Lewes Walks.

The Indian Chattri on the Downs

High up on a hill overlooking Brighton is one the town's most curious but least-known memorials, built to commemorate the thousands of Indians who died in Brighton during the First World War. They were brought here owing to the fact that the Royal Pavilion was then used as a hospital for the wounded, chosen on the grounds that the soldiers would feel more at home there. Despite these rather misplaced good intentions the wounded were more than a little bemused at

having been stationed in what looked like an Oriental Brothel and, of course, bringing Sikhs and Hindus from every caste all under one roof meant the atmosphere was not exactly convivial.

The 4000 who died here had their ashes scattered into the sea. The Chattri was built as a memorial to them in 1921, and every year there is still an annual pilgrimage organised by the Royal British legion and the High Commissioner for India.

Directions

Take the A23 out of Brighton, follow the A273 to Hassocks and go through Pyecombe. Take a right down Mill Lane and follow until you reach the windmill carpark.

From the carpark go past the Old Barn Farm and golf course, and keep following the path until you reach a signpost. Go through the gate, keep the large clump of trees on your right and keep following the South Downs way. (It's probably best to take an OS map, however, as these directions come from some illegible notes I scribbled years ago and it's easy to miss the Chattri, as it is hidden by trees until the last minute. The reference is TQ304111.)

SPORTS CENTRES

Stanley Deason

Wilson Avenue (01273) 694281
Open weekdays 8.50am-11pm,
weekends 9am-8.30pm

Offering squash, table tennis, badminton, basketball, volleyball, gym, astro-turf pitches, circuit training and aerobics.

King Alfred Centre

Kingsway, Hove (01273) 290290
www.kingalfredleisure.co.uk

Tropical style pools, badminton, table tennis, martial arts classes, gymnasium and crèche. See website for details on pool opening times.

Moulsecoomb Leisure Centre

Moulsecoomb Way (01273) 622266

Offering Badminton, table tennis, basketball, roller-skating (skates not supplied), indoor hockey, gymnasium and aerobics.

Norman Cook's three-a-side football team

SKATE, KITE AND BOARD HIRE

Pulse Station (Rollerblading)

23-25 Kings Road Arches
Open 10.30am until no one wants any
more boots. Open June-Sept.

Solomon semi-soft boot skates for hire. £3.50 p.h., £50 deposit required.

Oddballs Active Sports

West Pier Upper deck, behind the Rock
Shop. (01273) 777511
Open 11.30am-5.30pm (or thereabouts)
www.oddballs.co.uk

Skate hire, scooters, longboards, mountain boards, kites and flexifoils. You can even have a free bounce on their pogo stick whilst waiting.

SWIMMING

Saltdean Lido

Saltdean Park Road, Saltdean
(01273) 880616
Open end of May to the end of September
every year 10am-6pm every day
£3 adults, £2 kids

This original open-air Art-Deco swimming pool (and cover star of the first Clearlake album, 'Lido') is only a 15-minute drive from Brighton. In the last few years the pool has been lovingly restored and has an outside area with plenty of tables, chairs and spots for sunbathing and lounging. Highly recommended.

Prince Regent

Church Street (01273) 685692
Open 7am-9.30pm most days

Across the road from the Pavilion, this large pool has plenty of space, some good diving boards, a big slide, a gym, a sauna and sunbeds.

At weekends splashing around time for kids is between 9.30am and 4.45pm on Saturday, while on Sundays adults can do lane-swimming 10.30am-9.30pm. The boards are also in use for most of the day during weekends and early weekday evenings. Throughout the week there is an adults-only early swimming session from 7am-9am. For more details it's best to phone, as timetables change quarterly.

My only gripe with the place is their insistence on playing local radio all the hours god sends. I like a swim to get away from it all, not to listen to Phil Collins and adverts for double-glazing. I did once complain, but was rudely informed that the radio was not for the swimmers but to keep the lifeguards from getting bored. You just can't beat good old English customer service.

King Alfred Centre

Kingsway, Hove (01273) 290290
Open 7.30am-9.45pm
www.kingalfredleisure.co.uk

Preferable to the Prince Regent, owing to the fact that it's usually less busy, the water is warmer, it feels cleaner and they don't have local radio blaring at you. And, if you're driving, they've got a cheap carpark (40p) just round the back. It's also due to be rebuilt some time soon so it's best to phone ahead to check it's not a building site.

The Sea

It's free and there's lots of it. A visit to Brighton is not complete without at least getting your feet wet. It's traditional to swim twice around the West Pier before breakfast here, but for newcomers a couple of lengths of butterfly will do. Be careful when the currents are strong; every year someone gets swept away by a surprising freak tide.

For more information, see the chapter on the Sea.

Evening Anus

www.cheekyguides.com

30p

MAYOR SHOWS CRACK IN UNDERCLIFF WALK

Volks Railway to be turned into mobile nightclub

Residents today expressed their CONCERN over the council's decision to close down one of Brighton's best-loved features, the Volks Railway, and turn it into yet another seafront club. Built in 1886, this miniature railway line played a pivotal role in preventing the German forces from invading Britain in the Second World War and up until recently was used for taking visitors to the Brighton Marina to educate them in the horrors of town planning.

SPEWING

When confronted with the notion that another club in Brighton is going to attract yet more moronic stag parties and pissed up Londoners at the weekend, a council spokeman said:

'maybe so, but it'll be Brighton kebabs they'll have bought to spew on the pavement not London ones, and that's what matters.'

SAI BABA
Read his new gossip column on page 22

GIANT METEOR CRASHES INTO THE MARINA CAUSING OVER £4,000,000,000 OF IMPROVEMENTS!

FOR FULL STORY SEE PAGES 12-13

The spotter's guide to

Last year, when the Brighton and Hove buses got the idea of sticking the names of over 50 famous people with local connections on their buses, it meant that celebrity spotting in this town took a whole new twist.

No longer are you obliged to spend two hours in the rain outside the Brighton Centre just to catch a glimpse of Robbie Williams' flabby bottom. Instead, all you need is a pencil, a copy of the guide and a rudimentary knowledge of public transport. Just 5 minutes on Western Road and you could see Norman Cook, Winston Churchill or even Leo Sayer streak by, and nearly knock you over.

We've only included our favourite 15 here, but serious spotters can find the rest listed at the website www.buses.co.uk.

When you've spotted all 15, send in the completed sheet and the first 5 we receive will win a special Cheeky cagoule.

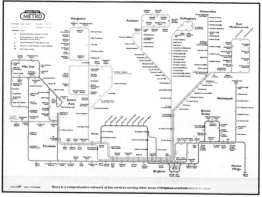

The territory of the Brighton & Hove bus

Brighton & Hove buses

- **Lord Attenborough** (Bus number 1) – starred in *Brighton Rock* and that thing with the gorillas.
- **Norman Cook** (3) – aka Fatboyslim but once the bassist in Blancmange.
- **Chris Eubank** (4) – star of coffee adverts and celebrated dandy.
- **Derek Jameson** (14) – having once been editor of the *Daily Express* and *News of the World*, Derek is of course only one notch above Peter Stringfellow in the ladder of celebrity fools.
- **Des Lynam** (15) – TV celebrity chef.
- **Annie Nightingale** (16) – Radio One DJ, celebrated for keeping the off-licenses of Hove solvent for the last 20 years.
- **Leo Sayer** (17) pint-sized singer shaped like a Bonsai tree.
- **The Who** (19) hugely successful Mod band whose singer Roger Daltrey once famously sang – 'Hope I die before I get old...', but then changed his mind and settled down into a life of fish-farming instead.
- **Sir Norman Wisdom** (20) – veteran comedian with a bad case of the DTs.
- **Prince Regent** (803) – a swimming pool.*
- **Charles Busby** (824) – small yellow man who spent much of his time hanging precariously from telegraph wires.
- **John Nash** (811) – celebrated country and western singer whose hit 'A cowboy from Whitehawk buggered up my patio', made him a superstar.
- **Stanley Deason** (827) – one-time maverick mayor, who in the early 70s famously elected Frank Zappa as the King of Hove.
- **Carl Vincent** (845) – known locally as 'Vinegar Vincent', Carl is best remembered as having supplied the voice of Pig in the children's program 'Pipkins'.
- **Charles Dickens** (828) – had a mate who knew someone in Brighton.

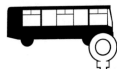

The male and female of the species

AMAZING BUS FACTS

- Often seen gathering in flocks at Churchill Square or North St.

- Predators: trucks and taxis.

- Prey: Cyclists, dozy tourists and prams.

*not sure why this one is here.

Weird Things To Do

Country and Western Weekends

For info (01273) 701152
Middle of May Admission free

Spend a day at Wild Park and you'll meet Red Indians in tepees, gamblers, cowgirls and cowboys. Also expect rodeo, live bands, frantic shootouts, birds of prey and err… owls.

Why spend time in a sweaty club drinking your money away when you could wear a raccoon on your head and be a Wild West hero? Contact Colin on the number above for more details.

Llama Trekking

For info call Steve or Sarah Young
(01273) 383807
Running Wed-Sun April-Oct, weather permitting, Llama for one £50
Share a Llama with a friend? (Ooh, suits you sir!) £75

Just you, the rolling hills, the sun beating down…and your faithful llama by your side. From April to October, this couple organise 5-mile rambles over the Downs, that includes food and a llama. You can't ride these magnificent creatures, but a packed lunch is included which is carried by your hairy friend. It may be expensive, but when will you get the opportunity again?

The llamas all have different personalities, and you can choose the likes of Lima, Basil, Frank (so called because of his blue eyes) or Sancho. But feisty Bunyip remains a favourite. As Sarah explained: *"He's just a really nice llama."*

Adventures Unlimited

64 Edward Street (01273) 681058
info@aultd.org www.aultd.org

I once spent a brilliant Saturday with a load of friends playing British bulldogs, hide and seek, lateral thinking games and clambering over assault courses thanks to these guys. Not only was it fun and fairly cheap, but we were also entertained by some shameless flirting between my friend and the organiser.

They also offer other outdoor pursuit days like canoeing, climbing, raft-building, pony-trekking and abseiling. And for the 8-18 market they run the '818 Club', which offers a mixture of outdoor pursuits & leisure activities similar to the above. All events take place outside Brighton, and transport is provided, should you need it. Book well in advance for summer events. Thoroughly recommended.

The Rabbit Roundabout

Follow the London Road out of Brighton, past Preston Park, and eventually you'll get to a big roundabout with a petrol station on your left. Look carefully, any time day or night, and you'll see the roundabout is home to hundreds of rabbits. Occasionally you might spot a huge pile of carrots in the middle that some kind soul has either expertly flung from their car or – risking life and limb – deposited there by running across the busy road and back. Marooned indefinitely, it'll only be a matter of time before in-breeding gets the better of these loveable floppy-eared creatures and we'll be seeing misshapen, idiot rabbits living there instead. The question is – how the hell did they get there in the first place?

Mountain Activities Ltd with Keith Fleming

3 The Twitten, Burgess Hill, West Sussex
(01444) 235258 or 07710 345322
keith@mountain-activities.co.uk
www.mountain-activities.co.uk

No relation to Bob – he won't be coughing all over you. Instead, Keith organises climbing, abseiling and other adventure activities in Sussex for groups (half or day sessions available). Longer courses (including mountaineering) for small groups are also available in North Wales, The Peak District and France. Keith also organises instructor training courses, technical advice on all related matters and Duke of Edinburgh Award Expedition programmes.

£150 per day for a minimum of 4 people, rising by £35 per extra adult. Tents are all provided for camping but are self-catering. £280 for a weekend, rising by £30 per extra adult. £5 each extra for bike-hire.

The Dolphin Derby

End of the pier

Complete with its own catchy theme tune, the Dolphin Derby is probably the greatest game ever invented and, more importantly, a chance for those of you on the breadline to earn some beer money. Spend a week on your hands and knees practicing rolling golf balls into paper cups and reap the rewards.

whenever you're getting demoralised with your job, just think of this guy

WHERE TO CONTACT THE DEAD

Brighton Spiritualist Church
Edward Street, opposite Devonshire Place
(01273) 683088

It all starts off surprisingly similar to a Christian service (not least because the hymns are the typical tuneless mumbling affairs), except, instead of God, one gives praise to 'the greater vibration'. Expect a bit more chat and another hymn, and then it all picks up when the guest clairvoyant comes on. Most of these guys are commanding speakers and come across in an American preacher style. There's a pep talk, some fabulous shaky hands business then, through the preacher, the dead will start to communicate with a few members of the congregation.

Don't always expect to be chosen, but, if you are fortunate enough, they'll ask you to speak so that the spirits pick up on your vibrations. What follows are nuggets of advice and information from the spirit world, channelled through the clairvoyant's voice, and all done to the accompaniment of the shaky hands (whether it works without these I don't know). The time I was picked I met my Granddad (apparently), and his message was – 'Stop worrying about your ears sticking out.'

Having never given much thought to the orientation of my ears, I did wonder what that was all about, particularly as I had never met either of my grandfathers.

Afterwards it's cheese, biscuits and a chat, a flick through Psychic News, and then a well-earned lunch at the Barley Mow.

Sunday services are at 11am and 6.30pm.

Séances

If you are serious about wanting to be involved with a séance group you can e-mail the Cheeky Guide with your name and phone number. We will pass it on to the group, and they will explain what is required. Unless you are staying in Brighton for some time though, this will not be possible.

If invited you will be expected to take the evening seriously, but I can guarantee you will have plenty of fun. It's all in the pitch dark and begins with singing a few old Musical Hall numbers such as Roll Out The Barrel and Daisy, Daisy to 'get the energy going'. Then, once the spirits have manifested through the medium, watch out for stuff moving around the room and hope that you don't spend the night with a chair on your head as one lady did.

Expect also to get covered in ectoplasm and have some questions ready for when you meet some of the fantastic characters such as James the Victorian transvestite comedian. And if you ask, the ghosts will tell you who your spirit guide is. Do I get a Buddhist monk or Native American Indian chief like everyone else? No, I get a chicken called Cyril.

At the end of the night not everyone will necessarily believe what they have seen, but it is, of course, something to tell the grandchildren.

Pets get their paws read for free every other Saturday at Margaret's

PALMISTS AND CLAIRVOYANTS

Margaret

64 Elm Grove (01273) 683623
Open Tues, Wed, Thurs, Sat 10am-3.45pm,
closed 11.45am-1pm

When you step in here be ready to take a time warp back thirty years or more. The walls are littered with fading newspaper articles and curling black and white photos showing Margaret on old TV shows. You feel like you're in a Rita Tushingham movie with Margaret looking and playing the part magnificently.

The readings take around twenty minutes in a tiny room at the back of the shop where she will read your palm or tell your fortune from a pack of cards. Along with the usual stuff like 'you know someone who reads The Daily Mail', Margaret also said some pretty accurate and insightful things the last time I visited. The readings range from £12 to £16. Go on, treat yourself to a seaside speciality from a true professional.

Paul Hughes-Barlow

295 Kings Road Arches, under the Palace
Pier (01273) 677206
Open Mon-Sun 12noon-6pm

The only palmist in Brighton I know whose room is full of interesting books rather than gypsy tat and the usual mystical paraphernalia. Friendly and honest about his profession and with a good knowledge of the occult sciences, Paul is easy to warm to, and has a reassuringly boyish laugh. Probably a good choice if you're looking for something beyond the usual nonsense. First sittings are a standard £15.

STUFF THAT LEGENDS ARE MADE OF

Tony Young Autographs

138 Edward Street (01273) 732418
Opening times seem to be akin to
MajorMajorMajorMajor's office in Catch 22.
In theory they're Mon-Fri 10am-12noon
and 1pm-3pm, Sat 10am-12.30pm

This tumble-down shop rescued from
the 1950s has a surreal and curling
collection of autographed photos and
bizarre oddities. Where else could you
get a copy of the homicide report of
the JFK assassination *and* a broken
banjo? Worth a visit for curiosity alone
but treat the owner with respect, he's
an old man and dislikes rowdy people
in the shop.

D & K Rosen Clothiers

Top of Church Street
Open Mon-Sat 10am-5.30pm

You don't have a look around here,
you have an adventure. The owner is
one of Brighton's most eccentric
characters, well-known for his bizarre
banter, and the shop is a haven for

second-hand suits, fez and other
gentleman's attire. Rumour has it that
it inspired the 'Suits You' sketch from
the Fast Show. Legends don't come
much better than this.

Kappa

Bottom of Trafalgar Street
Opening times defy logic

Run by Peter Grant, Kappa is not
only home to the world's largest
collection of valves, but also a
graveyard to all of Brighton's dead
TVs. Despite looking derelict inside,
the place is sometimes open, and
hidden away behind all the TV
carcasses sits Peter, a man who can
bring a 1950s Ukrainian radio to life
with just the wave of his magic wand.
When not performing implausible
feats on old electronic equipment,
Peter is invariably out and about
setting up pirate radio stations or
saving another Russian nuclear power
station from going under. If it's old,
electronic and knackered, bring it
here and Pete will fix it.

A SURREAL AFTERNOON IN BRIGHTON

Put on your silliest hat, pack up some sandwiches and head off to Number 64 Elm Grove, where you will need to part with £12 to discover what the future holds from Mystic Margaret. Try not to be frightened by her make-up and listen carefully to what nuggets of wisdom she imparts to you.

Wander up to the top of Elm Grove and reward yourself with a quick cuppa at Beckie's café, where you can pretend you are in a Mike Leigh film, or, if it's a good day in there, a David Lynch.

From here cross over and follow Tenantry Down Road for a stunning view of the coastline as you pass through Brighton's shantytown. The curve of houses you can see far below are Roundhill Crescent where the notorious baby-eater Genesis P. Orridge used to live, while the strange little huts on either side of you are occupied by Brighton's flourishing Amish community. Keep your walkmans well hidden at this point or you may have a bloodbath on your hands. At the end of the road take a left and look for the entrance to Woodvale Crematorium – the chosen resting-place of infamous occultist Aleister Crowley. This vast graveyard is remote and enchanting, and if Buffy Summers ever came to town, this would definitely be her hangout of choice.

Leave by the main exit at the bottom, and now start heading into town. Your afternoon should be rounded off with a pint in the Basketmakers Pub, tucked away at the bottom of the North Laine. Search the tins on the wall to see who can find the strangest message inside, and then leave one of your own. The best messages I find will appear in next year's guide.

A SPOTTER'S GUIDE
TO BRIGHTON CELEBRITIES

What better way to spend your afternoon than going all gooey-eyed and weak-kneed at having stumbled across your favourite snooker player? Brighton is home to an eclectic bunch of celebrities, and I wish you every success with your sleuthing.

STEPHEN BERKOFF

The bald-headed, champagne socialist playwright and actor can be spotted roller-blading outside his apartment in Hove, merrily effing and blinding as he glides along.
20 points

NICK BERRY

The shiny-nosed superstar can often be seen walking his four Scottie dogs on the beach in the morning. Don't start singing 'Every Loser Wins' as he is known to get aggressive and recently hurled one of his dogs at a journalist from The Argus, just for saying – *'Hello, hello, hello, what's all this then?'*
15 points

JULIE BURCHILL

Diminutive, irritating, squeaky-voiced journalist, renowned for her opinionated codswallop. Did you know she has a swimming pool and that Tony Parsons was crap in bed? You'll find her down the Arts Club having a good whinge.
4 points

NICK CAVE

The brooding Australian singer lives in deepest, darkest Hove (naturally), and can be spotted hanging around outside the King Alfred looking like a vagrant. Either that or he'll be in HMV buying Mr Bean videos.
18 points

STEVE COOGAN

Hangs out in the Hanover pubs, the Nelson on Trafalgar Street and just about anywhere that sells alcohol. If you're an attractive female it's best to wear heavily-protective armour when he's around, although he has recently started carrying a tin-opener.
10 points,
(25 if he doesn't try and mate with you)

DAVID VAN DAY

At one time the ex-singer of Dollar could have been found running his burger stall by Churchill Square. Now he's vainly trying to kick-start his flagging career in a Tony Blackburn sort of way.
13 points

CHRIS EUBANK

Easy to spot, owing to the fact that most of his waking hours seem to be spent driving his jeep, motorbike or tractor around the Old Lanes and waving at bemused strangers.
½ point

FATBOYSLIM

From Tarquin to Norman to Freakpower to Fatboyslim (and a host of other pseudonyms along the way), local hero Norman Cook can still be found DJing at the Concorde 2, supporting Brighton and Hove Albion, or inviting down a quarter of a million of his mates to urinate on the beach.
15 points

HERBIE FLOWERS

He's played with every rock god from Bowie and T-Rex to Lou Reed, and got paid a measly £12 for writing the bass-line to 'Walk On The Wild Side'. Herbie's probably best-loved, however, for writing the classic pop ballad 'Grandad'. See him down the Komedia doing his double bass thing from time to time. If you want a good Rock'n'Roll story, ask him about the time he was in The Wombles on Top Of The Pops.
10 points

THE LEVELLERS

Soap dodgers with integrity, The Levellers can be found in deepest Kemptown, hanging around their studio, the Metway, and making a racket.
10 points

MARK LITTLE

The only ex-'Neighbours' star not to have had a stab at a pop career, Mr Little can be found in the Old Lanes making documentaries about vegetarian cafés, doing the odd spot on telly, or getting into trouble for hurling abuse at audiences at the Komedia.
15 points

PAUL McCARTNEY

One of Brighton's newest residents, the former Beatle moved here with his missus, Heather Mills, and can be spotted cycling along the seafront, dining in one of the many veggie restaurants in town or having a crafty burger when no-one's looking.
100 points (1,000,000 if spotted in 'Yellow Submarine')

MRS McCLUSKY (FROM GRANGE HILL)

Better remembered as Bridget the Midget. I first spotted her at a Ken Campbell performance years ago and occasionally still see her at some of the more unusual theatre events.
25 Team points

JOE McGANN

TV heartthrob Joe McGann lives near the Seven Dials and recently made the local headlines when he was spotted in the Tin Drum pulling the legs off a daddy-long-legs and feeding them to his two-year-old son.
12 points

PATSY ROWLAND

Best known as the frustrated secretary in many of the Carry On movies, Patsy's main role seemed to be forever pursuing Kenneth Williams around the office desk for a snog and a grope. I just don't think you were his type dear. Usually spotted chasing thin, blond, gay men down St. James's Street in Kemptown...
17 points

GAZ FROM SUPERGRASS

The shy popster with the hairy face lives in the far end of Kemptown and can be spotted wandering about in his trademark flared pinstripes and leather raincoat.

15 points

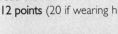

DAVID THOMAS
(FROM PERE UBU)

Strictly for the music lovers this one.
Look for him striding around Hove like some crazy Ignatious Reilly from Confederacy of Dunces. Hmmm I feel I've lost a few of you here, never mind, read on.

12 **points** (20 if wearing his infamous red plastic bib)

VICTOR SPINETTI

Best-known for his comic characters in the Beatles' films, and that famous scene from 'Return of the Pink Panther' where Spinetti, the flustered concierge, tries to deal with Clouseau's demand for a 'hcroom'. He can be spotted wandering around Kemptown dressed like some eccentric English gent, or in the latest farce at the Theatre Royal.

20 Points

MARK WILLIAMS (FROM THE FAST SHOW)

Found at Kambis grabbing a take-away kebab or hanging around pubs like the Lion and Lobster. Remember the Father Ted episode with Victor Meldrew before you go up to him and say 'Suits you Sir'.

15 points

If you've been missed out of our spotter's guide and feel that you ought to be included, please write to us finishing the following sentence -

I think I'm famous enough to be in your guide because ....

....

Please enclose £10 and a signed photo. If you are a local celebrity or just have been in The Bill a couple of times this will not be sufficient.

Things to do in Hove
when you're (not) Dead

BY DAVE 'BN1' MOUNFIELD

While Hove is now officially part of Brighton – and we're all meant to be one big happy family – it unfortunately remains the straight-laced and disapproving Maiden Aunt who tries to ignore sleazy old Uncle Brighton being sick under the sideboard at family get-togethers. Nevertheless, this 'small piece of Rhodesia on the South Coast', as Pete McCarthy once described it, does have some saving graces, so indulge us, if you will, as we endeavour to pick out a selection of interesting activities and places to visit in this civic equivalent of The Afterlife. But beware, gentle reader. In Hove, no-one can hear you scream.

Marrocco's
8 Kings Esplade (01273) 203764

Situated next to the soon-to-be-demolished-and-rebuilt-as-the-set-from-Space-1999-King-Alfred-Centre, this family run seaside café is endearingly chaotic and resolutely un-designer, with some very fine homemade Italian style ice cream, a job lot of pine fittings and some pretty good basic Italian dishes gracing its otherwise fairly standard café fare. To have a late afternoon perambulation along this stretch of the front, ending it here with a Knickerbocker glory and coffee while watching the staff run around in a permanent frenzy of Italian disorganization, is a real pleasure.

Gwyndwr Saloon
(The basement of Gwyndwr Mansions, by Hove Floral Clock)

Remarkably, this establishment is the oldest barbers in town, having kept it short and neat for a hundred and nineteen years non-stop. It is also the only barbers in the city with no vowels in it's name (well, the first bit anyway), and the only place I know where gentlemen can come for a Fifties style close shave. Situated in the basement of Gwyndwr Mansions in front of Hove Floral Clock, there are some nice steps down to a spiffingly old-fashioned window display for Pommade type products. Enter its portals and you will be delighted with the original thirties décor, with black and white tiles and Green Vitriolite. A very pleasant and humorous gentleman gave me a good cut on my visit, made all the more pleasurable by his heavily ironic use of the word "sir". As in "does *sir* think that?"

They've even had a book of poetry written about them by a poet in residence, which you can buy while you're there. It's not bad either.

Kings & Brunswick Lawn

The only bit of grass left on the seafront that the council hasn't dug up and ruined. And lovely it is too. This long stretch of lawn is ideal for picnicking, Frisbee throwing, or just lolling around. And when you get a bit peckish, the Meeting Place Café is nearby for a hot cuppa.

The Pussycat Club

(See 'Sex and Fetish' for details)

Where else can you see sweating IT workers stuffing ten pound notes into the g-strings of slightly bored but almost naked ladies? My trip here was dignified by an excited Arab saying *"So Beautiful! So Beautiful! I already go to toilet and masturbate five times!"* Sophisticated. Opposite the Gasworks on Church Road.

Canhams and George St. Butchers

48 Church Road (01273) 731021 & 49 George Street (01273) 731407

In a world where supermarkets are ruining quality meat production, good independent butchers are to be celebrated; none more so that these two fine establishments. Canhams offers heartbreakingly good meat pies and quality meat, while the butchers on George Street do an amazing array of sausages. A good enough reason to wander down this newly improved and pedestrianised shopping thoroughfare.

One Hove Place

Church Road & First Ave
(01273) 738266

While Brighton has over one million bars and pubs, Hove has hardly any, and still fewer you'd want to go to. An exception in this pub desert, however, is One Hove Place, boasting lots of designer oak panelling, a lovely large Italian sunken beer garden and a clientele of shifty-looking geezers with lots of gold jewellery.

Hove Floral Clock

This Civic wonder at the top of Palmeira Square is a clock made of flowers!! How crazy is that?!! For many Brightonians it stands as a gateway marker beyond which lie the cold, blasted wastelands of Hove Proper or 'Darkest Hove' as it is known. Even in the Spring, when its cheery, flower laden hands point to (usually) the wrong time, it seems to be a mute Memento Mori, saying "It's only a matter of time, Brightonian, before you grow old, and must perforce cross the shadow line, into Hove, and the arms of Death". It's very pretty though.

Hove Museum

(See museums in Wonderful Things to Do)

The Sea

Despite the fact that Brighton receives millions of visitors every year, you'd be surprised how few take the plunge and venture – beyond the occasional paddle – into the sea. Is it too cold, is it fear of sharks, turds and toilet paper, or are you all just a big bunch of Jessies? In an effort to encourage a few more of you out of the pubs and into the sea, this chapter gives the facts about sea water quality and explores a few ways to go messing about in the water.

Joe & Melinda's
WHERE TO SWIM GUIDE

Hove Beach

Hove is the gracious great-aunt of the south coast. So no surprise that Hove beach is clean and proper. Soft bowling greens and wide esplanades sparkle in the sun. Little flags flutter in the breeze and rosy-cheeked old ladies eat ice creams on benches. The best part is by the quarterdeck. A large groyne protects you from the predominantly southwest wind and it doesn't get rammed with tourists who, instead, make a beeline for the stretch between the two piers. This is also a good spot for families with ankle-biters who want to want to enjoy the sea, but without the bars, birds and blokes of Brighton beach.

Brighton Beach

Brighton beach in the summer is like a festival without the bands (and the toilets do sometimes beg comparison). Jugglers, drummers and fortune-tellers mingle with drinkers and dope smokers. Fat men seem compelled by some alien force to remove their shirts and try to roast themselves alive. The tacky (you love it), kiss-me-quick Palace Pier and its brooding forlorn twin, the West Pier, shimmer in the heat haze. On a hot July weekend, the beach is a carnival. A whiff of anarchy is in the air (or is that just the pot?). When the sun comes out, humanity throngs to the seaside in a great tide as if driven by a sudden ancestral urge – like lemmings. The only way to show gratitude for the sunshine so profound it goes beyond mere words is to strip to the waist and waddle around holding a plastic cup half-full of warm lager. The day usually ends with dizziness and a hysterical 'throw all the pebbles in the sea' competition. As for water quality, a former Beach Lifeguard says, *"it's fairly poor, though the council will lead you to believe otherwise."*

Saltdean

Take a coastal drive five miles west of Brighton to Saltdean. Early morning swimmers use the clean water all year round. There's a small pebble beach and Saltdean Lido provides a bathing alternative throughout the season.

Eastbourne

Blue Flag resort Eastbourne won the Best UK resort in 2001. From Brighton take a 21-mile scenic drive east along the A259. Great for windsurfing, canoeing, sailing, swimming or just watching the world go by, it offers traditional seaside atmosphere by the small, plastic spadeful.

Seaford

For crystal clear waters and plenty of space, keep on the A259 and head for Seaford. With ample free parking and an adjoining recreation ground with tennis, a pitch and putt, a café and a children's play area, this unassuming seaside town suits all.

Littlehampton

For fun head 22 miles west to Littlehampton, another Blue Flag beach. It has a large expanse of shingle beach with sand at low tide and a picturesque backdrop. Council initiatives guarantee cleanliness with the added bonus of the coastguard tower, an up-to-date first aid centre and a lost children unit. A must for families and suitable for all age groups, there's a modern funfair and theme-park close by.

Camber Sands

Finally for those in search of silky sand, travel 52 miles East to Camber Sands for the only sand dunes in Sussex and cafes and bars to keep you refreshed.

Eastbourne seafront

WATERSPORTS

Brighton Swimming Club
www.brightonsc.co.uk

Based at arch 250E down between the two piers, this 150-year old swimming club meets every morning at 11.30am (weather permitting) for a daily dip. New members are always welcome, though you'll be required to wear a coloured rubber cap, which might make you feel like a right Charlie, but is for your own safety.

Annual traditions include a big game of water polo down at the Marina and a very chilly annual Christmas dip. See website for more details.

The Brighton Kayak Company
185 Kings Road Arches (01273) 323160
Open all year round (for retail)
10am - 'whenever'
www.brightonkayak.co.uk
£8 per hour for kayak rental

Found under the promenade between the two piers, The Brighton Kayak Company hire out single and tandem kayaks, organise banana boat rides and parasailing. They also hire wetsuits, have full changing rooms and showers, and sell beachwear and wakeboarding gear. You can even book through these guys to do parascending and other action sports, both locally and internationally. All staff are qualified instructors.

Hove Lagoon
Western end of Hove promenade
(01273) 424842
www.hovelagoon.co.uk

Windsurfing, sailing, yachting and power-boating start at around £40 with an instructor for a two-hour lesson. Check the Hove lagoon website for more details.

Imaginary conversation between father and son Edible Crab:

Son?

Yes dad?

Sit down son, there's something I'd like to tell you.

Yes, dad?

You know how all these years your mother and I told you that 'edible' meant found under big stones…

ROCKPOOLING

Past the Marina on the way to Rottingdean there are some fabulous rock-pools where you can find edible spider and shore crabs, sea anemones, little fish and the occasional beached giant squid. If you're in the car drive to Rottingdean (just follow the coastal road heading towards Eastbourne), head to the seafront and turn right. From the Palace Pier it'll take 10 minutes to cycle and 30 minutes to walk.

Dolphin Spotting
Contact Stephen Savage
0777 3610036 (the dolphin hotline)

There has been an increase in the sightings of dolphins along the coast, in particular Bottlenose dolphins. I must stress that to spot one is rare but the best time to see them is high tide between May and September. Between the two piers and around the Marina are your best viewing spots.

If you do see one, phone this chap above and make him very happy; he's currently tracking all dolphin and whale activity along the South coast.

THE 'SURFERS AGAINST SEWAGE' CAMPAIGN FOR CLEAN SEAWATER IN BRIGHTON

The national environmental group 'Surfers Against Sewage' have had a strong local campaign in Brighton for over 7 years. They are calling for full treatment for the 95 million litres of sewage that is discharged untreated into the sea off of Brighton. That's 80 Olympic sized swimming pools of raw sewage every 24 hours!

A few facts about the quality of Brighton seawater:

• Brighton is one of the only major coastal resorts in the UK without full sewage treatment.

• The discharge in Brighton is currently in breach of European legislation.

• Inadequately treated sewage contains millions of viruses and bacteria, which can survive for days and days in seawater – swallowing one of these pathogens can cause illnesses from gastro-enteritis through to Hepatitis A and E.coli 0157.

• The most cost-effective, long term and safe sewage solution for Brighton is full treatment – UV (Ultra Violet) disinfection. It is tried and tested, economically viable, and used successfully by water companies across the UK.

• The quality of Brighton seawater is better on a sunny day when the sun's UV destroys many of the bacteria in the water.

If you would like to get involved in the local campaign to encourage Southern Water to provide UV treatment for Brighton's seawater, visit the Hemp shop in Gardner Street (North Laine) and pick up a letter to send to Southern Water MD Stuart Derwent. Or visit www.sas.org.uk

Many thanks to Richard Gregory for penning this article, and supplying the photographs on pages 10, and 67.

SURFING IN BRIGHTON

By shaggy, blond haired, Hawaiin shirt-wearing Marcus O'Dair

Despite the fundamental role that the sea plays in Brighton's identity, many people live here for decades without so much as dipping their toes in the water. The brave few who do manage a brief, ankle-deep paddle (and the wincing hobble across the pebbles that sandwiches such an experience) generally report back that it is, and I quote, "bloody freezing". When you combine the arctic water temperature with the numerous horror stories about the lovely things that float in the water, you might guess that Brighton's surfing community would be close to non-existent.

There is also, of course, the fact that most of the time there isn't a wave in sight. Brighton being Brighton, however, little things like this just don't put people off. In fact,

people have been surfing here since the mid-sixties, with some from that era still regularly in the water today. The surf community has been slowly growing over those forty years, and there are now perhaps 250 or 300 regular surfers, with a larger number who go in less often. Three main surf shops (Filf, Small Planet and Ocean Sports) support this thriving scene.

"But there aren't any waves!" you cry. Well, it's true that we don't have anything to make the Aussies envious. Most of the time the waves are no more than knee-to-waist high, although you do occasionally get head-high and above. There is also a problem with shape which, without wishing to get too technical, is due to the fact that our waves tend to be generated by windswell rather than groundswell, making them too choppy.

Whatever problems there may be with size and shape, however, surfable waves do occur with reasonable frequency. It's simply a case of studying the weather charts and knowing the right spots. The most important thing is not to be too fussy – if you wait for the perfect wave you'll be here a very long time. The most dedicated surfers manage an impressive average of three or four sessions a week during the winter months.

Er, winter months? That's right... while surfing here during the summer would fit in rather nicely with our reputation as the English San Francisco, it's sod's law that the best waves are usually between October and March. To keep warm, surfers rely on 5-mm-thick wetsuits, neoprene booties, gloves, and balaclavas, not to mention that self-warming device known to non-wetsuit-wearers as pissing yourself.

So forget about tanned surf dudes dressed only in boardshorts hanging round on the beach with bikini-clad surf chicks and ice-cold beers. You'll be shivering your arse off and struggling out of head-to-toe tight black rubber which, let's face it, is about as unsexy as it gets... to most of us, at any rate.

In a nutshell then, the waves are infrequent, small, and messy, the sea is dirty, and the temperatures would send an Eskimo running for extra thermal undies. As the title of a recent film about the Brighton surf scene said, it's Not California.

But Brighton surfers, many of whom have surfed all over the world, are passionate about the local breaks.

Yes, the waves are usually small, but they're good enough for several competition-winning Brighton surfers who are out there every chance they get. Yes it's cold, but people surf in the Outer Hebrides, in Sweden, even in Alaska (the boundary between surfing and masochism being decidedly blurred). And, yes, it's dirty – but hey, what do you expect in Brighton? See you in the line-up.

The main spots

The two main local breaks are the Hot Pipes and the Marina. The Hot Pipes, near Shoreham Power Station, has a friendly atmosphere and, for once in Brighton, easy parking. This fairly gentle beachbreak is a good spot for beginners.

The Marina, on the other hand, is ridden mainly by shortboarders. It's a fairly fast wave breaking over a shallow chalk and flint reef, and suitable for more experienced surfers only. It used to have a reputation as a fairly heavy locals spot, and it's still a good idea to show a bit of respect for the regulars.

Other spots include the West Pier (especially on a groundswell), the Wedge (primarily a bodyboarding break) and Shoreham harbour. Outside Brighton, check out Littlehampton and Eastbourne and, further afield, East and West Whittering and Camber Sands.

Surfing in Brighton?

Visit Richard Gregory's site *www.notcalifornia.co.uk* and download movies to see for yourself – it's not just extreme sport, this is art!

notcalifornia
this is surfing in brighton

SOUR ?

MISANTHROPIC?

TOUCHED BY THE UGLY STICK?

DO YOU HATE PEOPLE AND PEOPLE HATE YOU?

NOW'S YOUR CHANCE TO WREAK REVENGE ON THE WORLD, BY BECOMING A BRIGHTON TRAFFFIC WARDEN!

FEEL POWERFUL IN A UNIFORM!

BRING MISERY TO THE LIVES OF OTHERS! EVERY DAY!!

VICTIMISE PILLARS OF THE LOCAL COMMUNITY AS YOU SLAP TICKETS WILLY-NILLY ON BUILDERS' VANS, HEARSES, AMBULANCES, FIRE-ENGINES, AND ALL THE VEHICLES OF THE POOR FOOLS WHO PAID £1000 FOR A RESIDENT PARKING PERMIT BUT STILL CAN'T FIND ANYWHERE TO PARK!!!!!!

LAUGH MANIACALLY AT THE INJUSTICE OF IT ALL AS THE SCUMBAG COUNCILLORS, WHO DREAMT UP THE SCHEME, DRIVE BACK TO THEIR £500,000 HOMES AND PRIVATE GARAGES!!!!

SCREAM DEMONICALLY AS YOU DRINK THE BLOOD OF A FRESHLY CULLED NAKED VIRGIN AND INVOKE BEELZEBUB TO COME TAKE YOUR SOUL AND TRANSFORM YOU INTO A CREATURE OF THE NIGHT!!!!!

APPLICANTS WITH A CONSCIENCE NEED NOT APPLY

Shopping

Brighton can be a shopaholic's paradise, especially if you're a lover of antiques, fashion, jewellery, music, kitsch, glamour-wear and Retro clothing. And with over 700 independent shops in the centre alone, it boasts more per square mile than anywhere else in the UK. The most colourful areas with the best shops are definitely North Laine, Kemptown and the Old Lanes. For the less adventurous, Western Road and the Churchill Square Shopping Centre have everything that you'd expect to find in a high street.

The North Laine area is terrific, not only for its wide selection of Sixties/Seventies clothes and record shops but also for its unique offerings like the Seventies glam of Revamp, the Gothic weirdness of Arkham or the stylish wares found at Pussy. Get into the mood here and you'll find yourself going home with a 'Living Dead' doll, a Mod suit, a tie-dye candle and a pair of fetish shoes. And you only popped out for a loaf of bread. Kemptown too has an eclectic mix of shops, ranging from grubby but well-stocked second-hand places to gay clothes stores and poodle parlours, and the Old Lanes – though a lot less flamboyant and 'straighter' than North Laine – are renowned for jewellery, antiques, cafes and new clothes shops. Think of it this way; if North Laine was Eric Morcambe, the Old Lanes would be Ernie Wise. (With Kemptown as special guest Lilly Savage.)

And finally, before you rush off with your credit cards, don't get up too early! Shops here can open notoriously late (especially in North Laine) and not always at the same time every morning. So, do yourself a favour, have a long night out and get up at the same time as nearly everyone else here; around 11am.

RECORD SHOPS

Unless your idea of a good record shop is Woolworths, you owe it to yourself to buy a few cool and strange records while you're here. For a town its size, the choice in Brighton is superb, and many friends' bank accounts have come a cropper as a result. The North Laine area is a good starting point for second-hand and unusual vinyl/CDs at place like Borderline, Wax Factor and Edgeworld, while Essential Records in the Old Lanes is ideal for cheap, re-issued CDs.

Borderline

41 Gardener Street
Open Mon-Sat 10am-5.30pm,
Sun 12noon-4pm

Borderline has consistently stocked an amazing range of music ever since it opened, many years ago. The shop may be small, but by avoiding chart music and the obvious mainstream fodder, their stock is a carefully selected and extensive range of re-issued Jazz, Soul, Psychedelia, Exotica, Soundtrack, Electronica, Post-Rock and Indie. Most is on CD but there is a smaller selection on vinyl. If you can find a bad record here I'll change my name to Barbara.

Charlie's Orbit

95 St George's Road Kemptown
(01273) 571010
Open Tues-Sat 10.30am-6pm, Thurs 'til 7pm

Nestling in some improbable No Man's Land between The Wire magazine and a charity shop, Charlie's Orbit is a fantastic second-hand CD and vinyl shop on the outer limits of Kemptown, run by a man with a shock of curly hair that would put Tom Baker to shame. Having moved to Brighton from Scotland, and with an incurable passion for buying records, Charlie (or, rather, his girlfriend) decided the only solution was to open a record shop and the rest, of course, is history. You'll find Abba and the Carpenters sandwiched between weird Electronica, Post Rock gods and even old Shimmy Disc records, all of which show Charlie's rather eclectic tastes.

If you're a vinyl junkie, or simply looking for some rare gems, this is really worth making the trek into Kemptown for. You'll be made to feel welcome, and no doubt go home with a much sought-after bargain.

BPM Music

4 Bartholomew's (01273) 747400
Open Mon-Sat 11am-6pm, Sun 12pm-5pm

Dance Music specialists. I won't go on about the place as, the truth is, I know less than my dad does about this stuff.

Edgeworld

Upstairs above Re-Load, 6 Kensington Gardens (01273) 628262
Open Mon-Sat 10.30am-6pm,
Sun 12pm-4pm

Easy to miss, which would be a real shame, especially for anyone with a passion for small independent labels, or with tastes that lean towards Wire Magazine, Radio 3's 'Mixing It', or 'Careless Talk Costs Lives'. You'll find Lo-Fi, Mellow-Country, Post-Rock and Electronica here, and offerings from labels such as Pickled Egg and Domino. There's also a fair selection of CDs, though the stock doesn't seem to change that often. If you want to hear some of the stuff, there's a tiny listening area in the corner for vinyl, or simply ask the friendly (and refreshingly unpretentious) staff, Colin and Dave, to play whatever you fancy. Edgeworld is also a good spot for finding out about some of the more low-key gigs in Brighton. They'll even stock your own

CDs as well, if properly packaged. Mine's been sitting there for years.

Essential Music

15-16 Brighton Square (01273) 202695
Open Mon-Sat 10am-6pm, Sun 12noon-5pm

I buy a lot of CDs here, partly because the majority of the stock is under £7 and also because the selection is so varied. They've got a fine selection of re-issued Jazz, Soundtrack, Easy Listening, Sixties pop and Dance/Trance, while latest releases tend to be less than £11. You'd be hard-pushed to find better CD bargains anywhere else in Brighton, even from most of the second-hand places. Listening facilities are also available here, so why not come on a quiet afternoon and indulge in all those classic old albums you've always wanted to hear?

The Punker Bunker

Sydney Street, below Immediate Clothing
punkerbunker@aol.com
Opening times 11am-6pm Mon-Sun (but *'you can knock a couple of hours off either side, owing to the fat bloke upstairs'* according to its owner)

Located underneath Immediate Clothing, and run by local legend and 'Just One Life' promoter Buz, this tiny basement shop caters for anyone with a passion for Ska, Punk, Two-Tone and underground Punk Rock. Hanging onto those old Punk Rock ethics, its owner Buz is an eager promoter of live, noisy music in Brighton, sells all his CDs for a tenner or less, describes the Fish

the punker bunker
34 sydney street, brighton, bn1 4ep

Brothers as 'beautiful people' and discourages Nu-Metallers from visiting his shop. 'There are certain records I can put on to scare off the Nu-Metal kids,' he comments wryly.

You can also buy tickets for all Punk related gigs down here, buy yourself a badge that says 'Fuck Off', find adverts for local bands and learn all about the scene from Buz. Long many he reign.

The Record Album

8 Terminus Road (01273) 323853
Open Mon-Sat 11am-5pm
www.btinternet.com/~george.therecordalbum

Up the hill, just round the corner from Brighton Station, lies the Record Album; the oldest record shop in the country and a must for collectors of rare vinyl.

The shop specialises in all types of deleted recordings and rare one-offs, especially soundtrack albums, most of which are new or in mint condition, and the records that owner George sticks up in his shop window invariably reflect whatever movies are being shown on terrestrial TV that week. Don't expect to find a bargain; prices start around £10 and go up to £75 or more for that ultra-rare electronic 50s sci-fi B-movie soundtrack. George also supplies records to the BBC, theatre and radio and has an extensive mail order service. When asked by Mojo magazine why he doesn't stock CDs, George just shuddered and said – 'uh, those ghastly little frisbees'.

Recordland

40 Trafalgar Street
(01273) 672512 www.record-land.co.uk
Open Tues-Sun 11am-4.30pm
Sometimes closed for lunch 1.30pm-2.30pm

Now over 20 years old, Recordland is still going strong owing to its reputation for stocking an expansive range of CDs and vinyl from the 50s to 70s, with special emphasis on Jazz, Big Band, Easy Listening and Soundtracks.

It's owner Geoff is a friendly soul, and was once nice enough to play me a whole selection of Jazz records one afternoon when I couldn't decide what I wanted.

Don't forget to have a look upstairs too – there's a huge selection of old comedy records, from Woody Allen to Bernard Cribbins, tucked away underneath the central aisle.

Rounder Records

19 Brighton Square (01273) 325440
Open Mon-Sat 9.30am-6pm,
Sunday 10.30am-6pm

A first class record shop, offering discount CDs, a 50-50 split of Dance and Indie and the cheapest vinyl in town. And with Dave from the Gilded Palace of Sin and Detournmenet DJ Steve working here, these are staff whose discerning tastes you can trust. Rounder is also **the** place to come for tickets to local gigs, and, if you subscribe to their 'weekly' e-mailout, not only will you be treated to the acerbic wit of Steve Sexton, but you'll also be kept up to date on the best gigs in town.

Finally, remember to look out for the constantly changing graffiti round the back of the shop. It's all the handiwork of Warp/ Skint musician Req.

Wax Factor

Trafalgar Street (01273) 673744
Open Mon-Sat 10.15am-5.30pm

(See Bookshop reviews for more detail)

BIG GUYS

Borders

Churchill Square Shopping Centre,
Western Road (01273) 731122
Open Mon-Sat 9am-9pm, Sun 10.30am-5pm
www.borders.com

When all the rest of us are dragging ourselves out of bed, making strong coffee, lighting cigarettes and smearing marmite on the cat, these guys are up and open. Didn't anyone tell them that in Brighton no one even thinks about getting *out of bed* before 10am, never mind shopping? Still, that's crazy Americans for you*. They do, however, keep a fine array of books and CDs, have a small café upstairs, and stock the widest selection of magazines and spoken word tapes in town. This is also a good place for seeing small music performances and book readings – keep a look out for their monthly fliers for details.

Waterstones

71-74 North Street (01273) 206017
Open 9am-7pm Mon-Fri, Sat 10am-6pm,
Sun 11am-5pm
www.waterstones.co.uk

The Brighton branch of Waterstones has always felt more like a friendly local bookstore than a chain, and owes much of its success and popularity to its lovely manager Annie, who works hard to ensure that the stock here, as far as possible, reflects the true spirit

of the town. Many of the staff, too, seem to have their finger on the pulse of what Brighton readers are looking for, demonstrating that, with a little care and passion, a chain-store can still have a heart.

Sussex Stationers

37 London Rd, 114 St James' St, 55-56 East
Street, 55 Western Rd (01273) 204700
Open Mon-Sat 9am-5.30pm,
Sun 10am-5.30pm

Stocking the most popular books of the moment and somehow managing to offer them at an unbeatable discount.

LITTLE GUYS

Brighton Books

18 Kensington Gardens
(01273) 693845
Open 10am-6pm Mon-Sat,
occasionally open Sundays

A large selection of rare and unusual second-hand hardbacks (£90 for the collected works of Madame Blavatsky) and cheaper paperbacks (that usually sit in boxes at the front of the shop). Brighton Books is also home to some eccentric characters; there's Simeon (the last of the famous Brighton shop cats), a friendly black Tom who will greet you at the counter and rub himself against your chest to entice you into making a purchase and – on some days – local legend and king of

*Saying all that, I've just noticed Waterstones
open at 9am too...

charity shopping, Mr Stephen Drennan. Stephen's 'Little Book of Charity Shopping' can still be purchased from the till here, along with its sequel and a selection of his lo-fi comics. If he's wearing a badge, playing a bizarre record and sporting a black rollneck, you can rest assured that all is well in the universe.

City Books

23 Western Rd (01273) 725306
Open Mon-Sat 9.30am-6pm,
Sun 10.30am-5pm

Established now for 18 years, this is Brighton's biggest independent bookshop and favourite haunt of Nigel Richardson (author of Breakfast in Brighton). A proper local bookshop, it's the kind of place you find yourself leaving after an hour because you fell into a conversation with the owner about the merits of having Chris Eubank made into sandwiches. Having been accidentally missed out in our first edition of the Cheeky Guide to Brighton, they taunted us by hiding our books underneath unsold copies of the 1985 Michelin Guide to Yugoslavia. Despite this, I still urge you to give

them your support and just hope that one day they'll find it in their hearts to forgive us…

Colin Page

36 Duke Street (01273) 325954
Open 9am-5.30pm Mon-Sat

This former 19th century baker's is officially Brighton's oldest bookshop with all the trappings of the dusty, antiquated kind once frequented by JRR Hartley, complete with spiral staircase at the back. Set up in 1975 by John Laska and his twin brother Stephen, the shop specialises in antiquated and rare books, but, for the general buyer, always has a box of interesting paperbacks outside and a basement of hardback fiction and factual books ranging from history to the occult. It's also a popular haunt when the luvvies are in town. The likes of Stephen Fry and Simon Callow are old regulars, as are old-school politicians like Dennis Healey ('the ones who still read' quipped Stephen). A treat for the serious book collector.

Practical Books

14/14a Western Road (01273) 734602
(See Mind, Body, Spirit)

Two Way Books

54 Gardner Street
(01273) 687729

Frozen in time since 1982, this singular bookshop must be the only place in England still selling Paul Young and Van Halen annuals. If pictures of David Lee Roth in spandex pants aren't your bag, they also do a nifty selection of old comics ranging from Dr Who to Tractor Weekly. Mix that with more bizarre stuff like shelves of Mills and Boon, Giles compilations and several discreet piles of porn and you'll probably wonder how they make a living. Barbara Cartland or back issues of Razzle anyone?

West Pier Books

Underneath the West Pier (or what's left
of it) Open Fri-Sun

At weekends, when the weather is
good, you'll find these guys down on the
seafront. Run alternatively by local
filmmaker Mark Keeble and 'Polak' Pete,
West Pier Books hold a good collection
of second-hand paperbacks with a slant
towards cult fiction. Brighton's answer to
Steed from the Avengers, Mark can be
spotted at country fairs or whizzing
around Brighton in his red MG, sipping
champagne and blasting out Easy
Listening music. I really should get round
to including him in the Eccentrics
chapter one of these days…

Wax Factor

Trafalgar Street (01273) 673744
Open Mon-Sat 10.15am-5.30pm

If second-hand books on the occult,
drugs, philosophy, Sci-Fi, Eastern
mysticism and music are your bag then
this is the place for you. The window
display alone should be enough to pull
you in as you drool over all the
Crowley, Philip K Dick and Burroughs
books. They have a pretty good
selection of fiction here too, which is
just on your right as you enter. If that's
not enough, they stock one of the best
collections of second hand CDs and
vinyl in Brighton, with 7inches and CD
singles in the basement. Be prepared for
a good half an hour in this place; if they
haven't got what you were looking for,
you'll probably end up leaving with what
you didn't know you'd find.

David's Comic Shop

5 Sydney Street (01273) 691012
Open Mon-Sat 9.30am-5.45pm,
Sun 11am-5pm

Independent comics, graphic novels,
roll-playing figures, four shelves of
Manga and home to a Brighton legend
known simply as 'Smelly.'

GROOVY GIFTS & COOL THINGS FOR THE HOME

Blackout

53 Kensington Place
Open Mon-Sat 10am-6pm

The shop's angle is kind of fashion-folk-art mixed with kitsch religious imagery. If you're a Goth, keep away; they have a policy of selling nothing black here, colour is the order of the day (hence the name). Typical stock in the past has included a Tibetan baby carrier, fluorescent loo brushes, Virgin Mary ashtrays and plastic Hindu Gods. They also do a great selection of their own designer T-shirts and have some of the most original jewellery in town.

EM-Space

20 Sydney Street (01273) 683400
Open 10am-6pm Mon-Sat,
occasionally Sundays

Run for many years now by Kathy and Janine, EM-space specialise in design-led gifts with a slant towards cards and books, artists' sketchbooks and beautiful traditional photo albums (the ones where you add the sticky corners).

Don't miss the gallery at the back; it contains lots of very reasonably priced work from local artists, including that of resident artist Jim Sanders, whose art has taken a completely new direction since he discovered the joys of absinthe.

Fossil 2000

3 Kensington Place (01273) 622000
Open Tues-Sat 10am-5.30pm (6pm Sat),
Sun-Mon 11am-4pm
www.fossil2000.co.uk

Run by Denise, this lovely shop just off the beaten track in North Laine has an incredible collection of ammonites, trilobites, fossil plates, crystal-growing kits for kids and lots of other pre-historic relics. Denise mentioned to me that if you want something specific it's worth asking, as they can 'get their hands on most things', which made me wonder whether she had won a strip of Lyme Regis in a poker game. Prices range from a stingray's tooth for 20p to a Triceratops's horn for £1,200 or even an Amethyst Geode for £7,500! More unusual, perhaps, is their collection of flies in amber, beetles in treacle and woolly mammoths in a tar pit.

Glazed Expressions & Painting Pottery Café

31 North Road
(01273) 628952
Open Mon-Sat 10am-6pm Sun 11pm-6pm
Thurs late night, first in the month
www.paintingpotterycafe.co.uk
Prices for the ceramics start around £3 for
tiles and eggcups

Abiding by the philosophy that everyone is a painter, Glazed Expressions is a painting and pottery café where for a £5 studio fee you can try your hand at decorating plates, mugs, eggcups and tiles. They will ply you with coffee, hot chocolate and teas for as long as you want, and also glaze and fire your finished masterpieces. The late-night Thursday sessions are especially worth attending, as food is laid on and you can bring your own booze. So, men, don't be surprised if, after 14 cans of Special Brew, you wake the next morning to find 8 new eggcups sitting on your kitchen table, each crudely adorned with pictures of your own genitalia. Nonetheless, this place is also popular with families and children.

Icon

28 Gloucester Road
(01273) 698487
Open Mon-Sat 10am-6pm, Sun 11am-5pm
www.iconshop.net

Modern and Retro style furniture, funky bread bins, poufs, the Cheeky Chimp range of body products (including chocolate soap) and a cool range of artwork from Bazooka Joe Pop Art to iconic portraits by renowned local artist Dixon. There are even plans for Icon to publish their own magazine on style and interiors.

When Vogue reviewed the shop they described it as: 'Perfect for Austin Powers Wannabe!' Spot on.

Idlewild

64A Dyke Road (01273) 774401
Open 12pm-5.30pm weekdays,
10am-5.30pm Sat

This quirky gift shop in the heart of the Seven Dials stocks a colourful collection of cards, children's toys, mini piñatas, candles, mobiles, photo frames, tins of sweets and more besides. Kids with pocket money to blow can find anything from creepy crawlies (15p) to Miffy toys, while, if you're looking for an unusual gift for someone, the choices here won't break the bank.

Nilaya

38 Kensington Gardens
(01273) 697096

Jewellery and bags from Paris, boutique sellings, designer accessories and lingerie. A shrine to love, luxury and beauty. The vision of Miss Jessie Dook. No relation to Daisy Dook.

Pardon My French

104a St George's Road, Kemptown Village
(01273) 694479
Open 9.30am-5pm weekdays, 10am-5pm
Saturday www.pardonmyfrench.co.uk

Run by an eccentric French (or possibly Belgian) lady, this is a cornucopia of luxurious French items with an eccentric slant. Items include watering-can handbags, hot water bottles with boobs, plates from Provence, and enamel signs with such messages as 'Chat Genteel', or (my favourite) 'Attention! Chien Bizarre'.

Pussy Home Boutique

3a Kensington Gardens (01273) 604861
Open Mon-Sat 10(ish) -5.30pm,
Sun (in summer) 12noon-4.30pm
www.pussyhomeboutique.co.uk

Cross the sexy glamour of Betty Page with the slick design of Frank Lloyd Wright and the cool sounds of Stereolab, and you're beginning to get an idea of Pussy. Often imitated in Brighton but never equalled, this stylish and saucy boutique boasts a wonderful selection of cool furniture, chic and erotic books (such as the very popular 'Big Book of Lesbian Horse Stories'), jewellery, exclusive Paul Frank monkey stuff, and T-shirts. And their range of offensive cards, one of which includes the caption *'Jesus Loves Everyone. Except for You, You Cunt,'* are as popular as ever. Run by Nicki and her faithful sidekicks (including the ever-welcoming Jamie), the gang seem to spend most of the day nattering with half of Brighton over a cup of tea and a fag, yet still manage, unfailingly, to have the best window displays in town. Nicki also has a great talent for predicting trends. Spot something unique in Pussy, and, chances are, you'll see it in next month's issue of Vogue.

STOP PRESS
BIG NEW PUSSY HOME
BOUTIQUE OPENS UP
IN THE OLD LANES!
3 Bartholomews
(01273) 749852

Rin*Tin*Tin

34 North Road (01273) 672424
Open 11am-5.30pm Mon-Sat

A fascinating collection of memorabilia from the Thirties to the Sixties. Stock includes old comics, barbers' chairs, Felix the cat toys, old Brighton postcards, radios and original old adverts.

Silverado

3 Kensington Gardens &
30 Meeting House Lane
(01273) 326756
Open 10am-5.30pm Mon-Sat

Owned by the former keyboard player from Men at Work, Andrew Bird, Silverado offers beautiful and stylish silver jewellery, including rings, pendants and earrings. Look out for Andrew in his cork hat, wandering the Lanes whistling 'Down Under' with a nostalgic look in his eyes.

Tickled

(See Sex, Fetish and Body Modification Chapter)

Wallis Macfarlane

14 St George's Road Kemptown
(01273) 297088
Open Mon-Sat 10am-6pm

Now in its sixth year, this gift shop, deep in Kemptown, sells a variety of exquisite and unusual gifts, including a wide range of aromatherapy oils, soaps of the world (scented with everything from coffee to prawn cocktail), and original pots and cushions by local artists. Describing Kemptown as a cross between Coronation Street and the Left Bank, it's two owners Jonathan and Roland are firm believers in strengthening the Kemptown community and it'll warm the cockles of your heart to see the genuine friendship they have with many of the shopkeepers in the area.

Unhappy teachers take note, they both gave it up several years ago and seem utterly content.

"The only paperwork I do any more," said one of them gleefully, whilst wrapping a bar of chocolate soap.

Yasher Bish

98 Gloucester Road
Open Mon-Sat 10.30am-5.30pm

Specialists in all things Turkish, from ornate backgammon sets, prayer rugs (£15) and goat-herders' bells to a wide range of colourful and very beautiful rugs. Upstairs is packed with original old Anatolian pots, some over 100 years old, but still with that faint but lingering smell of olive oil. And, back by popular demand – the kitsch classic Mosque alarm clocks for only £12!

The Workshop Pottery

94 Trafalgar Street
Open Tues-Sat 9.30am-5.30pm
www.workshoppottery.co.uk

Run by Peter Stocker, this shop has been in the North Laine an incredible 24 years, even surviving a busload of Crusties crashing through its window in 1994.

Peter still remembers the days when North Laine was an area that just sold stuff like work boots and maids outfits, while scruffy urchins would roam the streets shouting – *'Coo! Ta mister,'* when you threw them a tangerine.

Of course, nowadays, the boots are a fashion statement, the maids' outfits are sold for kinky purposes, and the scruffy urchins all now play in local band Cheetah. But I digress. The shop sells modestly priced and beautiful earthenware ceramics, all made on the premises, ranging from bowls and plates to more creative figurines and one-off vases.

SPECIALIST CLOTHES AND SHOE SHOPS

From safari suits for him to rubber cat-suits for her, Brighton boasts a meaty collection of retro, exotic and club-fashion clothes shops. Most are located in North Laine, so, if you want to get kitted out in something especially slinky for a club night or just want something new for the wardrobe, here's a selection of places to go.

Ghita Schuy

17 Street George's Road (01273) 885275
Open Mon-Fri 12-5pm, Sat 12-6pm

Hand-made shoes, made to order, from classic styles to the more extravagant.

One customer recently had a pair of shoes especially made for a party in Paris he was to attend, in honour of the fact that his friend there had recently purchased one of the original 'Ruby Slippers' from the Wizard of Oz. That's doing it in style!
Sandals start at £50, shoes from £250.

Jump The Gun

36 Gardner Street (01273) 626777
Open Mon-Sat 10am-6pm
www.jumpthegun.co.uk

The UK's **only** exclusive Mod shop, 'Jump the Gun' has been established in Brighton for over ten years now, and is almost as synonymous with the city as the Pavilion, clubbing, Chris Eubank and arson. This well-loved shop boasts a handsome collection of suits, shirts, parkas, Dr Marten's and coats for the dapper gentlemen, all at very reasonable prices (Parkas start at £55, shirts £40, suits around £200). The shop's two owners are brothers Adam and Jonathan, who still live and breathe the Mod life – arriving to work on Lambrettas, always dressing smartly, and nipping up Little East Street every lunch-time for a bit of 'How's your father'. OK, I made up the last bit, but suffice to say, they're the genuine articles, and are still passionate about what they sell. Even if you're not in the least bit interested in Mod fashion, but enjoy dressing well, I'd urge you to drop by here. Jump the Gun is as much about proper tailoring, quality garments, good treatment and looking sharp, as it is about Mod culture. Or, as Adam puts it,

"We want our customers to go away looking like a cross between John Steed and Sean Connery. But be warned; if you drink too much, you won't fit into these clothes!"

M-Store

37 West Street (01273) 323505
Open Mon-Sat 10am-6pm
Sun 11am-5pm

Fashion items with a surf and skateboarding slant from the likes of Mooks, Insight, Paul Frank and Parka rock, all at painfully hip prices.

Route One

3 Bond Street (01273) 323633
Open Mon-Sat 9.30am-6pm,
Sun 11am-5pm

The guys in here are friendly, sell skating clothes of the jeans-hanging-off-your-arse variety and have a decent selection of boards, wheels, trucks etc. They are also pretty knowledgeable on what the current scene is like and can tell you some of the better places to skate in Brighton.

Simultane Ltd

37 Trafalgar St (01273) 818061
info@simultane.co.uk www.simultane.co.uk
Open 11am-6pm Mon-Fri, 10am-6pm Sat,
12pm-4pm Sun

This Brighton-based fashion label have their own boutique in North Laine where – alongside their own collection – they sell previously unavailable labels like Ann Louise Roswald, Lulu Guinness and LK Bennett. They also have a wide range of accessories, jewellery and home-ware as well as a gallery and exhibition space for local artists and designers. Even their website is beautifully designed, with some suitably cheeky pictures of the gang when they were toddlers.

She Said (Erotic Boutique)

13 Ship Street Gardens (between Ship
Street and Middle Street) (01273) 777822
Open 11am-7pm Mon-Sat, Sun 12pm-5.30pm

Exclusive lingerie, corsetry, designer party and club wear, and erotic accessories. (For full review see 'Sex, Fetish and Body Modification'Chapter.)

Yamama

92 Trafalgar Street (01273) 689931
Open Mon-Sat 11am-6pm,
Sun 12pm-5pm

Colourful range of interesting and fair-priced clothing with an urban hippy slant. They sell great baggy trousers, hemp-style clothing, shirts and skirts for the bohemian traveller types, and henna tattoos.

X 2 Zee

27 Western Road
Open Mon-Sat 10am-6pm,
Sun 11.30am-5.30pm

A rather wild collection of boots and shoes adorns this shop, even if it does feel a bit 80s Goth at times. Expect anything from thigh-high boots to glittery DMs. They also do a rather odd collection of faded punk and metal band T-shirts. Where else could you still buy an Exploited T-shirt?

FATBOY SLIM'S

all-season Fashion tips

Hello! Norman 'FatboySlim' Cook here, with some top fashion tips! And I reckon I'm a bit of a style guru, because once we were watching 'What Not To Wear' and Zoë said: "You should be on this programme, Norman," so she obviously reckons I'd make a better presenter than them! So, without further ado, here's Norm's guide how to look and feel good, whatever the weather.

Summer

Summers in Brighton always remind me of being a kid. You know – deck chairs, buckets n' spades, weeing in the sea. Nowadays I spend my summers idling on the beach, pottering around the house listening to records, or even making my own by cobbling together a few R'n'B samples with a drum loop! No, really! It's as easy as that!!!

And what could be more ideal for those long hot, sticky months than to slip into a cool, thin, colourful, 100% cotton Hawaiian shirt? They're comfortable, stylish, eye-catching, and make you look like a real 'Funk Soul Brother.'

Autumn

Now a lot of people see this time of year as an excuse to sport chunky knitwear and such autumnal colours as burnt oranges, dark browns and reds. This is a terrible mistake! You wouldn't catch me going out in a snowstorm dressed all in white!!! Take a tip from me – dare to be different! Why not go for something colourful, and striking? Like a Hawaiian shirt, say! And, when everyone else is turning up to those Halloween parties in black (yawn!), you'll steal the show with a dazzle of colour on your back!!!

Winter

Like many people I tend to suffer from the winter blues, especially during the long months from January to March. If I look out of my bedroom window in the morning and it's cold, miserable and grey outside, my spirits start to flag and, before I know it, I'm comatose in front of the box with a jazz mag in one hand and a joint in the other, watching Kilroy talking to middle-aged housewives about teenage pregnancy. God, do I get depressed!! Until, that is, I remember my faithful Hawaiian shirt! Once I've whipped off my jim-jams and got that cool cotton and splash of colours on my back it feels like a little bit of sunshine has returned, leaving me with a rosy complexion and a chance again to face the world with a smile. I recommend you do the same. Magic!

Spring

Now during the 'rainy season', a lot of people favour waterproof coats with hoods. This is a terrible mistake. And can be extremely dangerous! Did you know that wearing a hood can reduce visibility by up to 37%?!! If, for example, you were crossing the busy A27 between Worthing and Shoreham, your so-called 'sensible' hooded raincoat might shield you from the wet, but would offer precious little protection when you failed to notice the 30-tonne Juggernaught hurtling towards you, smashing into you at a hundred and twenty miles an hour and crushing your head like an over-ripe melon.

So don't be silly – be safe!! Make yourself visible when crossing the road. Why not go out just wearing something brightly-coloured – something like, say, just for the sake of argument.....a Hawaiian shirt?!! Sure you might get soaked, catch a cold, or worse, pneumonia, but at least you'll be safe.

*Right – I'm off now;
I've got until tomorrow to write
a new album. Not a problem!!!
Praise you!!!!!
Norm xxx*

SECOND-HAND & RETRO CLOTHES

Circe's Island

22 Trafalgar Street

Decorated with plastic birds, palm trees and fishing netting hanging from the ceiling, Circe's Island sells second hand quality clothes, shoes and err…fireplaces. Most of the stuff is for women, and rather than being the usual collection of Retro denim jackets and Hawaiian shirts that clutter half the shops in North Laine, the preference here is for the exotic and glamorous. If it's made of feather, fake fur, sequins, satin or leather, they've got it here. And fireplaces.

Glamour Chase

St James St

Quality vintage clothes and accessories, ranging from the Thirties to the Sixties. They've got shoes, sunglasses, suits, hats (boaters and Trilbies), feather boas and handbags. The stock seems carefully selected and, as with Circe's Island, veers more towards the exotic than the usual Retro pop look.

Rokit

23 Kensington Gardens (01273) 672053
Open Mon-Sat 10am-6pm, Sun 11-5pm

For lovers of mutton-chops, Levi jeans and the MC5. This long-established retro clothes shop has always been a bit on the pricey side, but does stock a good selection of quality second hand gear, from jeans and cords to Hawaiian and Cuban shirts, from flares to track wear.

To Be Worn Again

51 Providence Place (01273) 624500 &
Sydney Street (01273) 680296
Open 11am-7pm Mon-Sat, 12am-4pm Sun

Hidden away just off Trafalgar Street opposite St. Bartholomew's church, this is the biggest second-hand clothing warehouse in Brighton. The stock comprises the usual 70s shirts, leather and suede jackets and paisley dresses, but, as there's more of everything, you're more likely to find something suitable for a night at Dynamite Boogaloo. Don't miss the backroom with a great selection of coats, including three-quarter and full length fake furs. The shop on Sydney Street also sells trainers, bags and retro furniture upstairs.

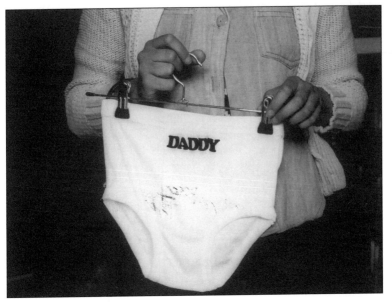

Yellow Submarine

12 Kensington Gardens (01273) 626435

Another terrific stockist of Retro gear ranging from the fifties to the Seventies, with the emphasis on old labels such as Lonsdale and Gola. They also do a neat line in leather jackets, pony vests, mittens, earmuffs and pin-stripe velvet suits (for about £75), and have a permanent sale on upstairs. The people who work here are an amicable bunch, and if you're part of the local band scene and have got a demo/ album that needs a bit of airing, bring it down; if they like it, they'll give it a good play. For lovers of fun underwear, they do a range of Y-fronts in lurid colours with slogans like 'Daddy', 'Mummy' or 'Donkey Dick' across the front. And should you be dragged here with by partner to get fed up waiting as he/she tries on yet another pair of Levis/ brown undies, you can lounge about upstairs on the cool leather chair and flick through their magazines. Watch out for Boris the spider on the stairs though!!

HIGH STREET STORES AND DESIGNER LABEL SHOPS

There are some good clothes and shoe shops around the Old Lanes for the ladies, with the likes of Nine West, Design Lab, Off-Spring and Morgan in Duke Street; Kookai, French Connection and Jigsaw on East Street; and Moist, Fat Face and Oasis in Duke's Lane.

If you're looking for the likes of Miss Selfridges, Hennes and Warehouse you'll find them up by Churchill Square, where many of the high street clothes shops for men and women are concentrated.

MUSICAL INSTRUMENT SHOPS

Adaptatrap

26 Trafalgar Street (01273) 672722
Open Mon-Sat 10am-6pm

A cut above the usual collection of ethnic instruments, this place sells a whole range of drums, koras, xylophones, singing bowls, old gongs, horns and many other exotic and strange instruments from all over the world. What's more, they don't mind you coming in and playing with them. Owner Les is helpful and will smoke an entire roll-up without taking it out of his mouth whilst offering advice on what to do if you've damaged your congas (ooh missus). The shop is littered with ads for music lessons, so, if you're sticking around Brighton and need that all-essential sitar teacher, this is the place to look. You'll also find out about workshops and gigs here, ranging from Zither recitals to Shamanic drumming weekends.

Music Exchange

2 Trafalgar Street (01273) 239356
Open Mon-Sat 10ish-5.30pm

Cheap and cheerful selection of second-hand guitars, amps and effects.

The Guitar, Amp and Keyboard Centre

79-80 North Road (01273) 672977
Open Mon-Sat 9.30am-5.30pm,
Sun 11am-4pm
www.gak.co.uk

Created from the barrow-boy charm of its haggle-friendly owner Gary, who turned up in Brighton ten years ago with just a broken banjo and the gift of the gab, and slowly built an empire. The shop now has everything you could possibly need in terms of acoustic and electronic instruments and equipment, and, despite not having any competition worth speaking of, still offers some terrific deals.

Will accept body parts as down-payment.

Acme Art

93 Gloucester Road (01273) 601639
Best to phone for opening times as they
seem erratic at the best of times
www.acmeart.biz

The world would be a duller place if
there weren't people like Chris
MacDonald. This ex-teacher found
happiness making strange sculptures
from original wood and metal objects
and has been established in Brighton
for umpteen years now.

There's something very cartoonish
and surreal about his work; it's the kind
of art you'd expect to find in Terry
Gilliam's house. The sculptures make
perfect unusual birthday presents, but
don't be surprised if they end up sitting
on your mantelpiece instead.

ChoccyWoccyDooDah

27 Middle Street (01273) 329462
Open Mon-Fri 10am-6pm
Sat 12pm-4pm, Sun 10am-5pm
www.choccywoccydoodah.co.uk

You'll forgive the ludicrous name the
second you walk in here and take in
that sweet smell of Belgian chocolate.
The display area is like a Doctor's
waiting room full of the most
outrageous, over-the-top chocolate
cakes you've ever seen. I've seen spiky
fetish cakes, ones covered in realistic
looking vegetables (including carrots
and cabbage!?), ones with willies and
more besides. If you can't afford a cake
(their top-notch wedding cakes can
cost up to £1000), they do gold coins
for 2.50 and Cuban cigars for £3.50.
'Head of Creativity' Dave Pop – who is
also renowned for his kitsch songs and
live appearances at various Brighton
venues over the years – does much of
the work here. If you want to show
him your appreciation, you can actually
buy a DVD of his greatest hits.

The Lanes Armoury

26 Meeting House Lane (01273) 321357
Open Mon-Sat 10am-5.15pm
www.thelanesarmoury.co.uk

Souvenir firearms and armour from all
periods of history. Get your granny that
old Vickers submachine gun she always
wanted, or maybe a Luger for young
cousin Donald. They also have Kentucky
rifles, Zulu war shields, Napoleonic
swords and even a helmet from the
Iraqi war. A Tudor suit of armour would
set you back around £20,000, though
the less affluent can buy a cap badge
for only £3. If the Ronnie Reagan
picture isn't up then nag them to get it
back on display as there's a good story
behind it.

The Olde Rock Shop

West Pier, Kingsway, opposite Regency Sq
Open winter 9am-5pm Mon-Sun,
summer 8.30am-late Mon-Sun

Of the dozens of gift shops that litter
the seafront, this one alone deserves a
mention as the building is a period
piece, has stood on the same spot for

over 126 years and can be spotted in the many films made here from 'Carry On Girls' to 'Oh, What a Lovely War!' They sell all the typical tourist stuff from sticks of rock to snowstorms, postcards, fridge-magnets and pottery lighthouses.

Top tip – their 'Seagull Poo' chocolates make good presents for kids.

Arkham

89 Trafalgar Street (01273) 628440
Mon-Sun 11am-5pm (closed Wed)
www.arkham-darkart.co.uk

Celebrating the darker side of life, Arkham stock a curious assortment of goods, ranging from clothes, jewellery and ornaments to sculptures and books. You can expect to find such curios as gargoyle sculptures, Edward Gorey books, coffin handbags, Living Dead dolls and Industrial, Goth and Nu-Metal CDs. It's a fascinating shop, even if you don't feel part of their vision. Imagine Jules Verne meets Cyberpunk.

Taylors (Tobacconist)

19 Bond Street (01273) 606110
Open 9.30am-6pm

A 'THANK YOU FOR SMOKING' sign welcomes you as you enter, and the selection of flavoured tobacco (including chocolate) and Cuban cigars reminds me why it took 10 years to kick such a pleasurable habit. Go on, have a fag.

Paul Bruton Army Surplus

Viaduct Road
Open 10am-1pm and 2pm-4.30pm Wed-Sat

The two masked dummies that stand guard outside this shop must be one of the most famous sights in Brighton. Both creatures have posed with innumerable tourists and even appear on an album cover by some obscure Scottish band. The stock in here is immense, and you can get kitted out in just about any uniform you fancy, from the pith helmet and khaki shorts style of 'It 'Aint Half Hot Mum', to the German guards in 'Escape from Colditz'. And the dressing booth is fantastic, but you'll have to go in to find out why!

BUY YOUR OWN FUCKING LIGHTER

The Sunday Market

Behind Brighton Station
Open 6am-12pm

As much a part of Brighton as the Pavilion, a Brighton weekend is not complete without visiting the Sunday car-boot at the station. The serious bargain hunters arrive before 7am, but, if you've had a bender on Saturday night, 11am is a more realistic time and you'll still get to see it all. It's the perfect excuse for walking up an appetite for late breakfast or early Sunday lunch.

Expect to find record stalls, videos, antiques, clothes, food, weird stuff and loads and loads of crap. One of the strangest stalls is the guy selling manky limbs from Victorian dolls. He's often there, so logic dictates that there must be a regular stream of people who need them. WHO ARE YOU???

One tip – don't be afraid to haggle, and if something seems too expensive, say so. If the stall owner won't accept your generous offer of 50p for the Rolf Harris stylophone, take satisfaction in rolling your eyes, huffing, then walking off. If it was a bluff on their behalf they'll run after you and beg forgiveness.

To find the market, go into the station, head right and continue until you get to the car-park. Keep walking and it's just behind there. But don't be too surprised if one day you turn up and there's a Sainsbury's there instead. No, seriously.

A Cheeky Tale

Once at the Sunday market, I found this old tin with a goofy looking vicar sticking out the top. If you turn the handle the head moves up and down. It might have cost 15 quid, but you just don't come across stuff like this every day.

Saturday in North Laine

Upper Gardner Street
Saturdays only 10am-4pm

Nothing to get too excited about, unless your idea of a bargain is a broken cine camera for £30. But you might find a good book or a cheap shirt and, besides, it's pleasant to wander down, and can be a good alternative to being squashed in Kensington Gardens on a hot, busy Saturday afternoon.

Fruit and Veg Market

Between the Level and London Road
Open Mon 7am-1pm Tues-Thurs 7am-5pm
Fri-Sat 7am-6pm

Your cheapest option in town for fresh fruit, veg, fish and other food. There are also plenty of stalls selling things like cut-price tins, and dairy products. Perfect for students, if you're trying to live in Brighton on a tight budget, or simply hate supermarkets.

The West Pier Market
Weekends only

If you slept through the alarm at 11am for the station car-boot sale, don't fret. A leisurely stroll down to the charred remains of the West Pier after lunch will more than compensate. Here you will find an eclectic array of stalls and friendly stall-holders, flogging everything from clothes, books and sunglasses to painted eggs and Sea Monkeys (remember the creatures that used to be advertised in the back of old 1960s Marvel Comics?).

Despite council grumblings, the West Pier market reflects much more of the personality of Brighton seafront than many of the other things built here. Any old seaside resort can have a glut of cafés and clubs on its seafront, but only in Brighton will you find chancers doing head massages, magic tricks, Tarot readings, writing on grains of rice (no, really) and selling bloody Sea Monkeys. And long may they reign. Take them away, and Brighton will turn into Skegness overnight.

FLEA MARKETS

Snoopers Paradise
7-8 Kensington Gardens (01273) 602558
Open Mon-Sat 9.30am-5.15pm

Brighton's largest indoor flea market. There are two floors of stock and a particularly good collection of Sixties clothes, Retro ephemera and furniture, but be prepared to pay through the nose. Don't visit if you have a heart condition – you may find yourself saying things like '*I threw one of those away last year and they're selling it here for £200!!!!*' or '*Sixty quid......... for* **that***?????*' But those with a keen eye might still snap up a bargain or two.

Well worth a visit, if only to see the sheer size of the place, marvel at all the tat, and thank the lord that it hasn't yet been turned into a café bar.

Kemptown Flea Market
31a Upper St. James's Street
(01273) 328665 Open Mon-Sat 10am-5.30pm, Sun 10.30am-5pm

Keep going up St. James's Street and you'll find this garish, pink, two-storey building just after the road bends. Sure, there's the usual overpriced tat but you might find some really unusual objects here and, dare I say it – the odd bargain?

There isn't much in the way of clothes, but there used to be a good stock of accessories for the house, like Sixties lamps. Stock, however, seemed a bit thin on the ground last time I visited, and the window display was decidedly flaccid compared to past classics such as the skeleton in the deck chair. Is it still worth the trek from the city centre? I really don't know.

I've survived a
WEST PIER
SEAGULL POO ©
"Bombs Away"
Contains 125gms℮ Chocolate Raisins
125g℮

CAFES & CAFE-BARS

Billies (C)

34 Hampton Place (01273) 774386
Open Mon-Fri 8.30am-5pm,
Sat-Sun 9am-5pm

Just up from Waitrose – at the very top of Hampton Place – Billies has developed a cult following amongst locals, largely thanks to its legendary breakfasts and hash browns, at which it excels. So popular are the hash browns here that, according to owner Carol, *'we've had grown men cry because we've run out on a Sunday afternoon.'* Though a small café with limited seating, there's never a huge wait here (rarely more than ten minutes), even at weekends. And it's child-friendly too. I don't know how Carol does it (she must have learned the secret of Dr Who's Tardis), but, even on a Saturday, when it's crammed with prams, bikes, canoes and tractors, there's always just enough room for everyone to lean back, stretch, rub their bellies after a jumbo breakfast, and wallow in a feeling of immense satisfaction.

The Dorset Street Bar (NL)

28 North Road (01273) 605423 L
Mon-Sat 10am-11pm, Sun 10am- 8pm

A visit to Brighton really is not complete without Eggs Benedict, a coffee and a pose outside the Dorset. As well as an ideal breakfast café, this place also manages to be an excellent snack bar at lunchtime and a sociable restaurant / drinking den at night. As well as offering a range of good beers, warm drinks and food – ranging from mussels and fries to some fabulous hot meat baguettes and a delicious seafood chowder – the Dorset also has an enviable location on the corner of North Road and Gardner Street and, on warm summer afternoons, you can sit outside and marvel at the misfits and style gurus parading through North Laine. Or, if you're local, it's unlikely you'll pass an afternoon without spotting a host of familiar faces passing by to have a natter with (unless you've got no mates, that is). Finally, be on your guard for the manager Mark, (recognisable for his spiky black hair); he adds a certain madcap feel to the place and, if he likes the look of you, will belt out a few old 50s numbers while you're slurping on your drinks.

Dumb Waiter (NL)

28 Sydney Street (01273) 602526
Open Mon-Sat 9am-6pm
Sun 10am-3.30pm

Despite being caught in its own little time-bubble from the late-Eighties, this laid-back family-run café actually makes a refreshing change from the transient and overly trendy nature of North Laine. The Dumb Waiter still seems to attract a fair number of Brighton's dying breed of dreadlocked, rolly-smoking New Age community but if that's not your scene, don't be unduly put off; it's still one of the cheapest places in town for grub, and does a cracking breakfast for veggies and carnivores alike – ideal for that Sunday morning hangover cure. The rest of the menu is straightforward nosh; baked potatoes, soup, sausage sarnies and some good puddings (including treacle tart and custard). There's seating upstairs, a couple of plastic tables outside by the loos and a notice-board for house-shares, man with van types, and lost cats.

Mr Cyclops enjoys a nice cuppa at the Dorset

Kai Organic Café (NL)

52 Gardner Street
(01273) 684921
Open Mon-Sat 9am-5.15pm
www.kaicafe.co.uk

Organic (and veggie) cafes in Brighton seem to come in two varieties; the vaguely hippy, or the polished, Habitat catalogue variety. Kai is definitely the latter – a stylish, smoke-free environment with wooden furniture and soothing piped music. On the menu are such offerings as homemade pizzas, hot bacon ciabattas, a pick and mix salad bar and some tasty cakes. The best seat in the house is – as with many North Laine cafes – upstairs by the window, where you can play 'spot the loony', as you tuck into your tasty grub. They also offer a take-out service.

NB Kai is one of only 8 cafés in the UK to be certified by the Soil Association as 'authentically organic'.

Guaraná Bar (NL)

36 Sydney Street (01273) 621406
Open Mon-Sat 10am-6pm, Sun 12pm-5pm
www.goguarana.co.uk

'Europe's first Guaraná Bar!' is the motto for this unique place in North Laine, which to most people (including myself), begs the question *'yes but what **is** Guaraná?'* Well, having done my homework, and sampled the stuff, I can tell you that it's a South American 'super-charged' natural energy drink, said to put a skip in your step and hairs on your chest. And very refreshing it is too. It is, however, just one of the **many** unusual and natural stimulating drinks and herbs on offer here. The closest comparison I can think of for this place are the Smart Bars of Amsterdam, for, along with serving wheatgrass, coffees and other freshly-made brews, they stock an incredible range of smoking paraphernalia (grinders, pipes, scales etc), American Spirit cigarettes, herbal highs (Druid's Fantasy, Bliss Xtra), nutritional supplements, mild hallucinogenics (legal of course), and aphrodisiacs.

Ideal for those in search of a healthy pick-me-up or 'mind-expanding' experience, without the usual teeth-grinding, bad trips and lousy comedowns. And yes, it does attract the odd Sydney Street nutter.

Frank-in-Steine (C)

By the fountain in the Old Steine, at Grand Parade (01273) 674742

Open 8am-8pm summer, 9am-5pm winter

Well, if your name's Frank, and you're opening up a café in a converted toilet in the Old Steine, what else could you call it – 'Some flushers do have 'em'? Not only have they got the Frankenstein motif everywhere, from the napkins to the mosaics and old movie posters on the walls, but go downstairs and you'll find a ghost train style cage with a life-size Frankenstein's Monster inside. Press the large white button and……..well, I'll not give it away, but if it does cause you to soil yourself, you'll be pleased to know the loos are close by. (Though the spider's web toilet seats might also cause undue distress to those of a nervous disposition.)

Along with Frankie, the two other café mascots are Patsy and Clarence, who can be found in the fishbowl to the left of the counter. No, they're not fish, but actually strange looking orange frogs whom, for eight years, the owners presumed female. That was until the spring of 2003, when tiny transparent tadpoles started appearing in the bowl. If you've got kids who can promise a good home to a cuddly tadpole or two, Frank, or his partner Tracey, will happily stick a few in a bag for you (the tadpoles, not your kids). Staying on the theme of kids, Frank-in-Steine is very child friendly; they even go to the bother of putting out boxes of toys and bikes on the grass for kids to play with, leaving you to relax, stuff your face, and have a crafty cigarette. Renowned for its chunky toasted sandwiches, which come in a variety of fillings (soon to include frogs legs), Frank-in-Steine also serves cold sarnies and wraps, Danishes and rolls for breakfast, coffee and juice, and even wheel out the ice-cream machine in summer.

With the exception of the Pavilion Gardens, I can't think of another café in town that comes close to capturing that lovely feeling of sitting in a park far, far away from Brighton's smelly buses, busy streets, and ugly traffic wardens.

Mad Hatter (C)

35 Montpelier Road (01273) 722279 L
Open 8am-8pm Mon-Sat, 10am-6pm Sun
(11pm alternate Sundays)
www.themadhattercafe.co.uk

The latest incarnation of this ever-changing corner café on Western Road, the Mad Hatter sells itself on being a young, 'funky' hangout with a New Age slant. The walls are covered with ads for Kung Fu lessons and Tai Chi classes, while upstairs they even have their own space for Kundalini yoga, meditation classes and other workshops. The café itself is spacious and colourful, featuring artwork on the walls from such local luminaries as Hardkandy's Tim Bidwell. The food is a fair selection of healthy salads, toasted ciabattas, pizza, cheesecakes and various teas and cold drinks, and the Alice in Wonderland theme is all pervading; look for the model of the Mad Hatter hanging over the counter and try not to cringe when having to order a 'Tweedledum' or 'Tweedledee' from the menu.

Other features include an outside seating area, where you can sit and soak up the sun and bus fumes; the strange old lady who comes in with her teddy bear (which invariably ends up balanced on her head); and a performance evening held on alternate Sundays, hosted by the legendary Dave Suit, offering a mix of music, performances and other 'happenings'.

As it is close to my house, I tend to eat at this café quite a lot, but do have some reservations about their culinary skills. The meals I've had here range from the tasty to the grizzly, and when, for example, I bite into a sandwich to find the avocado as hard as stone, it does make me wonder how much care and attention to detail is going on in the kitchen. And the occasionally dour and brusque service seems at odds with their 'shiny, happy people' image.

But, with just a bit of fine-tuning, and losing the 'Glastonbury on a come-down' moments, The Mad Hatter could be *the* place for spearheading a revolution to transform that raddled behemoth known as the Western Road into the new Sydney Street...

The Meeting Place (S)

Hove Sea Wall, Kingsway, right on the
seafront! (01273) 206417
Open 7am to sunset, all year round
(weather permitting)

Set up as a 'temporary kiosk' in 1935,
it seems that in the council
characteristically dragged their heels
in allowing planning permission for a
more permanent structure for this
seafront café, as the thumbs up only
came through *last year!* Not one to
miss an opportunity, its owner soon
had the place rebuilt......five metres
to the left, thus craftily relocating
from Hove to Brighton. The Meeting
Place ranks amongst the ten best
reasons for living in Brighton; it's
literally a stone's throw from the sea,
the views are terrific, it's far enough
away from the piers to avoid the
weekend crowds and, on a warm
summer morning, is the perfect spot
to have your breakfast, read the
paper in your pants and get a suntan.
Heroically it stays open throughout
the bleakest of winters, but, as it's a
Brighton tradition to make a
pilgrimage here on Christmas
morning for a coffee, you'll even see
queues then. The food is classic caff
grub – jacket potatoes, toasties and
chips, milkshakes, cakes, cakes and
more cakes. *The* place to come if you
want the traditional Brighton
experience rather than the designer
one. Highly recommended.

Infinity Café (NL)

50 Gardner Street
(01273) 670743
Open Mon-Sat 10am-5pm

This veggie/vegan café in the heart of
North Laine was born out of Infinity
Foods' incredible success, and has the
food to match. The menu is 95%
organic, the coffee is Fair Trade, they
offer a take-away option and, by
choosing to eat here instead of
Burger King, you'll be supporting a
workers' co-op. Expect queuing at
lunchtime, though you should always
be able to find a seat upstairs.

Red Roaster (K)

1d St James St (01273) 686668
Open 8am-7pm, Mon-Sun

If you're looking for the perfect place to fritter away an afternoon reading or chatting, and you're a genuine coffee-lover and smoker (the two always seem to go hand in hand), this independent coffeehouse at the bottom of St James' Street should be your number one destination. Being the only place in Brighton currently to have its own roaster (yes, it's red), its claims for providing the freshest and best coffee in town should be taken seriously.

As well as offering the chance to get high on coffee – in all of its flavours and cup sizes – Red Roaster sell Yogi teas (herbal drinks that actually have flavour!), steamed milk, breakfast patisseries, and baguettes, sarnies, ciabattas and salads for lunch.

This is also a great place to come and mix with a genuine cross-section of the Brighton community. You'll find students, foreign visitors, poseurs, gay men, mums meeting for 'baby chat', an inordinately large percentage of pretty girls, and always one disturbing-looking guy, chain-smoking and staring vacantly into space (but this is St James's St after all). There's even a piano in here which, sadly, doesn't get played, unless a drunk tramp happens to wander in (or was that Nick Cave?).

Come on a busy day, and the queue in Red Roaster can be a touch slow, but you could wile away your time admiring the owner's collection of coffee pots high up on the shelf around the back wall, checking the clientele to see if there's anyone suitable for flirting with, or getting someone to bag the sofa by the window for you. And keep your eyes peeled for curly-haired manager, Michael Keane, who is not only passionate about his work (he wrote his PhD on coffee-houses!), but also DJs for MFI at the Tavern Club and is a mine of information about leftfield pop, should you be overcome with a sudden need to remember the name of the bassist from the Woodentops.

A heated debate at Nia Café

Nia Café (NL)

87/88 Trafalgar Street (01273) 671371 L
Open 9am-11pm Mon-Sat, 9am-6pm Sun

With simple décor, candles, a commanding view of Trafalgar Street, laid-back music from the likes of Jeff Buckley, and inexpensive but delicious and imaginative grub, this café gets top marks all round. Attention to detail is excellent too; order a mint tea and it arrives, in a pot, made from fresh leaves. It's these little touches that separate Nia from many of the cheap and cheerful trendy cafés in North Laine that would rather lob a herbal teabag in a mug and charge you £20.

The food is Modern Continental (chicken breast in ciabatta, goat's cheese tart etc) but also on offer are more traditional meals, like bangers and mash. The breakfast choice (served until 1pm) even includes crumpets with honey and pancakes with maple syrup, which is ideal if, like me, your sweet tooth needs its morning fix.

Take your slippers, park yourself here for the afternoon with a paper or a friend and you'll realise why nobody gets anything done in this town.

Kensingtons Café (NL)

1 Kensington Gardens (01273) 570963
Open 9.30am-5.30pm Mon-Sun

Tucked away upstairs at the corner of Kensington Gardens, this is the first Brighton café I ever visited when I moved here and I still have fond memories of the place.

It hasn't really changed much in 10 years, it still serves everything you can think of on toast, does salads, jacket potatoes, a great breakfast, and, more recently, has started serving Mexican snacks, like nachos. The food is reasonably priced and hits the spot if you're after a decent café snack. Inside there's plenty of seating, including these Happy Days style booths at the bottom. The décor is simple, but, for reasons known only to themselves, a golf club and hockey stick appear to have been super-glued to the wall. On warm summer days, however, you'll probably want to plonk yourself on the balcony, read the paper, and drop coffee froth on the heads of passers-by.

The Tin Drum (K/ SD/ H)

95-97 Dyke Road (01273) 777575 (L)
43 St James's Street, (01273) 624777
10 Victoria Grove Second Ave, Hove
(01273) 747755
Open Mon-Sun 11am-11pm

With the success, five years ago, of their first café bar at the Seven Dials (which actually arose from the ruins of Brighton's dingiest and smelliest convenience store), the Tin Drum has gone from strength to strength, and now they've another two similar establishments in Kemptown and Hove. Priding themselves on their friendly service and relaxed style, these café-bars offer a mouth-watering range of modern European food, each with its own autonomous in-house chef. The décor for each is pretty similar – they go in for big splashes of colourful artwork on the walls, chilled-out music (though, ironically, it can, sometimes, be annoyingly loud), comfy seating areas, and table service – though the Kemptown chain has an additional offering of Sunday lunch Jazz and poetry and book-readings most Tuesdays to keep the natives happy.

The Sanctuary (H)

51-55 Brunswick Street East
(01273) 770002 L Open Mon-Sun
9am-11pm www.sanctuarycafe.co.uk

This well-established and chilled-out vegetarian café has been one of Hove's best assets for many years now; it's spacious, offers tasty grub and has a nifty basement venue, though the upstairs area has lost much of its character since being turned into a restaurant space (gone are the sofas and chess–playing hippies). On the menu there's a good range of salads, bakes, pies, pastas, soups and hot dishes of the day to choose from. It's all homemade, and very tasty too, though service and quality can be a little unpredictable. The last time I ate here my partner's meal arrived *so* long after mine that I'd finished eating before hers appeared, and when it did it wasn't properly cooked and she had to send it back. I'm prepared to give them the benefit of the doubt, however, and presume it was just a bad night for the cook (or maybe just a bad cook for the night).

On a better note, they offer a good selection of bottled lagers, have an excellent range of vegan and non-vegan cakes, and have recently started serving fish, so if you know any fish be sure to invite them along.

The Cella, downstairs, is an intimate space, host to many evenings of poetry, music and magic (see Entertainment Chapter). The likes of acoustic maestro Geoff Rob can be seen here, 'Creative Liquid' have their long-running monthly offering of spoken word, and my friend Denise swears she once saw an act here called 'Fish and Chip Strip', where a girl did a striptease, and proceeded to smear herself with…yes, you guessed it. But this is Brighton after all. Sorry, Hove actually.

Mock Turtle (OL)

4 Pool Valley (01273) 327380
Open Tues-Sat 10am-6pm, lunch served
11.30am-2.30pm

This wonderfully preserved, traditional teashop in the Old Lanes is rightly cherished for its dazzling range of cakes, speciality teas and more besides. (The Times recently included it in its top 50 teashops of Britain.) Its owners Gordon and Birthe Chater, a lovely old couple who set the Mock Turtle up over 30 years ago, use only local produce wherever possible for their menu, whilst their mouth-watering cakes, biscuits, soups etc are all completely homemade. Visit at lunch and be treated to their legendary omelettes, Welsh Rarebits and pork sausages, while afternoon visitors can simply stuff themselves silly with cream tea and choose from over 30 cakes and biscuits. Visitors returning to Brighton after many years have been known to kneel down and cry with happiness on discovering this teashop is still in existence. As Gordon said: 'Everything has changed around here apart from us'.

They also do take-aways. If you've got a sweet tooth, you may want to bring a wheelie bin.

Red Veg (NL)

21 Gardner St. (1273) 679910 **L**
Open 11am-9pm every day

A veggie take on your classic fast-food burger joint, this brightly-coloured, communist icon-themed café/takeaway serves chilli burgers, noodles, Jamaican rolls, goujons, plantain chips, and falafels and organic ales. Despite being veggie, Red Veg is still essentially a fast food joint, which is reflected in the quality of some of the grub (the noodles taste like spaghetti hoops with chilli powder and the veggie burgers taste like....well, Burger King veggie burgers), but for vegetarians in a hurry and in need of a protein fix, it serves its purpose.

Trogs Café (K)

24 George Street (01273) 687821
www.trogsrestaurant.com
Open Mon-Fri 11am-4pm, Sat-Sun10am-6pm

Despite its unassuming appearance in the part of Kemptown normally associated with pervy shops and old gay pubs, Trogs is a blessing for Brighton's environmentally friendly and health-conscious veggies. To get the formalities over with first, this café is vegetarian, organic, serves bread fresh from Infinity Foods, recycles all its waste, uses non-toxic cleaning products, is dog-friendly, and even feeds its scraps to rescued battery hens. And while its owner, Alison, clearly has irreproachable ethics where environmental and animal welfare is concerned, she is chatty, easy-going and extremely amiable, and *not* the Dr Marten-wearing dreadlock type who will kick you in the goolies just for wearing a leather jacket.

But I digress (as always); the food here really is something to behold. Serving an excellent range of healthy veggie grub, Trogs do soups, pizzas, veggie burgers and tasty (and very filling) tapas for only £5.50. Drinks range from smoothies to organic ginger beers and, for afterwards – and I pause here for effect… the homemade Mayan chilli chocolate cake is utterly divine! Whoever thought of adding chilli to chocolate cake was a genius – after the sweet, sugary rush of chocolaty goodness, the taste buds won't know what hit them when the chilli kicks in. Trust me, you'll not be disappointed!

As well as a café and restaurant, Trogs also serves as Brighton's unofficial animal rescue centre. Alison has collected many homeless creatures over the years and, currently, Trogs is home to two cats and a floppy Dalmatian, Pablo. If he's lolling around in his basket it usually means he's been out on the Downs with Alison and her (rescued) horse and, as a consequence, is utterly shagged out. Even the lady who brings Alison her eggs is an animal rescuer, liberating battery chickens from their prison, taking them home and giving them a new lease of life. Also, following the old adage that owners begin to take on the characteristics of their pets, she is, according to Alison, *'turning into a giant chicken'.*

If you find an abandoned hamster on your travels round Brighton, you now know where to bring it…

Wai Kika Moo Kau (NL/OL)

11a Kensington Gardens (01273) 671117
Open Mon-Fri 9am-6pm, Sat 9am-7pm
42 Meeting House Lane (01273) 323824
Open 11am-11pm Mon/Wed-Sat, 11am-6pm Tues/ Sun

This successful and popular veggie café has two locations in Brighton – one in North Laine and another in the Old Lanes (which has a smaller menu, is a restaurant, and is 100% organic). It's pronounced 'Why Kick A Moo Cow?', a title which prompted one of my friends to announce her intention of opening a meat-only café next door, called 'Why Not Kick A Moo Cow?'.

The food is a selection of burgers, pastas, breakfasts, curries and veggie grills, and they do a good selection of rather scrummy cakes. For a North Laine café they've got the right balance of style and atmosphere, with genuinely friendly staff who, after a couple of beers, will dance on request to old Motown classics. It's also useful to know that this is one of the few North Laine cafés to open really early. If you're prone to go for an early dip at the Prince Regent (as I am, occasionally), this is the only place open for miles around for a hearty post-swim breakfast.

Brighton's Best Chippies

Brighton has many advantages as a town, but really good fish and chip shops is not one of them. Perhaps it's the embarrassment of other, more exotic eateries on offer that have served to marginalise our humble national dish, or maybe it's the Bank Holiday crowds that allow poor-quality outlets to flourish. Whatever the case, to help you avoid a bad case of runs after sampling fish and chips from some of the more dubious outlets on the seafront, detailed below are (in my opinion) the two best chippies in Brighton. And yes, I **am** aware that we have a Harry Ramsdens...

Bankers

116A Western Road (01273) 328267
Open Mon-Sun 11.30am-9.45pm

An excellent take away and sit-down chippy on the high street, whose classic Sixties décor will make you feel like you're walked into some 'Kitchen Sink' drama. (In fact, thinking about it, it's actually reminiscent of the café that Rita works in, in 'Billy Liar'.) Bankers fish and chips are near-perfect, they offer decent portions for the price, and the fish can even be cooked in Matzo meal (a Jewish alternative to batter, and definitely worth trying). If you're still feeling peckish afterwards, *you are a glutton,* but I can recommend the cheesecake. Don't miss the indoor guttering effect above the counter. What's that all about?

Bardsley's

23 Baker Street (01273) 681256
Open Tues-Sat 10.30am-2pm, 4pm-8pm

While not in quite the same league as Bankers (plus they're a bit stingy with their portions of chips), Bardsley's offer top quality fish and chips and the option to eat in, if you want to avoid being dive-bombed by seagulls.

A Heart-Felt Defence for Greasy Spoons

(By lard-lover Brian Mitchell)

There is more to life than longevity, as the patron of the greasy spoon will surely agree. Brighton, once boasting an embarrassment of such cafés, now seems simply embarrassed by them. In my fifteen years here I have seen their number sadly dwindle (the closure of the legendary Clock Tower Café last January was a particularly severe blow), and, with it, the very café society that Costa and Starbucks are so eager to colonise. Below is a (wholly subjective) list of Brighton's top five greasy spoons. Lend them your support, and your custom, before this remorseless gentrification leads to their extinction, and we end our days forking out £5 for a cup of bloody latte.

The Brunswick Breakfast Bar
Brunswick Street West, Hove

Once upon a long ago, Brighton boasted two kinds of café – those whose walls threatened collapse under the weight of posters for gigs at the Richmond or Free Butt, and those festooned with garish, disturbing, care-in-the-community art. The Brunswick Breakfast bar, I am very glad to say, falls into the latter category. There are some truly awful paintings in here, including one that seems to be – and correct me if I'm wrong – a portrait of someone's arse wearing a pair of spectacles. Taking breakfast here is rather like dining in Tony Hancock's studio in 'The Rebel', only with, presumably, much better food than one might expect in a garret and a great deal more comfort. I love this place; it reminds me, as too few things do nowadays, why I came to this town and never wanted to leave. Oh – and the breakfasts are sublime.

Divall's Café
Terminus Road (01273) 328861 (opposite the station)

This would occupy second place solely for being the only café I know that still regularly serves mashed potato, but there are many reasons for this accolade: the choice of vegetables is unparalleled; the value exceptional, the staff warm and friendly, and the cryptic back-room, oddly congenial. When it closed down early in 1999, my life simply fell apart; its re-opening in time for the Millennium was a portent more propitious than any recorded in the 'Acts of the Apostles*.'

Mac's Café
30 Arundel Road (01273) 692621

My friends and I make trips to this place as some people take jaunts in the country. When I remember its existence and that, with only a little effort, I can actually go there, I am cheered up in a way mere Nature could never accomplish.

*Cheeky would like to warn its readers that reading aloud this last sentence with a mouth full of mashed potatoes in a busy Greasy Spoon café can have serious consequences.

Admittedly, it does look a tad soulless with its plastic seating and Spartan interior, but don't let that fool you: I have achieved the heights of ecstasy eating their home-made steak pie and seen the God-head in their bubble and squeak – Mac's truly puts the transport in 'Transport Café'. Also, as it is situated conveniently opposite Lidl, you can, after a hangover-cure fry-up, simply scoot across to stock up on more cheap booze for your next massive bender – like Holy Water from Lourdes. Make your pilgrimage today.

The Kitchen Café
Trafalgar Street (at the bottom)

The food here is invariably well prepared, and of an unarguably high quality. The roast dinners are satisfying and affordable. Two things conspire against a higher rating: firstly, the seating capacity, which is minimal and, secondly, a lack of proper provision for smokers; no smoking tables in a greasy spoon are like atheist pews in a church.

Mrs Hudson's
12 Sydney Street (01273) 671266

Teetering on the brink of teashop respectability, Hudson's presents a slightly up-market alternative for pie-and mash vulgarians. Presumably taking its name from Sherlock Holmes' landlady (who always made them a slap-up breakfast before a day's sleuthing), Mrs Hudson's is wonderfully antiquated compared to the rest of Sydney Street's more bohemian food outlets and boutiques. The upstairs room provides a welcome air of gentility; the reasonable prices, the amiable staff, and the much-feted homemade apple pie would ensure its inclusion in the most objective of top-fives. And if you fancy a bath after breakfast, it's the only café I know in Brighton to supply one.

NB *The Market Diner is not included in this list because, being an all-night café, it properly deserves its own category. Nonetheless, drunkards everywhere give thanks to the god of greasy spoons for creating it*

Vegetarian Brighton
By Joseph Nixon

A typical vegetarian

If you're a vegetarian, vegan, or even a fruitarian, one of the best things about Brighton is that it's possible to live an animal-products-free existence with great ease. Unlike certain towns in this country, which will remain nameless (although 'Mansfield' comes pretty close), you won't be met with a look of blank incomprehension if you request a veggie sausage in a café, nor burnt at the stake for witchcraft, effeminacy, and general oddness if you enquire about the possibility of a nut roast in your local (*"Aye, we'll be having a nut roast tonight alright. Fetch the flaming torches, Bert."*) **So** veggie-friendly is Brighton that I've seen clueless meat-eaters requesting roast beef being turned away from vegetarian pubs with a cry of *"Sorry mate, we don't do that sort of thing in here"*.

To anyone who, like me, spent his or her teenage years subsisting on a diet of burger-bar 'vegetarian specials' (a roll and salad, without the burger) or the ubiquitous restaurant 'veggie dish of the day' (always, **always** bloody lasagne or some bland pasta dish), this city is a godsend. It's great eating in a place with so many veggie-only eateries, as for once you'll be free of the paranoia (which secretly affects all vegetarians) that you'll accidentally be served a meat dish which you'll consume with relish, while saying *"bloody hell, these sausages are good. Almost like the real thing."*

The best thing about Brighton veggie grub is that the eateries don't conform to the 'vegetarian food must be worthy, earnest, bland, look like a beige cowpat, and taste like the contents of a lawnmower' rule. Some of the stuff on offer in Brighton looks and tastes so good that even your hardened carnivore mates might be tempted.

VEGGIE, ORGANIC & HEALTH FOOD SHOPS

Golchin's International

132 Western Rd (01273) 324514
Open 10am-9pm every day

My favourite vegetarian and organic shop. Situated at the point where Western Road starts to edge into the evil that is Hove, it's a little place heaving with veggie goodness, fresh vegetables, and those hard-to-find 'ethnic' spices and ingredients. They also have an array of Asian music tapes, if you're that way inclined.

Vegetarian Shoes

12 Gardner St (01273) 691913
Open Mon-Sat 10am-5.30pm

Yes, very funny, I know you don't eat shoes (unless you're Charlie Chaplin). This shop sells leather-free shoes in various styles, from Doc Martens to Birkenstocks. They've also got trainers made from hemp, so I guess you could smoke 'em if you got desperate.

Infinity Foods Cooperative Ltd

25 North Road (01273) 603563
Open Mon-Sat 9.30am-5.30pm,
Fri 9.30am-6pm

Brighton's much-loved health food shop stocks everything for your (healthy) heart's desire. Yogi teas, organic turnips, grains, nuts, seeds and tofu burgers all under one roof, and organic bread baked on the premises. Whether you're a veggie, vegan, or allergic to yak hair, you'll find something here to suit your palate. It's also handy for its notice board (if you're looking to share a room with a cat-owning, non-smoking vegetarian or need a lift to Belgium), and is a co-op too, so you can even feel saintly about shopping here.

VEGGIE PUBS

The George

5 Trafalgar St.
(01273) 681055
Food served 12pm-9.30pm Mon-Fri,
12.30pm-8.30pm Sat-Sun

Brighton's most notable veggie and vegan boozer offers good food in light, airy surroundings. The extensive menu includes such old favourites as sausages 'n' mash, Thai fishless cakes, nachos, fajitas, burgers, and (a rarity) tasty vegan puddings. Vegetarian beers and wines are also available, as are a selection of soya-milk coffees. Oh, and there's a beer-garden at the back. The only downside of this place is that when it's crowded (and sometimes, bafflingly, when it's not), it can take upwards of an hour for your nosh to arrive. So don't wander in for a bite to eat twenty minutes before an important meeting /appearing in court /getting married, etc.

The Golden Cannon

20 St Georges Road (01273) 607544
Sunday lunch served 12pm-6pm, £5.95

Though the ubiquitous modernisation of old men's pubs may justifiably be met with extreme consternation, the Golden Cannon – whose previous incarnation was a frankly terrifying place – is one of the few to have done itself proud. Like the Prestonville (below), it's not exclusively veggie, but the food here is excellent, surpassing traditional pub grub by a country mile. The Sunday lunches (with *three* fantastic veggie options) are enormous, almost exotic things; I've yet to find better in this town.

The Snowdrop Inn

119 South St., Lewes (01273) 471018
Food served 12pm-3pm, 5pm-9pm
Mon-Sat, all through the day Sun (provided the chef's up to it)

All right, it's in Lewes, but if you happen to be out there burning Catholics or sacrificing goats you should definitely give it a go. Veggie and vegan only, it looks like a cross between a haunted house and the abode of a mad toymaker and serves wonderful homemade pies (mushroom and stilton, mmmmm), pizzas, and Thai curries. Beers include the sort of real ales and ciders that are called things like Scuttock's Old Necessary and almost always leave you waking up the next morning in another country wearing a tutu and three crash helmets.

The Prestonville Arms

Hamilton Road (01273) 701007
Food served 5pm-9pm Mon-Thurs,
12pm-2.30pm, 5-9pm Fri, 12pm-8pm Sat,
12pm-4pm Sun

Whilst not exclusively a veggie pub, this friendly, charmingly old-fashioned boozer deserves a mention if only because they do a selection of **three** different nut roasts on a Sunday, which is three times as many as most watering holes do. Steer clear of the 'veggie burger' however, as it appears to be a slice of nut roast in a bun.

For veggie / vegan restaurants, see special section at the back of the 'Restaurant' chapter. For veggie / vegan cafés, read the reviews in the Café chapter for Trogs, Infinity, Kai, Red Veg, Sanctuary and Wai Kika Moo Kau.

Other good boozers for veggie Sunday roasts

The Basketmakers
12 Gloucester Rd (01273) 689006

The Shakespeare's Head
Chatham Place (01273) 329444

Coopers Cask
3 Farm Rd, Hove (01273) 737026

The Hampton
57 Upper North St (01273) 731347

The Sidewinder
65 Upper St. James's St (01273) 679927

The Great Eastern
103 Trafalgar Street (01273) 685681

The Lion and Lobster
Sillwood Street (01273) 327299

The Earth and Stars
46 Windsor St. (01273) 772282

VEGGIE BRIGHTON

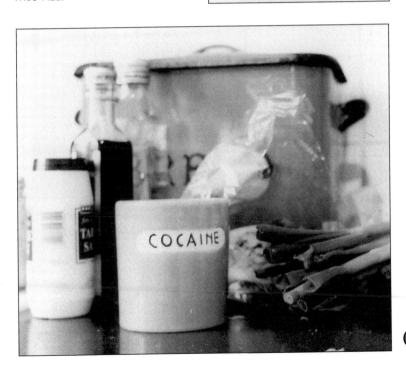

TAKE-AWAY

TAKE-AWAY

Nishat Tandoori (Indian/Goan)

58 Preston Street
(01273) 321701
Open Mon-Sun 5.30pm-12am.

Defintely the best Indian/Goan take-away in Brighton. I use these guys about once a month and have yet to be disappointed with the quality of their curries.

Piccolo

56 Ship Street (01273) 203701
Open Mon-Sun 11.30am-11.30pm
Pizzas are £3 before 5pm (if you collect),
5pm onwards, prices range from £3.50-£5

The pizzas here are tasty and cheap. I've forgotten the number of times I've used their fantastic take-away option, but really should try something else apart from their Hawaiian.

Kambie's (Lebanese)

107 Western Road
(01273) 327934

See restaurant section.

Famous Moe's

Brighton (01273) 676867
Hove (01273) 779779
Open 5pm-11pm, Fri-Sat 5pm-12pm

This well-loved pizza take-away has single-handedly kept Hanover's student population from dying of malnutrition for many a year now. The pizzas are good value and come with a better than average variety of toppings, together with some of the creamiest coleslaw I've ever had. Go for one of their cheap deals for two people and you've got the perfect excuse to be a greedy pig and tuck into banoffee pie after a whopping great pizza.

LATE-NIGHT EATING

Grubbs

63 Western Road, 13 York Place and
89a St. James's Street (01273) 691869
Open Sun-Wed 12pm-12am, Thurs 12pm-1am, Fri-Sat 12pm-3am

Grubbs do hot dogs, salad boxes and a wide range of vegetarian and meat burgers, starting at around £2 for a regular. But why bother with those when, for twenty pence more, you can have Barbecue, Malaysian, Tropical or Hawaiian?

You can sample a bit of Brighton nightlife here most evenings if you want to stick around and eat, though at two in the morning, it's not always the most convivial atmosphere. Be prepared for a bit of a wait though. Even when it's empty I've waited up to fifteen minutes just for one burger. And is it my imagination or do half the staff always seem to be nursing outrageous hangovers? Maybe you should ask them which parties they go to.

The Brighton Bystander

I Terminus Road (01273) 329364
Open Mon-Sun 8am-12am

Opposite the station, this greasy spoon café will deliver the goods if your taste buds are none too discerning. Quite a chilled atmosphere if you get a table, but don't let them rope you into giving a hand behind the till, as I've witnessed here on at least two occasions. It's also a good place for picking up magazines and fliers for local events, and a perfect opportunity to impress the staff by cracking the joke – 'Waiter, there's a flier in my soup'.

The Market Diner

19-21 Circus Street (01273) 608273
Open 8pm-11am Mon-Fri, 8pm-9am Sat,
8pm-6am Sunday

Found on Circus Street, just around the corner from the Art Block, the Market Diner is one of the most famous landmarks in Brighton's nightlife. This is your classic greasy spoon, boasting ashtrays made from the foil of Mr Kipling's apple pies, a near-legendary gut-buster and the added bonus of being open all night. This, purportedly, is to cater for truck drivers delivering to the fruit market in the small hours but, at the weekend, its clientele consists mostly of drunks, deranged lunatics, deranged lunatic drunks and incapacitated clubbers. It is, however, a must for that post-club hunger and **the** place to meet and socialise with dangerous people. And hats off to the staff here – they're like experts in linguistics. Not matter how off your head you are, they can *always* tell what you want!

NB. My friend Duncan recommends that you ask for a cup of tea without a fag end in it.

WHERE TO BUY MILK AT 4 AM

BP Garage / Safeway

Kingsway, by King Alfred Centre in Hove

Again a bit of a way out, but more likely than Asda to have (as in the Eddie Izzard sketch) a string of people asking for: *"Twix, Mars Bar, eight bags of Monster Munch, loaf of bread and err......a packet of king sized rizlas please."*

One-stop Shop

West Street

At least I think that's what it's called. Anyway it's open on West Street twenty-four hours a day and sells fags, papers, corner-shop and booze. Working here on a Saturday night must be the pits though.

Three 2 Four

Next to Kambis, Western Road

Round the clock grocers / newsagent. Essential when you're craving a fry-up at four in the morning. *"And...errr...a packet of King Sized Rizlas, please..."*

RESTAURANTS

There are over 400 restaurants in Brighton, with cuisine ranging from African, Mexican, Asian, Soul Food, Japanese and Lebanese, to Cajun, French, Italian... even English. So after all this hard work, not to mention putting on 400 pounds in the process, I'll be very annoyed if you end up in McDonalds...

AFRICAN

Blue Man

142 Edward Street (opposite Amex)
(01273) 622885 Open Mon-Fri 7am-2.30pm, Sat 9am-3pm, Thurs-Sat 7pm-11pm
Kemias £12.50, shisha pipe with apple tobacco £3.50, party banquets £20 a head
Bring your own booze.

Set up a over a year ago by Majid and Georgie, this authentic North African restaurant, hidden away up Edward Street, is open all day, serving breakfast, lunch and, in the evening, kemias (tapas).

Taking its name from the Toureg (a tribe of Saharan nomads who only ever wear blue), this restaurant serves a plethora of tasty traditional dishes throughout the day, including goat and turmeric, lamb with chickpeas and prunes, potato bakes, Algerian omelettes and even pigeon (of the Wood, not Brighton, variety). There's a great choice of kemias, which include a good range of nibbles – sausage, salad, bread, and cheese – together with a main meat dish of your choice (I had goat – it was delicious). Also, while the portion of baklava and dates we got

for desert seemed meagre for the price, its bring-your-own-booze policy really does make for an inexpensive evening.

Besides the food, its other strengths are the colourful style and laid-back ambience of the place. As Majid said: *"I don't believe in having formal rules for a restaurant. You eat when you're hungry, you sleep when you're tired."* In fact, if you wanted to put your head down after a meal I'm sure he wouldn't mind; there are lots of cushions and pillows in Yema's room at the back and they're more than usually accommodating. When I came with a group of six, one of our party, Martin, enjoyed their sausages so much, all he wanted for dessert was more sausages (if you knew Martin this would come as no surprise), which they obligingly provided, for the princely sum of 60p!

While so many Brighton restaurants think that slinging a few sofas around the place and playing chilled-out dance music makes for a relaxed atmosphere, Blue Man shows how to do it in style. Recommended.

The Nile House

Preston Street (01273) 326003
Open 6pm-12pm Mon-Sun
Zegni (chicken in chilli with tomato sauce
served with rice) £8.50, Tabikh Alyoum
(lamb stew with seasonal veg and rice)
£6.50, lentil stew dressed with caramelised
garlic and two pitta breads £4.50

One of only two Sudanese restaurants in the country, The Nile House does a unique line in North African cuisine with a resolutely Sudanese character. The menu confidently straddles the meat, fish and veggie realms, with most dishes accompanied by hot pittas and spicy basmati rice. I must recommend the inappropriately named Foul (sesame oil-fried dark broad beans with grated feta cheese and crushed chickpeas) and the Karkadeh (dried hibiscus flower tea), a traditional Sudanese thirst-quencher that really hits the spot. Being on Preston Street, this place is also good for bargain three-course specials.

AMERICAN / CAJUN / SOUL FOOD

Blind Lemon Alley

41 Middle Street (01273) 205151
Open Mon-Sun 12pm-11pm
www.bluescompany.co.uk Two courses £9.95

This intimate restaurant in the Old Lanes serves tasty Southern food – in particular, homemade, char-grilled burgers (meat and veggie). The hidden entrance makes it a bit tricky to find (which is good news if you like to avoid over-touristy places), though as it's very small, it's still best to book ahead. The bad news is that legendary Blues guitarist and singer Phil Mills is not around on Sundays any more (after ten years of singing 'woke up one morning and my girl was gone', he decided he needed a holiday), but the good news is that they've finally painted the ladies.
Top tip – The best seats are in the room upstairs.

Momma Cherries
Soul Food Shack

11 Little East Street (01273) 774545
www.mommacherries.co.uk
Brunch served 11am-2pm
(full American breakfast £6.50)
Dinner served Mon-Thurs 5pm-11pm,
Fri-Sat 11am-midnight, Sun 11am-9pm

All hail Momma Cherries, the little restaurant with a big personality – a fact which is apparent even before you step through the door, owing to the giant mural that dominates the façade of the restaurant, depicting Momma, in her chef's hat, about to utter her hearty greeting of *'Goodgoogamooga!'* For this bijou, two-storey 'shack' thrives on the eccentricity and humour of its creator, Momma (a.k.a. Charita), and is warmly decorated with fairy lights, cosy tables and pictures of black icons, ranging from Malcolm X to Gary 'Whachu lookin' at Willis?' Coleman (the little fellow from Different Strokes).

Britain's only Soul Food restaurant, Momma Cherries serves up hefty portions of tasty, traditional Southern fare such as Southern fried catfish, buffalo wings and Brother Brian's pigs' feet. But the choice doesn't stop there, the menu is vast, taking in such classic American and Cajon dishes as blueberry pie, meatloaf, fried chicken, pan-fried red snapper, burgers, jambalaya and fish platters, all served in gargantuan portions, very reasonably priced and ready to be washed down with jugs of refreshing, homemade lemonade.

In fact, Momma's menu alone merits a visit, for, within its pages, you'll find history lessons, poetry, photo collages, advice for diners (*'..read the menu in your best American accent. Think of a Southern Baptist preacher....let the energy flow.'*), and even translations of such less familiar American terms as:

Jelly *(jam)*
Jello *(jelly)*
Biscuit *(bread)*
Small *(medium)*
Medium *(large)*
Large *(huge)*
Spicy *(real hot)*
Hot *(have some water nearby)*

During the day, you can drop by for brunch or a full American breakfast (it requires three weeks down the gym to work off, but is worth every minute), while, most evenings, Charita usually has something special organised. Mondays, in the school dinner's tradition, are for 'second helpings'. (Requiring **third** helpings isn't a problem either; Charita **loves** seeing people with a healthy appetite. Don't eat simply out of greed though, as *'momma doesn't like waste'.*) Later in the week there are games and music nights, with Momma's partner Goatée Phil indulging in his passion for New Orleans Funk and sweet Soul music.

Truth is, Charita and the gang like any excuse for a party. Halloween, Christmas and Fourth of July are all celebrated here, but the truly unmissable event is Thanksgiving, which Charita describes as an evening of *'giving thanks and pigging out'.* In the past she has had diners standing up and holding hands, while her mother (a seventy year old Baptist minister), via the wonders of telecommunication, has blessed the food from her home in the States. This is followed by a 'cabinet reshuffle', in which diners are split up and re-seated, to encourage mingling.

This, of course, is all a reflection of Charita's personality. Effervescent and larger than life, she is theatrical, ever-cheerful and even prone to burst into the occasional song. Not surprising when you learn that, for many years, she has been a professional singer and even provided backing vocals for the Sopranos theme tune with the band Alabama 3. On a typical evening she will cheerfully buzz around the tables asking – *Y'all OK? You wan mow vegetables, you wan mow chicken? You*

just ask honey!' or regaling visitors with tales of her cheeky antics, such as the time she blagged her way backstage at the Theatre Royal to meet Huggy Bear, claming to be his long-lost cousin!

Brighton may pride itself on the current glut of poncy, stylish restaurants serving 'modern cuisine' on big white plates, but, to be honest, they add little to the true spirit of this town. For character, cheekiness and damned fine, gut-busting grub, Momma Cherries is peerless.

Top tips:
• Thanksgiving at Momma Cherries is a night you'll never forget. While it lies at the end of November, I'd recommend booking in August!
• Get to the gents before everyone else; you can read all the jokes on the wall and go back armed with a few corkers. I particularly like the one about the pope.

CHINESE

Brighton Pagoda

Brighton Marina, West Jetty, opposite the
Seattle Hotel (01273) 819053
Open every day, 12pm-1.45pm and
6pm-10.30pm Set menu £18-£25 per head

This can claim, without fear of
contradiction, to be Brighton's only
floating restaurant. There is no point in
living if you don't experience the odd
sensation of slurping good Chinese
food as the waves rock you to and fro
(unless, of course, you're the kind of
landlubber who only has to look at a
boat to start re-enacting the mushy-
pea puking scene from the Exorcist, in
which case this really isn't the place
for you).

There are no quirks to the menu, but
the fare is surprisingly above average,
given how cheap it is – you might
expect to pay double for the
ambience alone. The waiting staff can
be incredibly pushy on a Saturday
evening, but, if you don't panic, they'll
let you go at your own pace, so that
even this becomes part of the charm.
A wonderful place to surprise
somebody with – the lower deck is
especially romantic for newfound
loves. If you want to impress without
breaking the bank, this exotic little
one-off is just the ticket.

China Garden

88 Preston Street (01273) 325124
Open every day 12pm-11pm
Sweet and sour fish fillets £8.95, sizzling
king prawns £9.95

If you were to judge this place by its
décor it'd probably not fare well. It
may look flash, but, with the exception
of the monographed carpet, much
effort seems to have gone into styling
it on the interior of my old, grey,
1980s Renault 5. This was probably

the height of fashion 15 years ago but it
wouldn't go amiss to remove some of
the Athena pictures and have them
quietly put down. Fortunately, however,
the food here is of such high quality
and the service so good, that to avoid
this place for the sake of a few tacky
features would be a real shame.
Having eaten here several times with
large groups, I can vouch that everyone
has savoured every morsel, from their
hors d'oeuvres platter right through to
the toffee banana at the end, and the
food has received nothing but glowing
praise from all concerned. Everything is
fresh, full-flavoured, and far removed
from the typical stodgy Chinese take-
aways we've grown accustomed to.

Top Tips – watch out for the pianist at
weekends, he's lovely to listen to when
you're in the waiting area, but don't get
a seat near him when you're eating, as
he tends to get over-excited when
playing 'Windmills of My Mind' and it
could interfere with your digestion. Try
instead to get yourself a sea view, as
the restaurant overlooks the charred
remains of the West Pier.

– If you're a veggie you'll need to ask
for the special vegetarian option, as it's
not on the menu.

Blanch House

17 Atlingworth Street (01273) 603504
Open Wed-Sat lunch 12pm-3pm, Tues-Sat
dinner 7pm-10pm. Average price £50

A step-by-step guide to the Blanch
House Experience...

1. *Make a reservation.*
2. *At the appointed time buzz on the
   unassuming front door and be met
   with a big, knowing, 'Welcome to
   Blanch House!' smile.*
3. *Enjoy a truly excellent cocktail while
   perusing the menu in the living-room
   style bar (it was, presumably, once a
   living room).*
4. *Be escorted into the big, white, chic,
   ultra-modern restaurant.*
5. *Enjoy high-quality gourmet food
   served on huge white plates.*
6. *Be treated like royalty.*
7. *Retire to the bar.*
8. *Have another cocktail.*
9. *Have another cocktail*
10. *Get the bill.*
11. *Have a heart attack.*

Yes, this place is not cheap, but for
that once a year (or once a lifetime)
experience, it's unbeatable. Your
evening will be full of neat touches:
the cocktails are delivered with
professionalism; your white wine is
poured, then whisked back to the
chiller, then poured again just before
your glass is quite empty; the
espresso is good (blimey!) and there's
even a friendly, fluffy dog, called
'Poolux', to charm you to bits, though
that will already have been taken care
of as your hosts will have told you
how beautiful your (obviously
inexpensive) dress or necklace looks.

One for very special occasions or
as a weekly treat (if, unlike me, you
earn a respectable wage).

Harry's

41 Church Road (01273) 727410
Open Mon-Sun 9am-10.30pm
Breakfast serve until 4pm: 'Greedy
breakfast' £6.35, chicken brochettes £5.95,
beef, steak, kidney and mushroom pie
£7.65, bangers and mash £6.95, jam roly-
poly and custard £3.45

Remember how in The Beano every
week one of the characters would
foil a couple of burglars (dressed in
black striped shirts and carrying a bag
of swag) to be rewarded with a slap
up meal of bangers and mash at the
local nosh-up? This is a posh version
of that restaurant, serving hearty,
meat-heavy, traditional English dishes
and old classics like Jam roly-poly for
afters (but, unlike the ones you had at
school, the custard isn't lumpy, and
Simon Timmins won't have flicked
one of his bogies in it when you
weren't looking). Particularly
recommend are their breakfasts
(served until 4pm) and if you come
on Christmas Eve as I did one year,
you can expect the full works, with all
the trimmings.

Prompt Corner

36 Montpelier Road, Brighton
(01273) 737624
www.promptcorner.com
Dinner served from 6pm, Sunday lunch
1pm-4pm. Sunday lunch £9.50, Escargots
£4.25, fillet of sole £9, Beef Wellington £12

Since its grand opening in 1946 by actor Bob Dean, Prompt Corner has continued to uphold and cherish its theatrical theme. When current owners, Ken and Alan, took over in 1979, they decorated the place with hundreds of photos of Hollywood stars from the Thirties to Sixties. Sure, there's a picture of Tom Cruise in here somewhere but, as one customer grumbled – 'he just doesn't belong here.'

And I know what he means. For it is the elegance, style and relaxed pace of this 'golden era' of the movies that are evoked by the ambience of this restaurant. From the moment you step in and Ken greets you, takes your coat and sits you at the bar for an aperitif, you can actually feel time slowing down a pace and putting its feet up. Almost nothing has changed here since Alan and Ken took over; in a town of transience and ever-changing fashion, Prompt Corner is a rare and almost surreal delight, reflecting a by-gone era when style meant Lauren Bacall, not some floozy from Big Brother.

The cuisine is classically English (with a few French numbers thrown in for good measure) – plenty of steaks, fish and seafood dishes to choose from and the likes of chocolate pud and ice cream for afters. Having sampled their snails, chicken in mushroom sauce, scampi and sorbet, I found them all to be of exceptional quality. Together with the lilting tones of old songs from the Forties and impeccable service, it's easy to imagine coming here for a five-course meal and wiling away the hours trying to name all the Hollywood stars who grace their walls.

Unsurprisingly, Prompt Corner has had more than its fair share of celebrity customers over the years, from Joan Collins, Frankie Howerd and Jon Inman to Cynthia Payne. (*"She gave me one of her 'luncheon vouchers'* commented Ken, *'but I never used it."*)

In fact, Alan and Ken have some great tales to tell about some of their famous customers (make sure to ask Ken about the time David Blunkett popped in) and the two of them together make a great double act, Ken being the foil to Alan's wry, but good-natured quips. Ken has a wonderful way of floating around the restaurant – adjusting a napkin here, picking up an empty glass there – and there's a distinct air of the Peter Sellers about him.

Like all good places with a theatrical connection, Prompt Corner has its own resident ghost. The mistress of a Jewish landlord, she is said to have hung herself at number 37 (now the area where the bar is) and while no-one has seen her directly, Ken said: *"Sometimes I think I'll see a shadow over someone's shoulder and presume a customer's gone off to the toilet, but when I look there's no-one there!"*

For those who love Brighton as much for places like the Mock Turtle, The Colonnade Bar and Pavilion as for its trendier clubs and bars, this restaurant is a sheer delight.

FISH AND SEAFOOD

English's

29-31 East Street (01273) 327980
www.englishs.co.uk Open12pm-10.15pm
Mon-Sat, 12.30pm-9.30pm Sun
Pacific Oysters £6.95 per half dozen, grilled

English's has, for countless years now, enjoyed a reputation not only as **the** seafood restaurant in Brighton but, for many, as **the** restaurant in Brighton, full stop. And I, for one, am not about to disagree. Unchanged since it opened in 1946, and housed in three old fishermen's cottages in the Old Lanes, English's is both an eat-at-the-counter Oyster Bar (which still has the original, marble counter-top) and high calibre seafood restaurant, with an extensive a la carte menu and weekly specials that have been known to reduce grown men to tears. From seafood chowder, pan-fried scallops, Dover sole and grilled turbot, to sea bass, Lobster Thermidor, jellied eels and medallions of monkfish, all the food here is sublime.

You can do English's for a modest price (main courses range from £10-£20), but, chances are, you'll get carried away and opt for the deluxe seafood platter, which will have you delirious with joy when you spot it being wheeled to your table.

This restaurant has, however, many other appealing qualities besides the food. The Edwardian décor and red velvet furnishings are thoroughly charming, the journey up two flights to the ladies' offers terrific views of Brighton and there are some nice touches to the service – I love the fact that the waiters present the desserts on a silver tray to help you select your choice.

If you are seated near the window in the Red Room, have a good look at the mural closest to you. The original owner, Clifford Lee Jones is the guy pictured holding a glass of wine. Look carefully at the other characters, however, and you'll notice they all look strangely similar.

Apparently the artist could only afford one model, hence the eerie 'Boys from Brazil' experience.

Although, from the outside, English's appears very formal, this belies a more friendly interior. Sure, you'll probably watch your manners if you're sat inside, rather than out, but it actually isn't the stuffy *'Certainly sir, whatever sir requires, sir'*, type establishment that some imagine. And the clientele, rather than being confined to snooty suited types, ranges from young couples and seafood fanatics to flirty gay men trying to chat up the waiter with phrase-book French (despite his obvious Italian accent) and groups of old duffers sitting around, puffing on cigars and swapping anecdotes about going to school with Dennis Compton.

Fashions come and go in Brighton, but sitting by the window of English's, slurping on a bowl of lobster bisque, eaves-dropping on three old queens on the table behind and watching the plebs eating pizza at the restaurant next door, has to rank in the top five quintessential Brighton experiences. But remember, you most probably didn't hear it here first.

The Regency

131 Kings Road (01273) 325014
Open 9am-12pm Mon-Sat, 9am-10pm Sun,
main courses range from £5-15

This distinctive seafront fish restaurant wouldn't look out of place in a 70s Carry-On movie. Everything on the menu is of good quality, and I'd particularly recommend their seafood platters; they're excellent value and the calamari can be chewed without having to take out dental insurance. From £5 for the basic haddock and chips to £15 for the Dover sole, if you're after an inexpensive sit-down fish and chip dinner with plenty of choice and a sea view, forget Harry Ramsden's and come here instead.

Curiously, the restaurant next door, the Melrose (01273) 326520, has similar prices, menu and style, so I've never been able to figure out why the Regency is always much, much busier. Some friends reckon the food is better in the Regency but, having eaten at the Melrose twice in the last year, I have nothing but praise for the place. Added to the facts that the Regency has lost some of its charm since refurbishment, and that their eccentric waiter (the one who wears thousands of badges on his waistcoat) has defected to next door, I'm beginning to prefer The Melrose instead. But then, being British, I'll always champion the underdog.

FRENCH

La Fourchette

101 Western Road (01273) 722556
Open 12pm-2.30pm and 7pm-11pm,
closed Sun and Mon lunch
Two-course £19, 3-course with pudding
£23 Typical main course: veal sweetbread
with pommes dauphines and baby veg, wild
mallard with hot apples and celeriac

Decorated in a French farmhouse
sort of way (framed bunches of hay
on the wall and stray chickens all
over the shop) this small, high street
restaurant offers classic French dishes
with a sophisticated touch.

The menu has some excellent
choices (for carnivores) such as skate
with veal juice, scallops with leek and
saffron sauce, and escalope de fois
gras with caramelised turnips, all of
which are mouth-watering and
tender. I happened to visit with two

French ladies, whose critical palates
were delighted with the food, while I
was simply delighted with the two
French ladies. Be careful, however,
when tucking into your meal; the
food presentation comes from the
Le Corbusier school of piling
everything in one enormous tower.
Stick your fork in at the wrong place,
and, as in Kerplunk!, everything rolls
off onto the table.

This restaurant's only drawback is
its size; the more portly gourmands
might find it a squeeze in here, while
the monstrously large menus and
small tables meant that all three of us
managed to knock cutlery on the floor.

That aside, this is a place of
exceptional quality food. As my
escorts confirmed – you won't find
better French cuisine anywhere in
Brighton.

The Gingerman

21a Norfolk Square (01273) 326688
Open Tues-Sat lunch 12.30pm-2pm,
dinner 7pm-10pm, three-course £25

Local chef Ben McKellar has turned this unremarkable building in a quiet side street into a celebration of modern French cuisine. A small room, simply decorated, reflects a purist approach, beautifully executed. From the fresh-baked rolls served with olive oil and balsamic vinegar on arrival to hand-made petit-fours, the attention to detail throughout the meal is consistently designed for inconspicuous pleasure.

Meat features heavily on the main courses, with creations such as pork fillet with figs and squab pigeon on celeriac puree, but rather than going overboard on eclecticism, Ben's real strength lies in the intelligent perfection of his sauces. He has a rare ability to make cod or spinach taste divine.

Three courses here will set you back about £22 and the wine list is well-balanced if somewhat narrow in its restrictions to French wines.

GREEK

Ipanema

121 Western Road, Brighton
(01273) 779474
Open 12pm-11pm Mon-Sun
Spanish and Greek meals £15-20 per person

The Ipanema is a restaurant that oozes Mediterranean warmth, courtesy of the charismatic staff and liberal supplies of Sambuca. The new bit, upstairs, is an expansive Spanish tapas bar with a wine list to match – ideal for big groups and 'fruity red' experts alike. Downstairs is the original Greek part, presided over by Dimos, who was his country's entry in the Eurovision Song Contest sometime in the Eighties. He still plays and sings in the restaurant at weekends and is an ideal accompaniment to the vast armoury of 'small plates' on offer. Mass breakouts of group singalongs, table-dancing, and even the occasional bout of plate-smashing are well-known and encouraged in here.

INDIAN JAZZ FUNK FUSION

Black Chapati

12 Circus Parade (01273) 699011
Open Wed-Fri 7pm onwards,
Sat 6.30pm onwards

It's ten years since Steve Funnell burst onto the Preston Circus scene with this incongruously located temple to bold, fusion cuisine. In the early days it was brutally minimalist, and some will remember him lecturing the entire restaurant on exactly what they were eating. Any diners spotted talking amongst themselves during these sermons would be asked to share the joke with the rest of the class.

Today the approach has softened: mellow yellow décor, chairs that it's possible to stay on for more than half an hour and only an occasional sight of the red face through the kitchen hatch. But there's still a stern feel about the place; the first line on the menu is an admonition to smokers.

It's all about the food, really. Steve's approach to the blending of Asian and European cuisine is unique and a consistent gusto runs through the menu, which, in pleasant contrast to current vogue, is framed in understated language. The spices lightly sear across the roof of your mouth and the range of ciders is as good an accompaniment as the small, well-chosen list of wines.

The message would seem to be 'serious diners only', but there is enjoyment to be had from the sense of occasion, the delicately handled service and the uniqueness of the place. I have to add, though that last year, one visitor was so annoyed by the way he was spoken to by the

waiter (I believe the 'C' word was used!) that he felt compelled to send me an angry two-page e-mail about it. Be warned, you may be in for a Basil Fawlty experience. Enjoy the ride.

Bombay Aloo

39 Ship Street (01273) 776038
Open Mon-Thurs 12pm-11pm, Fri-Sun
12pm-12am, Happy hour 3.15pm-5.15pm
www.bombay-aloo.co.uk

This family-run buffet restaurant has been around for years now, and is terrific value for money as it's an all-you-can-eat vegetarian Indian buffet, including Bajis, salads, dips, and main curries with rice, for only £4.95. Make sure to ask for the comments book at the end; there are some corkers in there including, my favourite, *'I luv your grub, had a fat poo afterwards'!*

They've now got a sister shop in Kemptown (Bombay Mix) for the meat-eaters, with meat and veg all-you-can-eat for £6.95. Starve yourself for three days and clear them out.

Indian Summer

Kingsway, Hove (01273) 773090
Open 6pm-10.30pm Tues-Sat, 6pm-10pm Sun
8 East Street (01273) 711001 Open 12pm-
10.30pm Tues-Sat, 12pm-10pm Sun
All meals around £8

About as far removed as you can get from those clichéd, cheesy restaurant ads from Seventies cinema. You remember, the ones with sitar music, psychedelic wallpaper and grinning young couples who look like they're on medication. Instead, Indian Summer has minimalist furnishings, trendy young staff and offers traditional Indian cuisine. In fact, you won't find a single curry dish on the menu here; the cuisine is comprised solely of authentic Southern Indian food served in the traditional way; three distinct courses, each with accompaniments (followed by European deserts). Particularly recommended are the masala dosas (rice and lentil pancakes served with two different chutneys) and the pakora dishes – all cooked in exquisite coconut sauces.

ITALIAN

La Capannina

15 Madeira Drive (01273) 680839
Open every day, lunch 12pm-2.30pm and
dinner 6pm-11.30pm Average prices: Pizza
£7, meat dish £10, fish, £12

You'll be hard pushed to find a proper Italian restaurant in these parts that can match La Capannina's high standards. It's a family-run place that simply sets its store by doing things the Italian way. The restaurant itself is atmospheric, romantic and as authentic as they come. The menu is vast, the food top quality and the portions gargantuan.

The only problem is whether or not to have a starter; it may leave you unable to tackle the main course without bursting at the seams. Unsurprisingly, La Capannina has a large fan base, so it's advisable to book ahead during busy times. Incredible good value considering the standard of cuisine and service; this genuinely ranks as one of the best – you'd be mad to miss out.

Alfresco

The Milkmaid Pavilion, Kings Road
(01273) 206523
Open Mon-Sun 10am-Midnight

Looking like it's out of some cool, Sixties, Italian movie, Alfresco is an enormous glass-panelled building with a commanding view of the beach and a spacious round balcony on the first floor (which means no fighting for the precious sunny spots during those two minutes of heat in the summer).

While the building and location are top banana, the food is decidedly bland – the usual array of pizza and pasta dishes that most genuine Italians would turn their noses up at. Fact is, I had one of the worst meals of my life here last summer; the mussels were bad, the mozzarella was off, and the gaggle of surly staff seemed to prefer loitering by the bar to acknowledging my frantic gestures that the food in my mouth appeared to have turned to Space Dust.

The sad truth is that they really don't need to try hard. This restaurant is in such a prime spot that it'd be full of tourists all-year round, even if it only served dog-food.

Top Tips – Come and sit on their balcony in summer, but stick with the drinks menu.

JAPANESE

Moshi Moshi

Bartholomew Square (01273) 719195
Open daily 12pm-11pm
Tapas / sushi £12-£15

After establishing three successful sushi bars in the Big Smoke, Moshi Moshi demonstrated a new level of ambition by taking on the 'Curse of Bartholomew Square' and winning. Ignoring the obscurity that has swiftly followed any attempt in living memory to set up a working eatery in this windswept graveyard of civic space beside the Town Hall, they demolished the old rotunda and started afresh.

The result is a sort of sub-007 screened cube, the entrance an opening fully fifteen feet wide, with temperature cunningly controlled through a system of under-floor heating.

First impressions are stunning; between wooden slatted floor and textured red ceiling a great conveyor belt snakes around light rattan benches and a long bar.

As you sit, you are faced with an endlessly renewed, slow-moving display of small plates containing colourful samples of sushi, sashimi, tempura and other delicacies. The simple beauty is that when something tasty-looking passes by, you pick it up. It may turn out to be pickled octopus with horseradish, but you can always hide it in your pocket if you don't like it.

You can also order off the menu. Sushi sets on stylised chopping-boards, bento boxes (a double decker starter and main course), seaweed-wrapped tamaki rolls and teriyaki combinations. Each table holds a jug of soy sauce, red-hot horseradish and plenty of lovely gari (sliced pickled ginger) to cleanse the palate.

Though wine is available, you can indulge yourself in a choice of hot and chilled sake, sake sours or Asahi beer. Service is focused on guiding you through the unfamiliar experience, and thoroughly professional. You are never committed here; you can as easily leave after a nibble as submerge yourself in a three-hour blow-out.

This may not be Japanese cuisine at its zenith, but the food is surprisingly good value and the belt makes for top entertainment; simply spike the drink of the person next to you, stick a cuddly toy and a set of steak knives on the belt, and you should be able to convince them they're on the Generation Game.

Sapporo

38 Preston St (01273) 777880
Open every day 12pm-2pm, 6pm-11pm
Teppanyaki £8, average meal £14 per head

Stylish but expensive teppanyaki bar in a street of many restaurants. (Teppanyaki was apparently conceived during the American occupation of Japan after observing the GI barbecues. They went one better and developed a delicious and theatrical version where the customers sit around a huge hotplate while the chef juggles pepperpots, knives and chairs over a sizzling selection of meat and fish.)

The set menus are on the last pages and, for £29, the Sapporo Feast consists of sashimi, tempura and miso soup, followed by a blur of beef fillet, salmon, squid, whole prawns (the tails are exquisite) and buckets of fried rice. Wash it all down with warm sake and heartily congratulate yourself.

LEBANESE

Kambie's

107 Western Road (01273) 327934
Mixed grill £7, chicken shawarma £5.75, kibby basayniyeh (ground lamb with cracked wheat with pine but sand onions) £5.75

This place is a real favourite of mine; the mood is lively in the evenings and the food, while inexpensive, is very tasty. Try their meat grills, Falafels, or side dishes like batata harra (sautéed potatoes with coriander, garlic and lemon).

I came here one night when a group of us shared a seemingly endless platter of different Lebanese dishes and, at the end of the night, we got to smoke the Shiha (pronounced sheesha). The tobacco is flavoured with strawberries, so just one puff and – if you're a ex-smoker like me – you'll be craving those Marlboro Lights again. It's bring your own booze here as well, which always helps keep the price down.

A few years ago there used to be a band of musicians who occasionally dropped into Kambies to play Eastern European folk music. Knowing they did requests, my girlfriend handed over a couple of quid for them to come over and embarrass me with a short serenade while I ate. Instead, bizarrely, they played 'Happy Birthday' to *her*, and everyone in the restaurant joined in. She now has two birthdays a year, like the Queen.

MODERN CONTINENTAL

The Saint

22 St James St (01273) 607835
Open Tues-Sun, 12pm-3pm, 6pm-closing

A haven for those with a more discerning palate and a welcome retreat from the lunacy of St James St, the Saint takes a bistro approach to its English/Continental menu and offers a superb range of meat, fish and vegetarian dishes, all at relatively modest prices. Or, to quote its affable chef, this is," *unpretentious post-modern cuisine, without a twist!*"

Inside, the Saint is deceptively spacious, with a modern design, soft candlelight, friendly but unobtrusive staff and a gentle soundtrack from the likes of Sigur Ros, Lambchop and Goldfrapp – ideal for an intimate and unhurried meal.

If you're doing it in style, you'll want to begin by sampling a few of their cocktails. Their own 'Saintly Cocktails' section has a few tantalisingly named brews, such as 'Salty Dog and 'Dicky Wibbly' (which sounds like a medical condition for gentlemen who can't 'perform'). Once you're suitably loosened up by seven or eight of these, you'll no doubt be ready for food.

Keeping with the pious theme, the menu is split into 'Sermons', 'Hymns' and 'Prayers'. Typical dishes include confit of duck and salad of crayfish for starters, lime-infused, poached organic salmon for main (recommended), and Mediterranean figs or sticky toffee pudding for desert. And you won't be disappointed; the cuisine is stylishly presented, the meat and fish dishes juicy and tender, and the deserts very rich and satisfying. Just pray that after all this, the buttons on your trousers won't fire off and land in someone's soup...

Top Tip – The brown leather booths at the back are ideal if you're after an intimate meal for two.

Preston Street

Despite the glut of restaurants in Brighton, if it's Saturday night, you're out in town, and have forgotten to book somewhere to eat, you'll be in trouble. One of your best bets is to head for Preston Street (which runs from Western Road to the seafront), as it contains more restaurants per square inch than anywhere else on the face of the earth, all of **varying** quality. There are four Chinese restaurants, two steak houses, Italian, Italian, Japanese, Indian, and even a 'Cheeky Chicken', if you've lost the will to live.

Café Paradiso (Alias Hotel Seattle)

Brighton Marina (01273) 679799
Open 7am-10am breakfast, lunch 12.30pm-
2.30pm, dinner 6pm-10.30pm
Main course approx £10, no set menu

*'Somewhere decent to eat in Marina
shocker!! "I went there of my own free
will"* claims man. Yes it's true; there is
finally a reason to go to the Marina
outside of attending the Annual
Concrete Enthusiasts' Conference.
Situated in the extremely hip Hotel
Seattle, this is a special place to bring
your jaded, seen-it-all London friends.
The food, a mix of contemporary
English and Mediterranean cuisine, is
excellent and reasonably priced
(particularly early bird special menu, 6-
7pm), with an emphasis on fish, fresh
from the boat. The service is also very
good – friendly and helpful, and the
wine list extensive. But never mind all
that, just look at the place! If the late
Stanley Kubrick and Terry Gilliam had
put their heads together they couldn't
have come up with a more flamboyant
design.

You initially approach Café Paradiso
through a lift, in front of which is a golf
buggy from cult TV series The Prisoner,
surrounded by vaguely unsettling
mannequins. Then you walk along a
wide, white corridor full of Japanese
lanterns with Kabuki music playing in
the background, slowly approaching a
huge, wooden, perspective bending
sculpture that makes you feel drunk.
Then its down some stairs, decked out
in a vast Space Invaders painting, and
finally into the enormous, cavernous,
Neo- Brutalist dining room; one giant
wall of plate glass looking out onto the
boats and sea, the remainder a riot of
Sixties and Victorian furniture,
innumerable chandeliers, bamboo,
mirror mosaics and industrial 'Brazil' air-
vent pipes and girders. To quote that
bloke from the Fast Show, 'brilliant!!'

The Seven Dials Restaurant

1, Buckingham Place (01273) 885555
www.sevendialsrestaurant.co.uk
Food served 10.30am-10.30pm
Two-course dinner £19.50

Since it opened in 2001, The Seven
Dials restaurant has enjoyed
overwhelming success. Winning
awards and public acclaim – and
much of it through word of mouth –
this former bank (and once, ironically,
a Burger King) offers impeccable,
friendly service with colourful and
imaginative food combinations (black
pudding and scallops anyone?).
Its owner/head chef, Sam Metcalfe,
spent years honing his craft in a
number of top London restaurants,
before doing the sensible thing and
relocating to Brighton. You can see
heart-warming pictures of him and
his family on the stairs down to the
basement, though who the bizarre
photos on the doors of the Gents
and Ladies are of is anyone's guess!

The menu here is Modern
Continental, with an emphasis on
Italian and French cuisine, and the
dishes are beautifully presented, with
quality to match the price. On the
menu, when I visited, were the likes
of crab risotto for starters and grilled
halibut and roasted New England
lamb for main, both of which were really
filling. But make sure to leave space
for desert; their homemade Earl Grey
sorbet was a real taste revelation.

In summer, diners can opt for
eating on the terrace, marvel at
Sam's herb garden and meet some of
the Seven Dials regulars, still pleased
as punch to have an eatery of this
calibre in their neighbourhood.

RESTAURANTS

133

True, this restaurant is very grown-up, but it has a refreshingly unpretentious ambience; you won't get a contemptuous stare from the waiter if you order red wine with your halibut or slurp your soup. In fact, this is an ideal place to bring family, friends or – if you want to make a good impression – a date. And should things go really well, you can even return here to get married in 'the Vault' downstairs!

THAI ORIENTAL FUSION

Aum Thong

60 Western Road (01273) 773922
Open Mon-Sat 12pm-2.30pm & 6pm-11pm, Sun 6pm-10pm
Thai Green curry £7.50, squid in spicy sauce £9.95, stir-fried crabs claws £8.50

You know you're in an authentic Thia restaurant when the menu says things like: *'Thai food is always cooked with real hrebs.'*, or, my favourite,' *if you fell you don't like Thai food...'* which perhaps is some kind of ancient proverb.

The menu here is immense, and particularly extensive on seafood dishes, with all main courses around £6-10. While the mood can seem a little lacklustre during the day, in the evening it's perfect, with subtle lighting, a warm atmosphere and genial staff.

Much of the food is of an excellent standard; the Tom Kha Hed soup is dynamite, as are many of the curry, meat and seafood dishes. The duck, which is always tricky to get right, might be a bit foamy and fatty for the more delicate palate. Not fancy, but certainly authentic.

Sawadee

84 St James St (01273) 624233
Open Mon-Sat 5pm-11pm,
lunchtime at weekends
Set menu for two £31, vegetarian £25.50

Don't let the colourful paintwork and professionally styled menus put you off – this is no McThai for Western numbskulls. The food is as bright and cheerful as its surroundings, with a plenitude of options for people who don't like meat. Make sure you order a starter, as they're all delicious. Sawadee is a slightly more modern counterpart to its neighbour, Muang Thai (tel 605223), and its nice that St James's street can boast two authentic and inexpensive Thai restaurants with enough character to make you want to visit each time and time again.

Restaurant * Cocktail Bar * Summer Terrace

Chill-out in Brighton's stylish restaurant & cocktail bar. Escape the seaside crowds and relax on the outdoor Terrace or inside in the serene restaurant or cool bar.

Modern Asian Food * Sumptuous Cocktails * Fine Wines

Late Bar & Live DJ's (Thursday - Saturday)

Open 7 days a week

dadu
Opposite the historic West Pier
124 Kings Road, Brighton
Tel: 01273 72 25 25

Bali Brasserie

Kingsway Court, First Avenue, Hove
(01273) 323810
Open 6pm-10.30pm Sun-Fri, until 11pm Sat

Found at the far end of Hove and done out in wicker, bamboo and plastic plants, this place is straight out of 'Love Boat' and 'Fantasy Island'. If Barry Manilow lived in Hove, this is where he would eat.

The ambience is completed at weekends by live music in the bar from Gloria (or sometimes Mike), who sits on a stool singing old numbers from the likes of Nancy Sinatra and Lee Hazelwood to backing tapes, uttering such gems as – *'If anyone has a birthday out there, come on up and we'll sort you out with something reeeaal special.'*

A word of warning, though, kitsch fans – even at the weekends, it can be pretty dead in the bar, so I recommend it only as a place for big groups. It'll help if you get dressed up, come en masse and create the atmosphere yourself. Incidentally, the food is Indonesian and Malaysian. It's good, but a bit pricey. 'Look boss, it's de plane, de plane'…

Krakatoa

7 Pool Valley (01273) 719009
Open 6pm-11pm Mon-Sun, main course
£6-£10, vegetarian and seafood dishes only

If you want delicious, quality, Southeast Asian food in comfortable surroundings, then come to Krakatoa, plonk yourselves downstairs and enjoy the ride. If, however, you are of a more adventurous disposition, you owe it to yourself to venture upstairs, where you have to take off your shoes (it's obligatory – so wash those feet and don't be wearing the novelty socks Auntie Flo bought you for Xmas) and see how you fare sliding your legs under their low, low tables. You can now simultaneously test the myriad flavours on offer and the limits of your bone structure. All this contortionism is, however, strangely relaxing – mentally, if not physically – which means it's the ideal place for dinner with your best buddy, or as the perfect icebreaker on a first date. Their meat-free cuisine is a real adventure, although be careful if you can't eat nuts as these appear to be in just about everything. The menu has plenty of tantalising options – I always opt for the Japanese salmon or the swordfish with bananas and pak choi – but, despite my conventions, it'd still be nice to see a few new dishes from time to time.

The only real quibble with this place comes from it being a victim of its own success; if you don't like to be hurried, you might give weekends a miss, as it can get very busy and the staff obviously feel the pressure to turf customers out after 'first sitting' for the next onslaught of hungry souls.

That aside, this is the place to come if you fancy an evening of quality Asian food, fun and yoga all rolled into one.

VEGETARIAN

Bombay Aloo
(see Indian restaurants)

Terre À Terre
71 East Street
(01273) 729051
Open Tue-Sun 12pm-10.30pm,
Mon 6pm-10.30pm

This is the Brighton veggie restaurant that always gets mentioned in all the national broadsheets and was even voted the country's best independent restaurant for vegetarians by the Vegetarian Society. It's not heart-stoppingly pricey, but don't expect much change from £50 for a meal for two. The food is beautifully presented fusion cuisine and, from its very beginning round the corner in Pool Valley, this stylish restaurant set the standards for vegetarianism with a difference, proving that a meal can be delicious, sophisticated and look appetizing, even without meat.

Brighton's most celebrated vegetarian, Brian Mitchell, looks forward to another nut cutlet.

They also do a healthy children's menu that isn't burger and chips, and includes such favourites as organic pasta and pesto and pic'a'stics (thin slices of raw veg with creamy cheese and chives dip), proving that, with a little imagination, kids don't have always to be plied with sausage and chips to get them to eat in a restaurant.
Gluttons beware, Terre À Terre is not a restaurant for those who want to binge, but for those who like attention to detail and care over their dishes.
Top tip – Book way in advance; it's ridiculously popular.

Trogs Restaurant
24 George Street (01273) 687821
www.trogsrestaurant.com
Open 7pm-10pm Wed-Sat

Nothing to do with the Sixties band who spent their days effing and blinding in West Country accents, Trogs moniker originates from when it was housed underneath a seafront hotel, and its former owner – in comparing his underground existence to that of a troglodyte – coined the name. True, it's a rather bizarre choice for a vegetarian restaurant and, when it's current owner, Alison, took over seven years ago, she did consider changing it (to Trolls, Scabs or Mongs), but with the name already established, so it remained. It seems fitting, therefore, that having relocated to Kemptown in 2003, Alison chanced upon another underground location to house her restaurant. Down here she has given the walls a liberal coating of mauve, added some metal furniture and Moroccan style lighting and made the best anyone could of this small basement. It feels a little gloomy when you first arrive, especially if still light outside, but you soon get used to it, and the old, spiral staircase is a nice feature.

All the food on offer here is fully organic, vegetarian or vegan (see café review for more details), with plenty of tasty options, such as tandoori tofu steak topped with korma, pan-fried halloumi wigwams with capers, homemade soup, and fudge profiteroles in butterscotch sauce, all presented in a modern style. The prices do seem steep (starters and desserts are £7, with main courses at around £14), though you can opt for a more reasonable three-course deal for £23.

While the prices and presentation of the food here may be comparable with Terre À Terre's, Trogs is anything but a formal restaurant. It's no faint praise that it has a fair number of loyal regulars, some of whom come on a weekly basis. One couple famously celebrated five Valentine's, a

wedding, and two anniversaries here – in a row! This is as much due to the effervescent staff as the food; whether you're being looked after by Jodie, Neel (see Heroes Chapter) or Alison, you're bound to be in for a fun evening. In fact Alison is a true Brighton character; she'll feed your dog, hang around your table for a natter and tell you stories about her latest animal rescue mission.

While not in the most blessed of locations, if Trogs maintains its standards of food and service, newcomers may understand why this restaurant is not a one-night stand affair.

For more information on Vegetarian Brighton, see section in Cafés Chapter

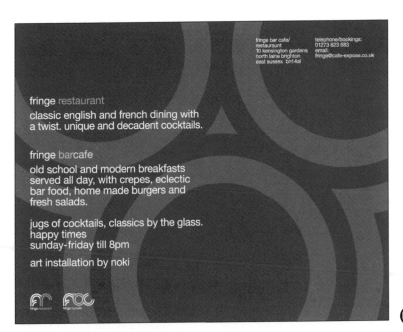

Watering Holes

Chances are that, during your time in Brighton, you might be tempted to pop for a swift half somewhere, so you'll be pleased to know that we have enough pubs and bars in the city to satisfy even the thirstiest of Glaswegians.

From the tiniest (the Hole in the Wall) and the tackiest (anywhere on West Street) to the most flamboyant (Regency Tavern), it's all on offer here; you're only problem – as with everywhere else in England – are the Draconian licensing laws. But there are even a few tips in this chapter for getting around those.

Over the last few years, however, Brighton has seen a glut of modern pubs take over in the city centre, all catering exclusively for a very young market. So exclusive in fact, that there was a shameful incident a few years ago when a 50 year old man (accompanied by his son) was ejected from the Polar Central on Queen's Road for being 'too old' and 'not trendy enough'.

Owing, therefore, to the plethora of naff chains and trendy bars that can found throughout the city centre, West Street and the Old Lanes, below is a carefully chosen selection of cool pubs and bars that cater for all you fresh-faced hipsters, but are still welcoming to the merely young at heart.

Cheers. Or 'Bottoms up', as they say in Kemptown.

FASHIONABLE DRINKING DENS

Alicats (S)

80 East Street/ Brills Lane (on the seafront, underneath the Prodigal) (01273) 220902
Films shown Mon-Sat 6pm, Sunday 5pm

Erring on the right side of dingy, Ali Cats is a cool, secretive underground bar, hidden up an alleyway, just off the seafront. Its clientele are a young, discerning and attractive crowd, while the bar, with its under-lit tables, sofas and futuristic lampshades, is a cross between a hip, New York basement club and the bar in 'A Clockwork Orange'. Quite simply, there is nothing else in Brighton quite like it (more's the pity), though someone does owe it to the girls to put more than one cubicle in the ladies loos*! Other nice touches here include the tiles (depicting images of Brighton from the Forties to Sixties) set into the bar, and every evening they show a cult film. At weekends, unsurprisingly, Ali Cats gets very busy, and claustrophobics may have a 'Charles

Bronson in the Great Escape' moment, owing to the stuffiness and lack of light, but its usually more sedate during the week. As one friend said: *"If Kelly Osbourne or Johnny Depp were in town, they'd drink here"*.

*Though, if there is a monstrous queue, you can always pop next door to the Prodigal

Barley Mow (K)

92 St George's Road (01273) 682259
Food served 11am-10pm

The Barley Mow is the Michael Palin of Brighton pubs; an all-round good egg, thoroughly entertaining and prone to the odd bit of silliness. The pub boasts a tuck-shop behind the bar, heated beer-garden, homemade food, a quiz every other Thursday, and – whey-hey! – Roast Dinners until 10pm! Fans of Lill, the landlord's 'Irish terrier wolfhound thing' (as described by manager, Julia), will be relieved to know that she still pays a visit most Sundays, as well as popping up in adverts for the pub in local magazines. But to solve the riddle of why *"where is Muriel?"* is written on the wall here, you'll have to visit, have a few jars, and ask the landlady.

Coopers Cask (H)

3 Farm Road, Hove (01273) 737026
Food served 12pm-9pm Sun-Thurs,
12-7pm Fri-Sat

Chocolate and love-hearts at the bar, free tampons in the ladies, excellent food, table service, music mags to look at and sweets at the end of the night? Seems like someone's been doing their homework on how to create a good atmosphere.

In fact this charming bar may be a trek into Hove, but is worth searching for its pub grub alone, as the ingredients are fresh, they offer homemade baked bread, the portions are incredible and it's so damned cheap! Of course I'm not the only one who thinks this, hence the fact that Coopers is rammed at mealtimes. If you're popping here for food, you'd best arrive early, as seating is very limited, or you may find yourself eating your lobster in the ladies.

Dr Brighton's (S)

16 Kings Road (01273) 328765

An excellent all-round Brighton pub, and particularly popular at weekends, especially with the pre-club crowd; Revenge, the Honey Club and The Beach are all within a 5 minutes walk. As well as a superb collection of new world wines, a pool table, a cute fish tank and DJs at weekends, Dr Brighton's shows off what this town does best by effortlessly blending a friendly, party atmosphere with a mixed gay/ straight crowd (despite the 'No Camping' sign above the bar!) If you're ever stood up here – or left waiting for friends – you can even pass the time reading all the trivia written on the columns in the centre of the pub. Originally based on the theme of infamous drinkers (Dorothy Parker, Oliver Reed etc) it has since expanded to include odd titbits of information (discover what a Hag Fag is!) and stories of weird deaths (find out about the man who was crushed to death by elephant poo). Dr Brighton's even claim to do the town's longest running drink's promotion, 'Prescription', which they rediscovered in some 80-year-old documents about the pub. The deal is that you get a large 'brand' measure with a mixer for £3.40 (though I suspect back in the 1920s it was a bit cheaper). The perfect pre-club, seafront bar for the more discerning.

The Eagle Bar & Bakery (NL)

125 Gloucester Road (01273) 607765
Food served Tues-Thurs 12pm-9pm,
Fri-Sat 12pm-8pm, Sun-Mon 12pm-6pm
(pizzas until 10pm)

Formerly the George Beard, the Eagle is a welcome addition to Brighton's modern breed of pubs, having won the Food Pub of the Year Award, in 2002, not to mention earning itself a place in a new book called 'the Strangest Pubs in Britain'! The former is due to the fact that the grub here is simply excellent, with daily specials, quality pizzas every Sunday and Monday, and a whole range of imaginative and tasty dishes, the latter owing to the fact that it actually has its own bakery **on the premises** (next to the bar in fact). They offer three styles – including Country Italian and Whole Grain – all made using artisan techniques (elbow grease and sweat), which can be purchased on the premises. Owned by the same chaps who run the Hop Poles, this place similarly has friendly service, a young clientele, plenty of seating and, of course, pride in its menu.

Non-smokers might be heartened to know they're planning to turn the upstairs into a non-smoking area – another Brighton first.

Earth and Stars (NL)

Top of Church Street (01273) 772282
Food served 12pm-8pm

Brighton's most environmentally friendly pub, the Earth and Stars is carbon-balanced and unbranded, has solar panels on its roof and prides itself on being 100% organic, from the beers, wines, soft drinks, peanuts and roast dinners to the floorboards, loo paper and staff. Ask for a pack of fags and, naturally, you'll get American Spirit.

Instead of Stella, Hooch, Guinness and the other usual suspects, The Earth and Stars sells unbranded organic drinks, which the obliging staff will let you sample first.

The pub, not surprisingly, attracts a young, eco-friendly crowd and is popular for its Sunday roasts (chicken, beef or nut), so it's best to arrive early if you're feeling peckish, otherwise it can get a little overcrowded. The rest

of the time, however, this pub is pretty quiet, which surprises me. Is it too far off the beaten track, is it too expensive (£5 for a large glass of wine, £2 for a can of soft drink), or is everyone scared off by the unfamiliar brands? Whatever the case, it deserves your support. On the subject of all things organic, I'll leave you with a story…

A few years ago I was in Cambridge, loitering by the fruit and veg section in Sainsbury's. There was a special offer on – that week only, organic mushrooms were half the price of the polluted, pesticide-riddled ones they usually sell. An old couple approached this section and the old guy said to his missus, '*Shall we try these organic mushrooms?*' A look of utter astonishment and fear crossed his wife's face and she pulled him away, muttering, '*Oh no, Albert. Please. Get the **normal** ones.*'

The Fortune of War (S)

157 Kings Road Arches (01273) 205065

This long-established seafront pub gets ridiculously busy during the summer weekends as it is always appropriated by hoards of visitors. In fact, be prepared to experience such a long and frustrating wait at the bar that you'll wish you'd simply gone to the off-licence and headed straight to the beach instead. Come off-season during the day, however, bag yourself one of the much-coveted window seats with sea view and you'll discover that it's actually quite a charming bar.

The Hampton (C)

57 Upper North Street (01273) 731347
Food served 12pm-3pm, 5pm-8pm Tues-Fri, 12pm-8.30pm Sat, 12pm-6pm Sun

Designed in a modernist, Scandinavian style, with lots of indoor stonework, stripped wood, geometric shapes and huge panoramic stills, The Hampton is laidback, stylish and a popular student haunt to boot. Visit on a Sunday for a superb roast, bask in the courtyard on a summers evening with a jug of Pimms, or drop acid and spend the evening staring at their giant photo of the Alps, actually believing yourself to be:
a. Heidi.
b. Goat Peter.
c. A Goat.

The Hop Poles (OL)

13 Middle Street (01273) 710444/ 710010
Food served 12pm-9pm weekdays, Fri-Sat 12pm-7pm, Sun 12pm-9pm

As with the Coopers Cask (these guys used to own it), the Hop Poles thrives on a tradition of quality food, sweets behind the bar, table service and a gay-friendly attitude. The pub is popular with a young, fashionable, mixed, gay/straight crowd and, unlike so many other pubs in its close vicinity, does not attract the weekend lager-louts. Being throwing distance from the Cinematheque, this makes a good spot for post-movie discussion over a pint and a bag of bon-bons, while its fair-sized beer garden can be a welcome retreat, should the music inside get a bit overbearing. They also seem to like any excuse to throw a party and, come St Patrick's, Halloween, Mother's Day or the semi-finals of the 'Yorkshire Indoor Bowling Championship', they'll be dancing on the tables and handing out the tequilas.

kept his tiny crowd enthralled with the tale of when his dog got its testicles stuck down the plughole. More recently I ventured up to witness two lesbians, tightly taped together, come writhing out of the gents toilets, closely followed by a girl flashing her tits at all and sundry. Another evening, there was a girl with a pen and paper, going round asking exactly how many teeth we all had. After collecting and processing her data, she stood on a table, announced the winners in the 'most teeth' and 'weirdest looking teeth' categories, and bought them both a pint. What was that all about? Someone please tell me this pub lies on a leyline or something, it'll make me feel better.

The Open House (PC)

146 Springfield Road (01273) 880102
Food served 12pm-9pm Mon-Thurs, 12pm-6pm Fri-Sun

Proving that with a little imagination Zel still have a few surprises up their sleeves, the Open House is a beautiful and stylish pub, situated next to the London Road Station. Expansive and decorated with colourful art (in collaboration with the Fiveways artists group), it has three main areas, one resembling a front room with sprawling sofas and paintings on the walls, whilst the main bit by the bar has big wooden tables and plays host to live music. If that's not enough they do Salsa every wed, live Jazz every Tues, have a table football game and one of the best beer gardens in Brighton.

If you don't live nearby, I recommend making the trip up the hill if you're in the Preston Circus area, or try it as a pre/ post movie bar if visiting the Duke of Yorks.

The Mash Tun (C)

1 Church Street (01273) 684951
Food served 12pm-5pm, Mon-Sun,

It's hard to believe that only ten years ago this place was a breath of fresh air to Brighton's pub culture. Nowadays the blend of sofas, big splashes of colour, loud music, continental pub-grub and young, Marlboro Lights smoking crowd - all spiky hair and bare mid-riffs – is **the** ubiquitous formula in Brighton. But the Mash Tun remains ever popular, as being central, spacious and with a 'chill-out' room upstairs it makes a perfect pre-club pub for weekend visitors and students.

I have to say, though, there's something strange about the little room upstairs, as I have had some singular experiences there. Many years ago someone used it for hosting literary events, and I remember one night listening to an old American writer, Jim Dodge, who

Palmer's Bar (C)

Queen Square (01273) 325812
Members bar with free admission

Once a brothel and an illegal drinking club, this tiny basement bar – hidden away near the ice rink – is one of the town's best-kept secrets. Offering tapas, cocktails, fresh fruit smoothies and low-key DJs spinning the latest in mellow Electronica, Palmer's Bar is the perfectly environment for an intimate, chilled-out evening. There are only a few tables so arrive early for a seat, as it can be a bit of a squeeze at weekends. And look for the framed pictures on the wall – they come from an old documentary about Fifties teenagers that was filmed down here. By chance I actually saw the documentary at the Cinematheque one year. Everyone had fuzzy beards and danced like they were on Happy Days. The beards may have gone but, otherwise, things don't change much in this town.

NB. Rumoured to be closing.

St James (K)

16 Madeira Place (01273) 626696
Food served 12pm-2.30pm every day

Situated in the heart of Kemptown, the St James' is a colourful and convivial boozer with enough originality to make it stand out from the crowd. The candles and fairy lights at night make the place really inviting, while little touches like the canned peanut dispenser by the bar, add a certain 'continental' charm.

The food, too, is enticing; a good choice of different Thai dishes are served daily, while on Sundays you can still get a good old roast with all the trimmings. The staff here are young and friendly and promote the place as a hang-out for students, the young-at-heart and the odd drag queen. Last time I was in, though, a girl tried to steal the book I was reading. What is the world coming to when even your trusty paperback is no longer safe from the hands of leggy young blondes?

Ok, we admit it, we've had a few...

The Shakespeare's Head (SD)

1 Chatham Place on the corner of New
England Road (01273) 329444
Food served Sunday 12pm-5pm
Free live music Sundays

There's a good ambience to this pub, with lots of seating, good beers, a permanent cloud of smoke in the air and a huge fat Henry the Eighth in the corner. For years he used to be chained to the ceiling of the Walmer Castle, until someone took him down to dust him one day and he ran off in search of a pub that would treat him with a little more respect. Saying that, he was kidnapped from the Shakespeare's Head last summer, though his kidnapper only made it to the Dials roundabout before having a heart attack and Henry's portly, peeling body is now back in its rightful place.

The Sidewinder (K)

65 Upper St. James's Street (01273) 679927
Food served weekdays Tues-Sun 12pm-3pm,
6pm-9pm

Is it just me, or does this place seem to be occupied entirely by Trustafarians, slackers and DJ wannabees, lolling around, smoking Marlborough Lights and swapping Glastonbury anecdotes? Being the exception to the rule in this neck of the woods, however, the Sidewinders trendy style works perfectly and, as well as the laid-back atmosphere, the pub provides excellent food, hip music, and a very large beer-garden.

Basketmakers (NL)

12 Gloucester Road (01273) 689006
Food served 12pm-3pm & 5.30pm-8.30pm
weekdays, 12pm-3.30pm Sat, 12-4pm Sun

Cherished by long-term Brightonians, the Basketmakers is simply a damned good local with no frills, no pumping music, no trendy lagers, no vile colours on the wall and plenty of decent pub grub. What is unusual about the place, however, is that the walls are covered, top to toe, with thousands of old tins, in which you can leave messages and, at the same time, look for any that have been left. I hid one in the Huntley and Palmers Dundee Cake tin (though I can't guarantee it'll still be there now), found another with the message – *'Ruth Hutt licked my face' (?)*, and recently discovered the bizarre drawing below in an old pipe tobacco tin. If you visit the pub it is your sworn duty to continue this fine tradition, particularly if taken with the urge to write fruity comments about the barstaff…

The Battle Of Trafalgar (NL)

34 Guildford Road (01273) 882276
Food served 12pm-2pm weekdays, 12pm-4pm weekends

Once the hangout for Brighton's theatrical types (possibly due to its close proximity to the original Nightingale theatre at the bottom of the road), the Trafalgar is a relaxed, spacious local with plenty of seats, a small beer garden and lots of lovely old theatre and comedy posters from days gone by.

The clientele and staff here have always been a friendly and mellow bunch, and the chances of witnessing a fight in this place is about as likely as Elton John's hair growing back of its own accord. The bar billiards table now has sadly gone (the manager told me it was broken but a cheeky local chipped in that it was due to 'cost-cutting'!) and the grub remains decidedly bog-standard, but, as good locals go, it's one of Brighton's finest.

Look out for the occasional visit from the landlord, he's the spitting image of Mr Fisher (the old head-teacher out of 'Home and Away') and is, according to one e-mail we received last year, *'a nice bloke, but steer clear from the subject of cricket, or you'll never get away'.*

Brighton Rock Beach House (K)

6 Rock Place (01273) 601139
Food served 11am-4pm, menu changes daily

Down one of Kemptown's many seafront side streets lies this relatively new pub. Decked out in a New England beach house theme (which works extremely well) expect friendly, camp staff, table service, excellent cocktails, scrummy food, cosy seating areas, loud opera after last-orders and a clientele that often includes young actors and musicians (owing to the fact that the Academy of Training, A.C.T., and Brighton Institute of Modern Music lie about 5 metres away!). Its owner, Neil Woodcock, adds a nice touch of finesse to his cocktails and, on a good day, will sit down with you, light a joss-stick and regale you with stories of the pubs three ghosts: an old lady, a coachman and a cat called Tiddles. On bad days, however, he gets stressed out and can be a bit of a grump!

The Cricketer's (OL)

15 Black Lion Street (01273) 329472

Brighton's answer to the Queen Vic, the Cricketer's is one of its oldest pubs (it even earned a mention in 'Brighton Rock) and is suitably decorated in red Victorian-style furnishings, old gramophones, ornate table lamps and wallpaper that'd make your granny blush. It is, however, best avoided at weekends when it's stuffy, uncomfortably busy and populated by blokes who wear their shirts out to hide their beer guts. Come instead on a quiet weekday, when it transforms back to a snug front room and you can bag the window seats by the trophy cabinet, or sit at the back and see how gaudy the furnishings really are.

The Great Eastern (NL)

103 Trafalgar Street
(01273) 685681
Food served 12pm-11pm Mon-Sat,
Sun 12pm-10.30pm

Located at the bottom of Trafalgar Street and the start of North Laine, this is another unspoiled Brighton pub with old wooden tables, shelves of books at the back, newspapers, friendly barstaff, and a genuine mix of clientele from students to beardy old men. (I even saw a vicar in here one Sunday necking a pint of Guinness.)

If you're coming for the night it often pays to get arrive early as seating is limited; the tables facing the bar can get a bit cramped if it's busy, while the big tables at either end of the pub are perfect if you're bringing a crowd for a good natter. The Eastern is also renowned for its pub grub, which ranges from classic to exotic food, and does one of the best (and cheapest) Sunday roasts in Brighton.

The Lion and Lobster (H)

Sillwood Street (01273) 327299
Food served 12pm-9pm (and they don't
scrimp on the portions either)

Though tucked away amongst the
maze of Hove's backstreets, the Lion &
Lobster should not be missed. As
many pubs in the city fall victim to the
modernisation process, this remains a
true traditional seaside boozer. Expect
psychedelic beer-stained carpets,
ploughman's lunches, sea faring tales
from salty old sea dogs, burned-out
clubbers in their late-thirties and an
absolute fog of tobacco smoke. On
football nights they celebrate in style,
with TVs in every corner and plenty of
beer and testosterone fuelled
'ooooohs, aaaaahhhs' and 'the referee
is a mong'. For the cool cats there's
even live Jazz on a Thursday, when the
Brighton All-Stars squeeze into the
corner and do their thing, and Irish
folk on Sundays. It's even a B&B on the
sly, which is invaluable if, at the end of
the night, you just can't face leaving.

The Napier (Ha)

Halfway up Southover Street
(01273) 601413

Maps of the British Empire on the
walls, Spandau Ballet quietly playing in
the background and a good pint of
HSB on tap…yes the Charles Napier,
along with the Greys and Geese, is
one of the few remaining locals in
Hanover that hasn't been handed
over to the student crowd. If there's
just two of you in for an evening's
natter, make for the yard of ale
hanging above the doorway by the
ladies, and grab the two armchairs by
the standard lamp. If it's warm,
they've got a sweet little beer garden
round the back, though look out for
the neighbour's cat, which is prone to
launch itself into your pint if you're
not careful*.

*A couple of year ago, the owner of the cat
emailed me to tell me its name, but sadly the email
got last down the back of the sofa. Can anyone
provide the pussy's name for the next edition?

Happy hour at the Napier

The Nelson (NL)

36 Trafalgar Street (01273) 695872
Food served Mon-Sat 12pm-2.30pm,
Sun 12.30pm-3.30pm Quiz Night Tuesday

Located half-way down Trafalgar Street, The Nelson is often overlooked, even by long-term residents, which is a pity as, along with the Great Eastern and the Basketmakers, this is one of the few really good locals in North Laine. With tobacco stained walls, a Sooty collection box, pork scratchings for sale, food 'like granny makes it', a mismatched collection of stools in the main bar, and an unspoken policy for conversation to take priority over music, the Nelson has been spared the makeover treatment and remains a cherished old-school pub. Manager and Cellar Manager, Sophie and Rob, will make you feel very at home and, if you're also a musician like Rob, you'll doubtless end up lost in conversation with him about guitar bands. In fact, the music selection in here is normally down to Rob too; expect to hear the sweet sounds of Belle and Sebastian, Neil Young, The Beatles; Crosby, Stills and Nash etc, his principle being – *'nothing modern, and always quiet enough so everyone can talk easily over it.'*

The Nelson also has a terrific reputation for its food, which is really top notch. Sunday roast is a lavish serving of roast and veg (and they do a tasty nut-roast for veggies) with crumbles and the likes of Spotted Dick and custard – of heroic portions – for pudding fans afterwards. The pub is also popular with the Brighton and Hove football crowd (hence all the photos on the walls), and still does its long-running Tuesdays quiz with cash prizes and free bottles of wine. Come here of a wet afternoon, sit down with a pint of Guinness, bangers and mash and a copy of the Argus and, within a few hours, you'll be shouting *'Come on you Seagulls'* in a genuine Brighton accent.

The Rock (K)

7 Rock Street (01273) 697054
Food served Mon-Sat 12pm-3pm,
6pm-9pm, Sun 12pm-4pm

Once renowned for its cabaret and music nights (local heroes David Devant and his Spirit Wife* started out here), the Rock, in the far-flung reaches of Kemptown, is one of Brighton's most spacious and convivial pubs. My mate Carl used to live near here, and it's always assuring to walk in to a friend's local and see them greeted by half the clientele. In fact, the manager, Fran, has a thousand and one stories to make your hair stand on end and will be cheerfully insulting if he likes you.

The pub is quite a way out in Kemptown, but, on a cold winter's night when you need somewhere to settle by the fire, have a game of chess and talk about the good old days, the Rock is perfect. (Saying that they've got a big beer garden which makes it a great spot in summer too.) The Rock also hosts an acoustic night every other Thursday, has a games room downstairs (with backgammon, cards, scrabble and chess), an upstairs room with pool and table football and a big beer garden. And, being a stone's throw from the very fashionable Sussex Square, don't be surprised to spot the odd celebrity skulking in the corner.

Brighton's answer to the Bonzo Dog Band, David Devant used to dress up as Cluedo characters and ride magic carpets on stage, while their 'Spectral Roadies' would perform magic tricks and grate carrots on the singer's head for the song 'Ginger'

Bedford Tavern (H)

30 Western Street, Hove (01273) 739495
Food served 12pm-3pm, (three-course
Sunday lunch served in the downstairs
restaurant downstairs

'A country pub in the heart of the town' says the sign above the door, and a fitting motto it is too, as this Brunswick local, run by David and Phil, is extremely welcoming, and suitably eccentric. Look for the paintings of the pub's two dogs, Libby and Emmie, on the walls, the collage of silly photos, and the strange picture with the slogan 'come on boys, mammas breasts are ready.'(?!) While the clientele of predominantly older gay couples seem to be hardy regulars, if you're a stranger, rather than getting the *you aint from round here, are you, boy?'* treatment, in the Bedford Tavern you'll be warmly received. I came last St George's Day with friends and we had a great evening; they'd laid on a terrific spread of creamy mashed potato, beef stew and sausages and there was a bloke by the bar dressed as a red, fluffy dragon. And, for those who recall last year's review – yes, they've cleaned the fishtank.

pubs

The Colonnade (C)

10 New Road (01273) 328728

This is the bar for the Theatre Royal next door. It's a wonderfully oddball place at the best of times and the atmosphere can range from that of a morgue to a Simon Callow party, with everyone throwing their arms around each other, shouting – *"Darling I thought you were simply wonderful"*. The wall are decorated with signed photos of cheesy celebs (Roy Kinnear, Jeffery Archer etc) who, presumably, have all performed at the Theatre Royal at some time, and it can make for a fun evening trying to remember the names of past TV stars, such as the bloke who played Eddie Shoestring.

While some people will really hate this place, others might find that it has a singular appeal (the last time I was in here, for example, the barmaid was playing War of the Worlds and the guy next to me was reading a Frank Muir book) and at least it's one of the few places in Brighton where you can pretty much guarantee a seat on a Friday night.

The Evening Star (C)

55/56 Surrey Street
(01273) 328931
www.eveningstarbrighton.co.uk

One of only two independent breweries in Brighton, The Evening Star is **the** place to come if you're passionate about your beer. As well as offering such heavenly brews as 'Dark Star', 'Golden Gate', 'Sea Cider', and the ever-popular wheat beer 'Spiced Vice', they also boast **nine** hand pumps (seven for the real ales, two for cider) and new ales on a daily basis.

True, this pub does have its fair share of real ale types (those who sport mangy beards and beer bellies and always win at pub quizzes) and it's a rarity to see large groups of ladies in

151

here, but if you're looking for somewhere to sample some genuinely excellent ales and true Brightonian hospitality, this place will not disappoint.

The Greys (Ha)

105 Southover Street (01273) 680734
www.greyspub.com
Sun breakfast 11am-12pm, lunch 12pm-2pm, evening meal 6pm-9.30pm Tues, Wed, Thurs & Sat

This tiny but celebrated pub has been an institution in Brighton for as long as I can remember. Although its famous Belgian chef has been replaced by a Brit*, the food here is still sensational, more akin to top-class restaurant nosh than pub-grub. Expect such delights as lobster bisque, homemade pates, desperate Dan style cow pie with horns (!), strawberry and claret jelly, and handmade coffee ice-cream. Despite its diminutive size, the Greys also puts on some excellent music evenings, with a slant towards Blues and Folk heroes, as well as performances by local storytellers Adam Acidophilus and Pete McCarthy, and such legends as John Otway. Combine this with the fact that there are new beers on tap every two months and you have a pub that really has no need of lava lamps and designer furniture to create personality. Inhabited by roguish landlord Mike and a motley collection of dysfunctional middle-aged drinkers, it does lean towards being a "locals' local", but new faces are made welcome, and the stuffing and mounting of American visitors is now kept to a minimum. The last time I was in, I overheard an old guy at the bar saying to his mate: '......*so she's embarked on this four-year aromatherapy course.........two years for each nostril.'*

*With a penchant for world dishes and traditional English food

Just had a knight Vindaloo – Now my mouth's on FIRE!

The Hand in Hand (K)

33 Upper St. James's Street (01273) 602521

The place for lovers of real ale, The Hand in Hand is still the only pub in Brighton where the beer is brewed locally. Instead of spending £3 on a pint of gassy piss, why not come here and treat yourself to a creamy pint of Brighton Bitter (only £1.70!), Olde Trout (named after the landlady), or, their best-seller, the 'Kemptown'. They also do a nice line in German beer, chocolate and hard-boiled eggs. Look for the newspaper stories that line the walls (Kennedy's assassination's up there somewhere), the naked Victorian ladies on the ceiling and the collection of ties, which were recently washed after nearly twenty years of hanging on the wall, collecting cigarette smoke and going mouldy.

A minor word of warning; The Hand in Hand is a very small pub, so don't always expect a seat, especially at weekends when their mass of regulars (middle-aged, beer bellied types who always win at pub quizzes) are in. During the week, however, you should expect your own table, and the chance to fall into conversation with a couple of beardy blokes about politics, holidays in Bavaria or real ale. If you want to spark a debate that the whole pub can join, ask why you can't buy turkey eggs*…

You might like to know that:

• You can take home 8 pints half an hour before closing.
• This is strictly a non-pulling pub!
• After 18 years, they've actually had the place re-decorated. But don't worry, nothing's changed!

The Heart and Hand (NL)

75 North Road (01273) 624799

An old-fashioned bar in North Laine, the Hand in Hand has, for as long as I can remember, been *the* hangout for many of Brighton's guitar bands, meaning that weekends in here can be like an informal identity parade of familiar faces from up and coming bands (British Sea Power), has-beens (Spitfire/ James) and stalwarts of the music industry (Stereolab). The reason for this is quite simple – the pub's famous jukebox, which features the likes of Love, The Electric Prunes, Scott Walker and Tim Buckley. Juxtaposed with the muso crowd, you'll find many North Laine traders, old school antique dealers, spivs and wrinkly old boys who look like extras from Eastenders.

**Even the butchers I've spoken too
seem mystified by this one.*

The Regency Tavern (C)

32 Russell Square (01273) 325652
Food served 12pm-2pm every day

One of Brighton's best-loved pubs where gay couples, locals, grannies, students and hammy old actors sit side by side. Done out in exotic gold leaf palm trees, plastic flowers and plaster cherubs, the Regency's interior could easily pass for a set from 'The Avengers'. Even the Gents is decorated with a glitterball and mirrored tiles. In spite all that, there's still something peculiarly Victorian about the place, which only adds to its charm.

If you're ever in for a friend's birthday (or your own, for that matter) make sure to tell the barstaff, as they like nothing better than playing their flamboyant, operatic version of 'Happy Birthday', and, before you know it, the whole pub will have joined in and you'll be arm in arm with some batty old Brunswick landlady, doing the Can-Can. If that's not enough, the Regency does one of the best pub lunches in Brighton and is haunted by several ghosts, which you can learn about from the ghost tours during the festival or, better still, from Jeff and Chris behind the bar.

Ranelagh (K)

2 High Street (01273) 681634

So I walk in here one Easter Sunday, to meet friends, and I'm confronted by two guys doing the can-can to the orchestra break in the Beatles 'Day in the Life' (?!), while at one of the tables near the bar, a guy is shouting, *"I've taken more acid then every fucker in here. And anyone who says not, is a fucking liar."*

Welcome to another St James St. anomaly. Sandwiched between gay bars and posh restaurants lies the Ranelagh, the last bastion of the 'pub drunk', the professional beer-belly and sozzled old musicians with corrugated faces. Come and meet an array of characters from friendly middle-aged blokes with pony-tails and leather waistcoats, to the kind of person one might simply describe as 'dangerous'.

The music theme décor ranges from the quaint to the naff, with albums stuck to the ceiling, pennies glued on the bar, banjos, guitars and accordions stuck everywhere, and a few dodgy photos and illustrations of old guitar legends on the walls. But the Ranelagh does still pay homage to its theme, offering live music every Sunday, from Boogie-woogie pianists to Blues guitarists. And this, of course, is the time to experience the pub at its best.

Otherwise, it's the perfect starting point for anyone brave (or foolish) enough to take the challenge of a Tuesday night 'alternative' Kemptown pubcrawl.

Every drinker's Utopia: A guaranteed lock-in on a Saturday Night

There is a pub in town that has a guaranteed lock-in every weekend, and usually stays open until the small hours of the morning. Last time I was there with friends, some smart Alec borrowed some lipstick from a female friend, and before we knew it everyone in the pub looked like Robert Smith for the night. If you get in touch and convince me you're not a copper, I might be kind enough to let you in on this secret drinking den.

Sumo and Cocktail Lounge Bar (OL)

9-12 Middle Street (01273) 749465
Open Thurs- Sat 12pm-1am
Thurs Free entry, Fri-Sat free before 9pm,
£2 before 10pm, £4 after 10pm

Mixing a futuristic and minimalist theme, this unique and stylish basement bar makes a worthy late-night drinking den. A lot of thought has gone into the place, with the emphasis on subdued music, table service, and cocktails, as well as a wide choice of beers. At weekends they've got DJs playing funky club classics and R 'n' B. It pays to get here early, not only is it cheaper, but you'll avoid those long queues – especially on Saturdays. The cocktail bar upstairs also has Internet access, so try not to knock your Martinis and fag ash down the back of their hard drives.

The Havana Club (S)

5b Regency Square
Open Fri-Sat 10pm-2pm
£3 after 11pm, free between 10-11pm
This is a members club but you can be
signed in for free on the night

A well-kept secret (up until now, that is), the Havana Club is a nifty late-night bar on the same side of the Square as the Pelirocco hotel and is ideal if you fancy somewhere calm to carry on drinking and while away the night, without all the hassle and expense of a club. It's even available – at no charge – for hire on Saturdays, has DJs playing Latin themed music and a free Space Invaders game by the toilets which, I'm assured, will be fixed soon.

Kia's Bar (underneath the Star of Brunswick) (H)

32 Brunswick Street East (01273) 771355
Open 11am-1pm, Mon-Sat £3

A rarity in Brighton, Kia's is an underground bar where you can carry on boozing until late. It can get a bit hot and claustrophobic down there if really busy, but, otherwise, it has a pleasant seediness to it. Food is served right up until 12.45am (burgers, chips etc). I'm also unreliably informed that the brilliant episode of 'Faking It' –the one where the bloke had to pull off being a drag act for the night – was filmed here too.

The Grosvenor Casino (OL)

9 Grand Junction Road (01273) 326514
Open until 2am every night

Free to get in (provided you've had the foresight to get a free membership card, which permits 6 guests) and the bar stays open until 2am. If cheap beer, gambling and breakfasts don't interest you, they also do a fine breakfast. (See Entertainment for more info)

A Pub Crawl in Hanover*

A host of fabulous pubs await you in this residential area of Brighton, and, if you're in town for more than a couple of days (or live here), I thoroughly recommend it. Your starting point is Southover Street, opposite the Level. Walk up a short way, wait for the smokers to catch up then start by visiting The Geese (Have Flown Over The Water).

This pub used to be just called The Geese, until the guy who re-painted the sign admitted that he couldn't paint geese and had just painted a stretch of water instead. Hence the name acquired the extra bit in parenthesis. But I digress; it used to be my local and is a small, friendly Irish pub with two resident dogs (CC and Murphy). Directly opposite is The Greys, another tiny pub, legendary for its food and music/ performance nights.

Continue up the hill from here and you'll find the Dover Castle, which is a popular student pub and does a great 'Reggae Roast' on a Sunday. Further up you'll reach the Napier. I have to say that the last time I tried this crawl I never got past the Napier as things had already started getting fuzzy, but I'm on my back after three pints so don't let my weakness dampen your spirits. This is a real locals' pub, with good beers on tap (my downfall!) and a garden round the back. Watch out though for the cat from the house next door leaping in your pint. Even further up the hill the crawl takes you to the trendy 'Pub With No Name', a favourite with DJs, the Skint crew and umpteen blokes with goatee beards. Stick on a woolly hat and anorak, give yourself a cool name like 'Loinclothsally' and enjoy the vibe. If you have drunk enough, the idea of 'doing aeroplanes' back down Southover Street should start to be appealing by now. Keep going until you reach Hanover Terrace. Circle for a while then parachute out.

As you walk down Hanover Terrace look out for house number 88. A student transformed it into a big smiley face a few years ago as an art project and it's stayed like that ever since (though it is in need of a lick of paint now). At the end you'll find the recently refurbished London Unity (now packed with students) and, further up, the Constant Service (now packed with students).

By now you should be so hammered that the munchies will have kicked in, leaving you no option but to scoff a pizza and Banoffee Pie at Famous Moe's on Southover Street. Doing aeroplanes will no longer seem quite so appealing after this, owing to alcohol-induced vertigo, tunnel vision, nausea and dizziness, so it's best to crawl home on your hands and knees from here or call an ambulance.

*See Watering Holes for more detailed reviews of some of these pubs

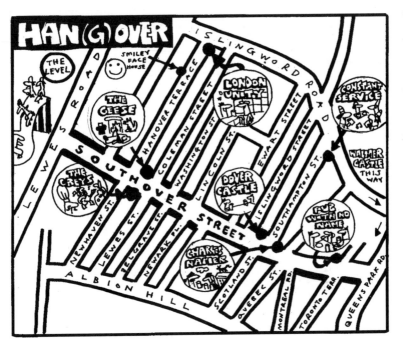

FOR A CRACKING PUB LUNCH WITH ALL THE TRIMMINGS...

Seven Dials: *Prestonville Arms (see veggie food section)/ The Shakespeare's Head*

North Laine: *Nelson/ Great Eastern/ Earth and Stars/ The Eagle*

Kemptown: *Barley Mow/ Sidewinder/ Brighton Rock Beach House/ The Stag*

City centre: *Regency Tavern/ Hampton*

Hove: *Coopers Cask/ Lion and Lobster*

Old Lanes: *Hop Poles*

Preston Park area: *Open House*

(See pub reviews above for more details)

WHERE TO BUY BOOZE AFTER 10.30 PM

Southover Wine Shop

80/81 Southover Street (01273) 600402

This is one of the few off-licenses in Brighton that stays open until 11pm. If that's not enough, they stock over 40 Belgian beers, have a great selection of spirits, sell fireworks all year round and even sell bread and milk as part of a special Sunday service.

The Booze Brothers

07887 483406

Brighton's most benevolent duo, these guys will deliver booze and fags to your door at any time of day or night, though you have to buy in bulk (to make it worth their while). Soon to be starting a sister company called the Louche Brothers, delivering ladies of the night, Class 'A' drugs and firearms on request.

discotheques

Home to the famous Zap Club, Ocean Rooms, Honey Club, Catskills records and Skint, Brighton's club/ DJ scene boasts everything from cool underground Jazz and Retro to House and Garage nights, as well as being home to the biggest gay club on the South Coast. Combine this with regular visits from big-name DJs, plus our own Norman Cook, and it's not surprising that Brighton's clubs are packed every night of the week. What other town can boast over 30 clubs, all within walking distance of each other, and most a stone's throw from the beach?

One of the very special things about Brighton is that, unlike so many other UK cities, the clubs here do not merely represent that weekend escapism from drudgery and boredom. If anything, some of the best nights are mid-week. Even Sundays are starting to become fashionable. Clubbing in Brighton seems nothing less than a shameless celebration of living in a party town, which is probably why carnival-type music, like Big Beat, Latin Jazz and 70s disco, is particularly popular here. And with special club nights, like Margot's Parties and Wild Fruit, the scene has a dimension of glitz and glamour that Manchester, even in its heyday could never have provided.

Please check local press for club-night details as they can change on a monthly basis.

Babylon Lounge

Kingsway, Hove (01273) 207100

No club adjoining Hove's bowling greens and lagoon will ever be cool, particularly when it resembles little more than a function room for weddings. That said, Babylon Lounge does offer decent Soul and Goth nights and hen-friendly male strippers every Friday (see Adonis Cabaret review in Sex Chapter). The rest of the time it contents itself with bog-standard student nights, Salsa classes and midweek sessions hosted by part-time Garage DJs from as far afield as Brighton.

Tip: Unless you live in darkest Hove, you'll need to get a cab here. I'd recommend paying the driver an extra quid to wait around an extra couple of minutes as, after a quick nose around inside, you *may* choose to make a sharp exit.

The Beach

171-181 Kings Road Arches (01273) 722272
www.thebeachbrighton.co.uk

Found between the two piers on the seafront, this spacious club, with a stylish Mediterranean flavour to its design, is one of the more popular of the many seafront nightclubs. Inside, the room has been divided into different sections, including a restaurant area off to one side, and a huge bar that looks like it should have featured in James Bond's 'Goldfinger'.

The Beach was once home to the 'Big Beat Boutique' but the Skint team upped and left when the Concorde 2 opened, so it's now back to party anthem knees-ups, Seventies disco and excellent House and Drum'n'Bass nights, and it seems ever popular for it. The only thing a bit disconcerting here is trying to find exactly where the dance floor is, as it's a bit ill-defined,

but it's a big club so don't worry, unlike many of Brighton's other clubs, you won't have to boogie with someone's armpit in your face. Attracting a friendly, unpretentious crowd, The Beach is a popular pick-up place. Get here early if you want to guarantee entry though, especially at weekends; it can be a lonnnnnngggggg wait in that queue sometimes, especially if you end up sandwiched between cackling hen parties.

Brighton Gloucester

27 Gloucester Place (01273) 688011
www.thebrightongloucester.co.uk

Despite a recent face-lift and slight
name-change, the Gloucester seems
destined to live on forever as a cheap,
cheerful, come-as-you-are club,
responsible for more unwanted
pregnancies and regretful *'Oh no, did I
really slam-dance to the Sisters of Mercy?'*
recollections than Brighton's other clubs
put together. Expect every musical taste
to be catered for here, from Seventies
and Eighties to House, Indie, Nu-Metal,
Nu-Goth, GothMetal, OldGothMetal,
QuiteOldButNotAsOldAsOldGothMetal,
and so on. Inside, the Gloucester is a
split-level funhouse with a dance floor
straight out of Saturday Night Fever,
and while some nights it's full to
capacity, on others there'll just be a few
Punks sat in the corner eating jelly. Even
the clientele here are an unpredictable
lot – everything from gangs of
teenagers from Crawley, to gaggles of
Secondary school teachers, who've
popped down here 'just for old times
sake'. Until you've been here twenty
times, fallen down the stairs to the toilet,
danced like a loony to Abba and been
chatted up by a fifteen-year old, you're
still a newcomer in this town.

Casablanca

2 Middle Street (01273) 709710

This club Specialises in Latin-Jazz and
Jazz-Funk, and is particularly refreshing
in that it has live bands at weekends,
and not just DJs. With such a strong DJ
culture here, you forget sometimes
what a pleasure it is to dance to live
music, especially when the bands really
know how to let rip.

The club has two floors, and while
it's a bit annoying that you can't take
your drinks between the two, the top
half is basically just a bar (with a naff
car theme), so I'd recommend sticking
to the downstairs bit. Shame that the
dance area is between the bar and the
exit, but if the funky music and those
horns don't move you to dance, you're
in the wrong city.

Dress code: flares, corduroy cap, goatee

Concorde 2

Miles from anywhere, Madeira Drive
(01273) 606460
www.concorde2.co.uk

Built out of the ashes of the Water Rats (a one-time greasy bikers hang-out), the Concorde 2 took over from where the original Concorde left off by specialising in live music, cracking clubnights (ranging from Reggae and Punk House to Hip-Hop and dirty acid Techno) and odd one-offs, such as the UK Air Guitar Championships. It's also the current home to the legendary Big Beat Boutique (every other Friday), though, if you want to come along and see the likes of Norm, Midfield General and the Lo-Fi's, you'll need to get here early, as this night still attracts very big crowds.

I have to admit though, as venues go, I've never been crazy about this place. Whilst they put on some cool club nights, the Concorde works far better for live music than the intimate, glamorous or pervy nights I've experienced here in the past (such as Vavavavoom! or Torture

Garden). If you are coming along though, for goodness sake, try and wear something that doesn't clash with the paint job.

Creation

78 West Street, Brighton (01273) 321628

Formally the Paradox, this place has always tried to take itself more seriously than The Event2 (just across the road), but being located on West Street, it is, of course, fighting a losing battle.

Full of weekend revellers in their late teens, Creation is a large multi-levelled club, with three dance-floors, cosy corners and paid podium dancers. It operates a seven-nights-a-week mix of chart hits, club classics and more specialised Garage / R'n'B nights, not to mention the famous Wild Fruit. That aside, it's still full to the brim with blokes who overdo it on the aftershave and girls who haven't yet learned that wearing knickers and a boob tube in sub-zero temperatures turns the skin blue and is strictly not a turn-on.
Dress code: G-string/ thong

Club New York

Dyke Road, Brighton (01273) 208678

Housed in what was once a church (and a crappy old club called the Shrine), this is now a place of worship for Salsa devotees, some of whom *can* actually dance. Essentially operating as an ongoing 24-7 Salsa lesson, this place runs classes most evenings, with a clubnight straight afterwards. The teachers are very good, the regulars are super-friendly (and often gorgeous) and the vibe is noticeably sparklier than most House nights in town. Two mid-size dance-floors hold the action and, if you're lucky, some sharp-dressed, swivel-hipped Mediterranean sex bomb will hold you up in the middle of it.

DISCOTHEQUES

The Escape

10 Marine Parade (01273) 606906
www.theescapeclub.co.uk

This cool Art Deco building, done out in mauve and sky-blue, and overlooking the seafront, is home to one of Brighton's most successful clubs. With winning formulas for music and promotions, two floors of music, a mobile nightlife guide and a terrace, the Escape attracts a young, to very young, horny crowd, who love getting tarted up and partying.

Despite countless refits (the latest being by the designers of Fabric) and changes of promoters, you can still count on this club if you like your music hard, loud and funky, and your fellow clubbers dressed up and 'with it'. **Dress code**: backless dress for the ladies, crotchless panties for the boys

A Cheeky Tale

If you look above The Escape you'll see a flat, which has a commanding view of the beach and, in particular, the phone box in front of the club.

These two guys I know, Mark and Bruce, used to live up there, and some nights after the club had almost cleared out, they'd ring up the phone box, wait for some inebriated clubber to answer, take a note of how he was dressed and then play these weird 50s adverts down the line to him. It would start with some cheesy music and then go –
'Hi, and welcome to the world of Lux soap, a new powder that'll get your clothes whiter than white.' – and then a different voice would say –
'You are wearing a red shirt, jeans, and a blue hat.'
Click

162

The Event 2

West Street (01273) 732627

The largest club in Brighton, popular with students, virgin clubbers, hen and stag parties, 'weekenders' and the under-twelves. Don't take the place seriously and you'll have a good time. It is, of course, a blatant meat-market, but the nights are generally cheap, unpretentious and unashamedly glitzy. Party tunes throughout the ages (plus a big nod to the previous week's *Top Of The Pops*) create the soundtrack, while the vast dance-floor is a sea of loved-up teenagers, all on the pull and sporting the latest in Top Man/ Top Shop fashion.

Funky Buddha Lounge

Kings RoadArches

(01273) 725541 *www.funkybuddha.com*

These two tunnels under Marine Parade have earned themselves a fearsome reputation for providing superb, cutting-edge beats for the smarter-than-the-average-bears of Brighton clubland. Each evening you'll find specialist nights, often run by local labels, dedicated to Raw Funk, Rare Grooves, jackin' Acid Disco and soulful Garage. This is a place to bathe your ears in the freshness and vitality of Brighton's beat underground (which isn't difficult, owing to the fact that the place is so narrow, you're never more than a yard from the nearest speaker). Don't come here for a quiet drink; these tunnels were made for the music.

Funky Fish Club

19-23 Marine Parade, underneath the Madeira Hotel (01273) 698331

Underneath the Madeira Hotel, this oversized school hall has been home for countless years to an evening of Northern Soul and Motown. Formally the Catfish Club, this night generally

caters for an older crowd, with regulars in their late twenties, thirties (and even forties) coming to indulge their passion for this music. The venue is awful, but it seems to be the only place in town where absolutely anything goes on the dance floor. So if you're tired of practicing those high-kicks at home, you now know where to go. The DJ banter here is a bit tacky but the crowd are a friendly lot, particularly the randy thirty-year olds. It also makes a pretty cheap Saturday night out compared to many of the other clubs in Brighton. Ladies, expect to be chatted up by visiting insurance salesmen staying in the hotel above, who will attempt to make conversation with opening gambits like, '*Oh, yes, I've always been a big fan of Diana Ross and the Pips.*'

The Honeyclub2
214 Kings Road Arches (01273) 202807
www.thehoneyclub.co.uk

This seafront club is a well-loved students' haunt during the week, and packed at weekends for its House nights. It's also popular with the gay scene, and is one of the few clubs in Brighton to open every day of the week. The party here never seems to stop and, with such full-on hard-edged Dance music playing every evening, it's only a matter of time before the poor building has a nervous breakdown. Attracting big name DJs now, The Honeyclub has moved away from being just 'cheap and cheerful', they've got a chill-out area upstairs and there are more places to sit down now and relax, watch the fashion gurus parading around in the latest cheesy high-street garb, or ogle at the sexy dancers.
Top tip – bring earplugs.

The Jazz Place
10 Ship Street, Brighton
(01273) 328439

Priding itself on being 'the world's longest-running weekend Jazz club', the Jazz Rooms has changed little since it opened ten years ago. It's still a poky basement with two tables, five chairs and a dance floor the size of a Persian Rug. In fact, the only thing that ever seems to change here are the posters on the walls. But it remains a terrific club-night and really packs in the weekend crowds – a friendly, straight-laced bunch, intent on sweating it on the dance floor to the Latin-Jazz-Salsa-Afro-Beats spun by Russ Dewbury and co.

Not just the Jazz Place, on Tuesdays it's also the 'Reggae Place', as it has been home to the excellent Roots Garden for almost as long as Russ Dewbury's Jazz nights. Laid-back, welcoming and even offering a free cloakroom service, this is one of the best clubs in town. Serious Jazzers, award yourself ten points if you recognise which Miles Davis album the colour scheme down here is taken from.
Dress code – flares, corduroy cap, Jazz dot*

That bit of fluff that grows below the bottom lip

dJ pROFile

Russ dewbury

Having helped develop the burgeoning Jazz Scene in London in the late-Eighties with Gilles Peterson, Russ Dewbury saw a chance to take things one step further with Brighton's open-minded music crowd, and moved here in 1987 to found his own club night – the Brighton Jazz Rooms – setting off a career that has included DJing, broadcasting, promoting and record compiling worldwide.

Since finding its natural home at the Jazz Place in 1991, Dewbury's night has continued ever since, attracting an easy-going crowd of all ages (a growing rarity in Brighton), and has now become the longest running Jazz Dance Club in the world. More importantly it has, as Russ succinctly put it, 'been packed the first night it opened and has been packed ever since.'

Born out of this scene, Russ also created the Brighton Jazz Bop, a mini festival that began in May 1988 with Art Blakey and the Jazz Messengers at the Top Rank Suite (now Event 2) and which has, over the years, played host to the likes of Marlena Shaw, Pharaoh Sanders, The Roots, Brand New Heavies, Roy Ayers and Jarimoquai.

Not content with regularly flying around the world DJing, Russ has also been responsible for the rediscovery and management of such artists as Jean Jacques Perrey, Fertile Ground and Terry Callier. More recently, he has achieved a long-term ambition with the release of his debut production project – Mitchell and Dewbury 'Rapping with the Gods' on Mumo Records.

Despite all that, you can find Russ DJing in his spiritual home, the 'Jazz Rooms', most months of the year, still wearing the same short-sleeved checked shirt and puffing away on a Silk Cut. *www.jazzbop.co.uk*

The Joint

West Street (01273) 321629

Despite its location on tacky West Street, The Joint has evolved into a super-cool Barbarella's den for retro enthusiasts. In recent times it has also become a magnet for some of Brighton's best alternative clubnights, such as DeTournement (No-Wave/Krautrock/Electroclash), Action-a-Go-Go (Sixties Psych'n'Soul), Glitter & Twisted (Punk/Electroclash) and, of course, the infamous Dynamite Boogaloo.

This club even has plenty of seats and a good L shaped bar where you get served fairly quickly. Expect to bump into a multitude of Sixties throwbacks, Mod chicks, blokes who claim to own every Flaming Lips album, and bewildered weekend revellers who thought it'd be a 'bit like the Event.' Highly recommended, even if you hate clubs.

The Ocean Rooms

1 Morley Street (01273) 699069
www.oceanrooms.co.uk

With three floors of eclectic décor, this is probably the strangest (and most glamorous) club in Brighton. While the dancing is reserved for the basement, the middle floor is a cool bar with murals and leather booths, and upstairs is a Gaultier-style cocktail bar with a distinctly brothel-red vibe and the biggest red-velvet settee I've ever sunk into. The club even has a quotation emblazoned across its front door, which is pretty tacky, but gives you something to think about when you're waiting for your burger at the Market Diner down the road. (Previous quotations have included: 'He's not the messiah, he's a very naughty boy', and 'Dancing is a vertical expression of a horizontal desire'). Musically, the ocean Rooms caters for big-name DJs and any type of House that is sufficiently dirty and sultry to ward off the handbag posses.

All things considered, it may come as no surprise that, in 2002, this club was voted best nightclub of the year by Theme magazine. The perfect choice if you're after a club where you can relax, chat and dance in style.

Tavern Club

Castle Square (01273) 827641

This place has been a popular spot for Indie music ever since Brighton's legendary Basement Club imploded after one of the DJs left a Shed 7 record playing all night by mistake.

The Pav Tav (as it's sometimes known) is basically a function room above a pub, but has enough character to suit the style of the club nights here. Subdued lighting, a wide bar and a few sofas make it intimate and friendly, and the Indie nights are always heaving. Every Thursday, 200 nicotine-stained, pasty-faced kids in need of a good square meal drag their skinny bodies down here for 'Mad For It' (MFI), to demonstrate how much they really can't dance. Friday nights, meanwhile, are home to the newer, noisier sibling 'Kick Out The Jams', while Saturday's long-running Sixties/ Retro night 'Pod', remains ever-popular with the kind of crowd who sport huge lambchops, do their shopping at Rokit and know *all* the lyrics to 'Forever Changes'.

Strict dress code: dyed black hair, skinny-rib T-shirts and trainers. If you're ginger, don't even try.

Volks Tavern

3, The Colonnade, Madeira Drive
(01273) 682828

This small, two-floor, DIY club may be slightly off the beaten clubbing track but, as a consequence, pulls in a friendly, intelligent crowd who come for the music, not the pose.

And, what's more, it boasts some very respectable credentials: great psychedelic Trance nights, Junglist mayhem (in the form of the long-running Lunarcy), frequent overloads of hard, dirty beats; the odd fetish night and even random, genuine, but legal, free parties.

The Volks makes for a sweaty night out, and it's well worth it when they open the doors at the end of the night, let the cool sea breeze in and everybody stumbles out onto the pavement in a messy, but satisfied state.

Dress code: vest and pants.

The Zap

189-192 Kings Road Arches (01273) 202407
www.thezapbrighton.co.uk

Under the arches, right down onto the beach, this was once the most famous club in Brighton; a cavern of cool, and a prime mover in the UK arts/culture scene. Name an influential DJ or fashionable band between the years 1984-1995 and they'll have played The Zap. Primal Scream came up with the idea for *Screamadelica* in here, for Pete's sake!

Although no longer top dog, and despite its ever-growing grottiness, these epic arches remain distinctly popular with teenage glamour pusses who like Seventies Disco and generic party anthem nights. And you can understand why – it's spacious (perfect for conducting endless walking circuits if you're bored), has two distinct dance rooms, and plenty of nooks and crannies in between for canoodling. But watch out for the floor in there; accidentally drop your tank top, and it will forever smell like a beer-towel and ashtray.

special club nights

Wild Fruit

www.wildfruit.com
First Monday of every month at Creation

Well-established and glamorous night for extroverts and anyone who fancies sticking on a frock, false eyelashes or anything that glitters. This club night was originally targeted exclusively at the gay scene but word somehow got around, and pretty soon everyone wanted to come. Still predominantly attracting a gay crowd, this is an evening of serious flirting, high camp, dressing up, and uplifting House and Garage music. If you've just moved from Skegness, prepare to be shocked.

Margot's Parties

Hanbury Ballroom £8-10 10pm-2am
www.margots.org

This popular and fun, kitsch themed clubnight at the Hanbury Ballroom is ideal for those who love any excuse for indulging in a bit of glamorous fancy dress. Previous themes have included 'Killer Heels and Cleavage', 'Fur' and 'Medical Mayhem'.

Pussycat Club

Every second Saturday of the month at Concorde 2

In its eighth year now and seeming more popular than ever, this colourful night attracts a mixed gay/straight dressed-up crowd, determined to prove that this is the best Friday-night club in Brighton. The music is hard, uplifting House, and Glam attire (or fancy dressed) is strongly recommended.

Vavavavoom!

Every so often

Last spotted at the Hanbury Ballroom
and Concorde 2…

Set up over 7 years ago by local diva Stella Starr, Vavavavoom! has grown to become something of a phenomenon. Based on the Fifties Burlesque tradition, the club night features saucy cabaret acts, strippers, go-go dancers, a live band, guest singers and many other surprises. Each event is themed and with a strict dress code, it is the punters who make the effort with their costumes that really keep 'Vavavavoom!' unique. Previous themes have included Voodoo Horror, Circus Freaks, Elvis and Underwater. This is a very flirty, sexy club where inhibitions are cast to the wind, while its gay, straight and fetish crowd demonstrate that the emphasis is on fun, not sleaze. Past highlights have included the three-breasted lady, live mixed-sex wrestling and Stella stripping whilst sprawled on a gigantic gorilla's hand.

At A Glance

Chart / Disco / Party Tunes: *Event2 / Creation / The Gap Club*
Drum 'n' Bass: *Beach / Pressure Point*
Easy Listening / Soundtrack / Lounge/ Retro: *Hanbury / The Joint*
Goth / Industrial: *Babylon Lounge / Brighton Gloucester*
Hip-Hop & Breakbeat: *Enigma / Pressure Point*
House & Garage: *Core Club /The Escape / Ocean Rooms / Snafu23*
Indie / Rock: *Gloucester / Pav Tav*
Jazz / Funk / Salsa: *Casablanca / Club New York / The Jazz Place*
Northern Soul / Motown: *Funky Fish Club / The Jazz Place*
Reggae: *The Jazz Place, Steamers / The Volks*
Seventies / Eighties: *The Beach / Brighton Gloucester / Creation /Zap*
Techno & Trance: *Honeyclub2 / Pressure Point / The Volks*
Electronica / Krautrock / Underground Pop: *The Joint / Hanbury Ballroom*

COMING SOON TO A VAVAVAVOOM NIGHT NEAR YOU

REVENGE
OF THE FURRY NIPPLE II

WITH
STELLA STARR AS THE NIPPLE TASSEL SWINGING HOT MAMA

cheesy, ❁ please! ❁

Despite its pretensions for being the South Coast's capital of cool, Brighton clubland has always housed a parallel universe of tacky late-night socials where Babycham, cufflinks, stilettos and Rick Astley records are eternally de rigueur. In case you're wondering, this is not a reference to such wilfully cheesy nights as The Gloucester's 'Back To School', the 'Agadoo' vibe of Creation, or any of those other nights that positively burst with self-conscious irony. These are nothing compared to the genuinely tasteless hilarity of Brighton's true 'Cheddar Fringe'. But you will have to hunt hard for this subterranean platter of naff disco culture, not because there's any shortage of it, but because a conspiracy of silence amongst Brighton's style police means that the really crap clubs are ostracised like embarrassing relatives from Bognor Regis and don't even get a mention in local listings anymore. If you're interested in experiencing a tacky night on the town, here are a few pointers in the right direction:

Caps
Western Road, Hove (opposite The Litten Tree)

Slide furtively through the doorway next to the conjoined kebab restaurant, and descend into a cavern of garish disco lights. Caps is home to a fascinating menagerie of local bachelors, Legal and General office party revellers, and youthful alcoholics who didn't make it to Threshers before closing time, all in regulation M&S shirt, creased slacks and polished slip-ons. Thankfully, the dreaming-of-bigger-things DJs have now dispensed with the Shania Twain end of cheesy tunesville, in favour of (almost-respectable) megamixes of soul and pop classics, meaning here is a highly enjoyable dancefloor to cut some funky moves with the regular posses of handbagged harridans and their squaddie boyfriends. The best thing of all about this club, though, is that you can order a kebab at the bar from the restaurant upstairs, allowing one the unusual cultural experience of munching a large doner whilst dancing to The Three Degrees.

Midnight Blues
In the bowels of the Grand Hotel

A terrifying jungle of glitterballs, plastic foliage and mobile disco fever. Originally conceived as an after-hours quarantine area for the Grand's slimier guests, this place now operates as a dream ticket for faux-bourgeois divorcees with cellulite, and lonely, bejewelled businessmen who can't dance. It's worth a visit if only to check out the sweaty, Phil Collins-obsessed DJs, who are in the habit of excitedly cradling their balls with one hand while pointing the other towards the ceiling and baying into the microphone: *"C'mon lovely laydeeeez, let's get on down! Whoa! Yeah! All-righty!"*

The Junction Club
Poole Valley (where the buses go to sleep at night)

Welcome to the Mecca of Brighton's tacky late-night establishments. As near as you'll get to a provincial meat market in Brighton, the Junction Club is guaranteed to incorporate all the sights and sounds of Cheeseville under one roof. Here you'll find women of a 'certain age' in mini-skirts (usually including a sizeable *Readers' Wives* faction) dancing round their handbags to 'Simply The Best', spats-wearing Paco Rabanne-scented gangsters groping their 'Sharon from Eastenders' girlfriends, and plump, mid-life virgins who specialise in dancing with gay abandon to Cyndi Lauper.

CINEMAS

See the latest Hollywood blockbuster on Friday night, a David Lynch film on the Saturday, then a documentary about Voodoo S&M on the Sunday. Here's how.

WHERE TO SEE THE LATEST BLOCKBUSTER

The Odeon
West Street (0870) 5050007

The biggest cinema in the town centre, and with the Event 2 nightclub next-door, handy if you're taken with the urge to snog a few teenagers after the film.

Virgin Cinema
The Marina 0541 555145

Eight screens and all the latest movies from Tinseltown. You won't find anything adventurous in their billings, and it is located below the multi-story carpark in the Marina, but, if you like modern swanky cinemas, you won't

be disappointed. Besides, if the film's crap you can always take a walk on the Marina breakwater and pretend you're in 'The French Lieutenant's Woman'. Judging from my last few visits here, this place is vying for 'Dirtiest Cinema of the Year Award'. At weekends (and during the week too) you may find yourself ankle deep in popcorn, teabags and litter. The fact that it seems to be run by disaffected teenagers has nothing to do with it…

Popcorn

I read somewhere that the reason popcorn is synonymous with cinemas is because when long feature films first started to be shown in the twenties, the cinema owners were afraid that their audiences would get hungry if made to sit still for over an hour. The cheapest, simplest solution to this was popcorn which, naturally, they gave out free. Nowadays we'll happily pay £10 for a bag of the stuff. Ooh, the irony.

INDEPENDENT CINEMAS

Duke of York's

Preston Circus (01273) 602503
www.picturehouse-cinemas.co.uk
Cheaper tickets Mon-Thurs before 6pm

Found at the end of London Road, this building is bright yellow and has a large pair of stripy legs sticking out from over the balcony. It's easy to miss however, as all the houses on the street have copied the idea, and now there are hands, elbows and feet sticking out all over the place, as far as the eye can see.

Having celebrated its 90th birthday in September 2000, the Duke's can claim to be the oldest independent cinema outside London, and shows a fairly wide selection of cult, art house and world films. It also has a nifty little bar and balcony upstairs and, rather than the usual cinema junk food, offers a selection of cakes and hot and cold drinks. The auditorium itself looks magical with coloured lights around the screen, and the red velvet seats are the most comfortable in Brighton. Thoroughly recommended for *all* movie enthusiasts and, if you fancy seeing one of their late-night screenings at the weekend, buy your tickets in advance; they often sell out.

Duke of York's Trivia

• The Duke's was originally built for theatrical impresarios Violette Melnotte and Frank Wyatt. Violette, always known to staff as 'Madame', was the archetypal iron fist in the velvet glove and, when one of the actors at the theatre gassed himself, she apparently instructed her solicitor to reclaim the cost of the gas from his estate.

• The Duke's famous legs once belonged to a cinema in Oxford known as 'Not the Moulin Rouge' and, every Sunday at 3pm, they do the Can-Can.

Cinematheque

9-12 Middle Street (01273) 384300
www.cinematheque.org

Upstairs at the Media Centre, this sixty-odd-seater cinema is the place for cutting edge, rare and experimental films in Brighton.

Run by Ben, Michael, Ian and Adrian (one tall, one short, one hairy, two bald), the Cinematheque offers an eclectic mix of documentaries, cult movies and rare oldies, while the programming is kept forever fresh and dynamic, owing to the passion and knowledge of its four organisers. While running the show in their characteristically laid back and informal manner, these guys still need a good kick up the arse when it comes to distributing their programmes round town properly (though it has improved in the last few months). That aside, I love this place to bits; look out for special events such as lectures from the likes of cult author Jack Sargeant, live musical accompaniments to old silent movies and – my favourite night of the year – the annual Laurel and Hardy Christmas special, which comes complete with mulled wine and home-made biscuits.

THE INNER WORLD OF THE ENGLISH

THEATRES

Brighton's Little Theatre Company

Clarence Gardens (01273) 205000

Founded in the late Seventies by Sid Little (of 'Little and Large' fame), this converted chapel, tucked behind the Pull and Pump, has been home for many years now to the amateur company who do everything from Aykbourn to Shakey. Avoid the back seats if you go – there are low slung beams that can obscure the view and spoil it – and keep a look out for Sid; he still pops up occasionally to see the odd farce, but has porked out a bit now and looks more like Eddie.

Gardner Arts Centre

Sussex University Campus, Falmer
(01273) 685861
www.gardnerarts.co.uk

This late, 1960s, purpose-built arts venue looks like it's straight out of an Eighties TV comedy drama starring Peter Davidson as a bumbling lecturer who wins the hearts of his rebellious rabble of students by accidentally turning up drunk and naked to one of his seminars. My fantasies aside, the Gardner Arts Centre is a large venue – with gallery space and a café-bar – which has really pulled out all the stops over the last couple of years to offer a wide selection of events. Their programme now features everything from alternative comedians, theatre and cult films to art exhibitions, dance groups and workshops.

The venue is seating only; perfect for dance and theatre, but it can feel overly formal at times for stand-up comedy and lively music events. All things considered, it's well worth the hike out of town if there's something good on and, afterwards, you can sneak into the student bar opposite for cheap beer.

The Komedia

Gardner Street (01273) 647100
www.komedia.co.uk

Impossible to miss, owing to the fact that its outrageous red lighting turns Gardner Street into an enormous brothel every evening. That aside, it's a blessing to have a theatre in town that doesn't churn out the usual old cobblers year in, year out. Instead, this is somewhere to come to see new comedy, contemporary theatre, world music and just about any other modern performance art you can think of. Prices can be a bit intimidating at times, but its usually worth the gamble, the quality of what's on here is normally very good. They also offer an excellent restaurant (The Curve Bar) and frequent late bars at many of the shows upstairs and down. Regular highlights include 'Voodoo Vaudeville' and the 'Joker Basement'.

The Nightingale Theatre

Located above Grand Central Pub, opposite Brighton Station
29-30 Surrey St (01273) 702563
alister@prodigaltheatre.co.uk

After many years in the wilderness, the theatre once described as 'Brighton's best-loved venue' is back. Though it was still being finalised at time of going to press, expect a wealth of unique and unusual shows, regular youth theatre workshops, touring companies and dance in this newly refurbished (and very swish) 40-capacity theatre space, all choreographed by resident company 'Prodigal Theatre'.

The Sallis Benney

Theatre University of Brighton, Grand Parade (01273) 643010
www.brighton.ac.uk/gallery-theatre

This place is as dead as a dodo for six months, but out of the blue it will have World Music, theatre and dance and then suddenly go back into hibernation again. It's like some drunk relative who's been woken up at a party and dances their way across the living room only to collapse unconscious in the kitchen moments later. Definitely worth keeping an eye on during the summer term, as all the performance-art students put on free events here for a couple of weeks as the final part of their degrees, before settling down to lives of unemployment. It's also the current home to the annual Occulture festival in July.

New Venture Theatre

Bedford Place (01273) 746118
www.newventure.org.uk

This converted school does about nine productions a year, usually covering more difficult and unusual plays than its diminutive rival down the road. I got into trouble last year for saying this place offered 'amateur theatre, done with luvvie gusto' so this year I'm not. Instead I'm going to say that it's community theatre of a very high calibre.

Scaramoush, Scaramoush, will you do the fandango?

Theatre Royal
New Road (01273) 328488
www.theatreroyal.co.uk

For the more conservative theatregoer. It may be the usual souped-up collection of farces, thrillers and musicals, but for that authentic old-style theatre experience you can't beat it. The auditorium is fabulous; plush red seats, 20p binoculars and viewing boxes. I once saw Barbara Windsor in the nude here, but that's another story. Dress code – loafers, slacks and a cardie. Monocle optional.

Compere of the Joker Basement and Arsenal fan, Guy Venables

COMEDY

The Treason Show
Monthly at the Komedia (01273) 647100

Packed with songs, sketches and digs at the usual suspects (the police, celebrities, Tony Blair, crap TV) the performances from this comedy team are fast moving, well executed and slick.

Far from being groundbreaking satire from the likes of 'The Day Today', The Treason Show follows the well-worn paths laid down by shows like 'Beyond the Fringe', and 'That Was the Week That Was'. The evening is perfectly split into two forty-minute performances, and although there'll be times when the slickness of it all seems more important to the performers than the humour, the pace of the show will leave you little time to dwell on the shortcomings of a sketch as seconds later you'll be bombarded by a cracking one-liner in the next.

The Krater Comedy Club
Weekly at the Komedia (01273) 647100

Usually running Saturday and Sunday nights, the Krater Comedy closely follows that tried and tested Jongleurs formula, found nation-wide. Regularly compèred by Stephen Grant, known for his speedy delivery, the Krater is unquestionably popular, but does, however, demonstrate the frightening lack of original material of most of the comedians currently trawling round the national circuit. Attracting stag and hen parties in their droves (a growing Brighton epidemic), this is hardly a discerning audience, but at least they don't seem to mind listening to men and women in their mid-thirties drone on about their pathetic sex lives. With moronic heckling and mobile phones going off every 10 minutes, this is my idea of comedy hell, but maybe I'm just a miserable bastard.

The Joker Basement

One Tuesday a month at the Komedia
(01273) 647100

Spawned from the ashes of the legendary Comedy Dairy, the Joker Basement has continued in the Dairy's long-standing tradition of playing host to a motley collection of near-genius yet dysfunctional 'care in the community' comedians – acts who are a far cry from the shirts-out-lets-talk-about-masturbation brigade that you typically find on the circuit, or down at the Krater.

This night's new compère is the marvellous Guy Venables – a bizarre cross between Arthur Daly, Terry Thomas and Sir Henry Rawlinson, and a talented cartoonist and drunkard to boot. Guy starts most evenings with a slide show of his latest escapades and pranks (skinny-dipping in the shark tank at the Sea-life Centre, subverting Argus headlines outside newsagents, hanging around Securicor vans with a camera and stop-watch etc) and then, later, for the joke competition, dishes out top quality prizes – ranging from hi-fis to Rolex watches – all pilfered by his mate Dodgy Dave. One month a friend of mine, Mark, won the 'home number of Brian Sewell!

Don't expect all the acts to be top quality here, Guy works hard on getting fresh talent each month so, predictably, there are still plenty of clichéd and amateurish performers, but it is the bizarre comic characters and strange and disturbing monologists that provide the winning formula for the night. Highlights include the musical, comedy genius that is Glen Richardson, the UK's best female comedian – Joanna Neary, local squaddie Sean Hard, 13-year old stand-up Crystal, and fable-man Adam Acidophilus (formerly Otto from the Simpsons, until he cut off his hair).

177

Comedy Profile #2 Guy Venables*

I have always held firm to the sensible notion that one should never trust a man who keeps firearms in his house, particularly one who uses a loaded air rifle as a toilet roll holder. But, knowing that Guy Venables has also sailed the Atlantic pissed as a newt, is the descendant of a famous pirate, a cartoonist for Punch and Private Eye, a prison escapee, did a skinny-dip in the shark tank at Brighton's Sea Life Centre, and once even appeared on 'Fifteen to One' sporting a tie covered with hardcore pornographic images, I'm prepared to make an exception.

Guy's recent arrival in Brighton was not only due to him taking over as compère at the Joker Basement Society, but also owing to him having outstayed his welcome in nearby Chichester (where he also ran his own comedy night). There he got himself into trouble by littering the town with a poster that read: *'Missing, three kittens in a sack. Unwanted Christmas present. If found, please drown.'* thereby incurring the wrath of the RSCPA. Following this he began erecting posters **below** his kitten ones, declaring; *'If this poster offends you, please call the number below'*. (The number was actually the contact for the local Jehovah's Witnesses, which incurred their rage too.) Add to this his fondness for leaving stickers that read *'Am I driving like a cunt?'* on the backs of Police Cars, and asking coppers for directions, thanking them with a hearty slap that actually deposits a gummed poster for his comedy night, and you can understand why he's much better suited to living in Brighton.

One scam that nearly was the undoing of Guy, however, happened in the States about ten years ago. Living in Canada, and being in possession of a diplomatic passport, Guy found that he could pass through the American border without trouble and so it seemed natural (for him) that he should use this to his advantage by doing a little drug smuggling.

On one trip down to Arizona, however, he decided to stop off in San Francisco for a spot of surfing and a drink or two. Several beers later he found himself careering down one of San Francisco's impossibly steep hills, whereupon he crashed into fourteen parked cars. When the police turned up they found *'two big bags of coke, seven bails of weed and two unlicensed guns.'* Guy tried to make a run for it but, being so inebriated, merely fell over. With drink-driving, destruction of property, resisting arrest and gun and drug charges being held over him, Guy knew he was looking at a minimum of 12 years hard labour. He spent two ('very unpleasant') weeks sharing a prison cell with a Mexican PCP addict, whom he nicknamed 'Aggghh!!' (it was all the guy ever said) and only escaped his fate when a moment of lax security arose outside the courthouse, enabling him to flee and eventually make his way back to the UK.

You'd think this would have been enough to frighten Guy into a life of respectability, but thankfully it hasn't. With the passing away of Brian Behan in 2002, Guy has proved himself to be a fitting replacement for the unofficial role of Brighton prankster. Just watch your back.

*You'll have to find a copy of the last edition of this book for #1

WOULD YOU LIKE TO PARTICIPATE IN NEXT YEAR'S BRIGHTON FRINGE FESTIVAL?

For more information go to www.brightonfringefestival.co.uk or e-mail your interest: fringe@brighton.co.uk or send a SAE to: Brighton Fringe, 42 Toronto Terrace, Brighton BN2 9UX

art.photography.music.nightlife.open houses.sculpture.theatre.dance comedy.film.animation.spoken word.literature.fashion.community arts.childrens fringe.design.street theatre.DJing.workshops

KOMEDIA
Cabaret
Comedy Music
Theatre

Gardner St • North Laine • Brighton
Tickets 01273 647100 www.komedia.co.uk

CABARET

Voodoo Vaudeville

Komedia (every three months or so)
(01273) 647100
www.voodoo-vaudeville.com
info@voodoo-vaudeville.com

Mixing old-style German cabaret with more than a touch of the bizarre, Chris Cresswell and his team have, over the last five years, created a surreal and anarchic world of 'glamour, art and filth' through this extraordinary show. This is Pontins cabaret as seen through the eyes of Lewis Carroll, where giant rabbits abound, ghostly puppets give acerbic advice to the audience, glamorous girls do teasing (and often hilarious) dances, and Chris and co ham it up and generally have ball.

Ever-evolving, Voodoo Vaudeville has been performing around the globe in recent years, but its spiritual home is still the Komedia, where it still appears, every few months or so.

Loyal followers of Voodoo Vaudeville may be perturbed to discover that former compères, Lennie and Morris, have been bundled off to a retirement home in Hastings, but rest assured, the anarchy, dark humour and spirit of Voodoo remains; Mitsy the cat will be popping up, Baby Warhol will be around to help with those little problems, there'll be a disco at the end and yes, you can all still join in with the Snake Dance. *Highly recommended.*

MAGIC SHOWS

The Great Velcro

Sanctuary Cella, Brunswick Street East
(01273) 770006 £3 donation
Last Wednesday of every month

This monthly evening of magic, hosted by the Great Velcro ('the name that sticks'), is currently the only monthly magic show running in the UK, and is a genuine treat. The intimacy of the Sanctuary Cella makes this the perfect venue; there are lots of tables and chairs near to the stage – ideal for seeing close up magic and card tricks. While some of the tricks are a bit unoriginal (metal hoops and handkerchiefs), there's enough variety to keep it interesting, particularly as there are usually guest spots each month from different performers from the Magic Circle. Its host has a wonderful style, mixing classic old tricks with charming anecdotes about his life and, at the end, you might even get the chance to meet Bridget, the, white fluffy rabbit who lives in his top hat. A unique and fun night out that won't break the bank.

GAMBLING

The Grosvenor Casino

9 Grand Junction Road (01273) 326514
Open 2pm-6am daily (4am Saturday)
Bar open until 2am daily (12am Sunday)

Having recently moved from its old long-term home by Brighton Station to a swankier residence, this casino has gone slightly upmarket since the days of the grotty psychedelic carpets and tiny bar. There are now automated roulette tables, a £2000 jackpot fruit machine, higher minimum stakes and the bar stays open longer. But, despite all that, it's still full of guys with strong aftershave trying to impress their ladies in white stilettos, and swarms of Chinese business with money to burn. Membership and entrance are still free (although it takes 24 hours for them to validate your ID) and, once in, along with the roulette wheels and pontoon tables, you can enjoy cheap drinking until 2am. The roulette tables start at 50p a bet and the Pontoon and Poker start at £1, but there are other tables with higher stakes if you're feeling brave. Alternatively, you can just watch the professionals in action and munch on the free sarnies. But did I really hear the desk-girl say 'Good Evening Mr. Paradise' to one of the regulars recently, as I was leaving?

International Casino Club

6-8 Preston Street (01273) 725101
Free 24-hour membership and free admission
Open 2pm-6am daily (4am Saturday)
Bar open until 2am daily (12am Sunday)

Taking itself more seriously than The Grosvenor, as you step in and hear the lilting tones of Phil Collins and Philip Bailey singing Easy Lover you'll realise that this place means business. Like the Grosvenor, the décor reeks of the Eighties, with mirrored walls, fake wood panelling and a clientele to match, though, with the bar in the basement and customers unable to take drinks to the tables, it's usually quiet down there, and has such a big telly that conversation will drain away as soon as you arrive and find yourself drawn into a documentary about Doug McLure.

The Greyhound Track

Nevill Road, Hove (01273) 204601
Box office: 0845 702 3952

With all the Parklife nonsense dead and buried now you can go to the dogs and have a laugh without feeling that you have to be ironic about it. It's a few quid to get in and the minimum bets are a pound. Forget trying to figure out how the betting works, just pick the dog with the silliest name, use the touts outside for better odds, watch out for the lasagne and you'll have a fun night out.

theatre dance comedy music film exhibitions art classes

Box Office 01273 685861
or check out www.gardnerarts.co.uk
Gardner Arts Centre, University of Sussex
Falmer, Brighton. BN1 9RA

The Music Scene

Let's begin with a couple of jokes...

Q. What do you call someone who hangs around with musicians?
A. A drummer.

Q. How do you know a drummer is knocking on your door?
A. The knocking speeds up.

And while I'm on a roll...

A bass player's girlfriend comes home to find him giving a particularly painful Chinese Burn to their ten-year-old son. She begs him to stop, and asks why he's inflicting pain on their loved one.
'Because he's de-tuned one of my bass strings,' he says angrily.
'But there's no reason to treat him like that!' she exclaims.
'Yes but the little bugger won't tell me which one it is.'

LIVE MUSIC VENUES

Upstairs at the Albert
Trafalgar Street (01273) 730499
While the downstairs bar remains ever popular with edgy, frazzled clubbers, the venue upstairs has had a new wind in recent years. In comparison to the spit and sawdust fleapit that is the Free Butt*, the Albert has seating, a decent PA and occasional candle-light; ideal for the American Country and leftfield type bands put on by local promoters Gilded Palace of Sin and Melting Vinyl.

Brighton Centre and East Wing
Kingsway, Brighton Seafront (01273) 290131
Fancy seeing Simply Red for £30 or would you rather have dysentery? Whatever your tastes, when the big guys are in town this is where they play.

* This is a *not* a criticism

The Brighton Centre is one of those horrible Eighties buildings you find in every large town or city, that somehow seem to have been fashioned on Gatwick Airport. Still if you've come to throw your knickers at Tom Jones, you're not going to care too much about the décor are you? (Saying that, the council are going to pull it down soon and, knowing them, replace it with something even more hideous.)

In a strange Russian Doll kind of way, the East Wing is a slightly smaller but equally featureless room for all those acts that couldn't fill the Centre.

Brighton Dome, Pavilion Theatre and Corn Exchange

Church Street/ New Road (01273) 709709

After a £22 million refurbishment, state of the art acoustic system and new bar area, the Dome is back, offering classical concerts, world music, comedy events and a plethora of big name artists from Ken Dodd to Lou Reed. At the Pavilion and Corn Exchange just round the corner, expect touring bands, more comedians, plays and world music.

Concorde 2

(See club section)

The Free Butt

Pheonix Place (01273) 603974

Not a sexual favour but a tiny, magical venue, tucked up a side street behind the Phoenix Gallery. The Free Butt has, over the years put on countless gigs of every description, from Ska to Indie to Hardcore, and is still the only venue in town where you can see a band most nights of the week (Wed-Sat). You still have to strain your neck half the time to see who's on stage,

but they have improved the PA now so that not every band sounds like a Butthole Surfers album being played inside a kettle. If you're in a guitar band and looking for somewhere to play, this will probably be your first port of call. Upstairs, the Penthouse is a small 'chill-out' room with a bar and the odd sofa, and is home to club nights such as the long-running Slip Jam (Hip-Hop), and other more experimental, Electronica type affairs.

Incidentally, I tried putting Free, Butt and Penthouse as key search words on the net for a bit of research, and (surprise, surprise) had to trawl through 4,000,000 hardcore porn websites before finding the relevant address. It was hard, but I got there in the end.

The Hanbury Ballroom

83 St George's Road (01273) 605789

Located out in the wilds of Kemptown, this building was once a mausoleum for a rather eccentric Brighton Pagan, but is now a multipurpose, 120-capacity venue, and one of Zel's best success stories. Lovingly restored to its former glory in 2001, the ballroom boasts a beautiful dome ceiling, adorned with bearded shisha-smoking mystics, willowy ladies holding chalices and a Celine Dion look-alike playing the clarinet. Look out also for the gold Buddha and wooden angel, which, along with the blood red painted walls, complete the mystical theme to the room.

Zel (who own it) have long claimed that they wanted to 'give something back to the community' and with the Hanbury they have more than kept to their word, by creating a flourishing venue that supports such diverse events as local bands nights, comedy events, DJs, Jazz clubs, Laptop Jams, special club nights and gigs from the likes of Melting Vinyl and Gilded Palace of Sin.

If you DJ, play in a band, do stand-up or fancy putting on something yourself, this is the place to try it out. And, to cap it all, there's also a cosy adjoining bar, which can be handy if you turn up too early and don't want to have to stand outside in the rain with your records, penny whistle and laptop.

The Marlborough Theatre
4 Princes Street (01273) 570028

Touching upon elements of Brighton's much-missed venue 'The Lift', this tiny and beautiful theatre occasionally plays host to such music nights as Club Quiet – where you can see shy Indie kids making strange, soft music with toy instruments. Go downstairs, in the break for a beer and, in perfect contrast, the bar will be rammed with feisty dykes, arguing over the pub quiz.

Melting Vinyl
Contact Anna (01273) 325955
Info@meltingvinyl.co.uk
www.meltingvinyl.co.uk

Groovy Northern lass, Anna 'eh-up' Moulson, has been beavering away in Brighton for many years now as a top promoter, and is responsible for some of the best gigs in town, as everything from Garage-Pop to weird Electronica come under her wings. To her credit, she arranged the first ever UK shows for The White Stripes, The Strokes and The Vines and has put on gigs from the biggest (Turin Brakes), the quirkiest (local all-girl classical ensemble 'Ptthh!) to the smallest (Danish duo 'The Midgets'). With a lack of good venues being an ever-growing problem in this town, Anna has applied a bit of lateral thinking recently and, as well as doing regular gigs at the Albert, Free Butt, Pavilion Theatre and Dome, she has put

Eee baa gum, it's Anna Moulson

on events at local churches, The Duke of York's Cinema and even Fred's old allotment shed in Peacehaven. Go to Anna's events and expect way-out sounds, Electronic pioneers, Lo-Fi, Punk and some of the coolest bands on the planet. Support this lovely lady. It would be awfully quiet in Brighton without her.

Everett True

While some might dismiss Everett as the archetypal drippy Indie kid who never grew up, it cannot be denied that his contribution to the music scene in the last two decades has been remarkable (and I'm not talking about that awful single he released in the Eighties). This one-time NME journalist, notorious for not mincing his words, was instrumental in bringing the Grunge scene to the UK (he spent the late Eighties hanging out in Seattle with Kurt And co) and has remained a fervent and verbal champion

of cutting edge, underground pop, always one step ahead of his peers.

While not exactly a local promoter, Everett is prone to DJing at the odd club night in Brighton, providing the perfect opportunity to hear lots of noisy all-lesbian Japanese grunge-core bands, or whatever his latest flavour of the month happen to be. More importantly it's actually in Brighton that Everett publishes his magazine 'Careless Talk Costs Life', employing talented local illustrators and writers in the process. While his style can be verbose, pretentious and childishly vicious towards anything remotely 'mainstream', if you're looking for a magazine that genuinely champions new and exciting music, and is light year away from that stodgy, tired, endlessly retrospective approach of 99% of all music mags (Mojo, Uncut, Q, etc), then I urge you to buy it.

THE GILDED PALACE OF SIN Presents:

THE

BROKEN FAMILY BAND

From Cambridge. John Peel faves and the UK's answer to CLEM SNIDE!

Plus:

THE SNAKES

Hot country-rock action from London!

Plus: Your host MY GOOD SELF and TOM SHERIFF's JUKEBOX of MISERY

FRIDAY 4th APRIL

THE PRINCE ALBERT
(Top of) Trafalgar Street, Brighton

Doors at 7:30pm

Tickets £5.00 + bf from Rounder Records (01273) 325440

The Gilded Palace of Sin - Autogenic for the people...

The Gilded Palace of Sin

www.thegildedpalaceofsin.com

If you like raw Country music of the Flying Durrito Brothers/ Will Oldham/ Sadies variety, then you will love The Gilded Palace of Sin nights in Brighton. I asked its promoter, David Morrison, about the night and this is the email he sent me…

The man leaned towards me and whispered "Do you like…banjos?" Instinctively, our eyes scanned the room to see if anyone had heard. I looked back at him and – gulping - nodded. "What about nasal, whining Americans complaining about drink, death, divorce and life on the road, to mournful, traditional tunes, often featuring pedal-steel guitars and fiddles?" I could see my trembling hand sliding across the table to grab his, but could not stop it. "I…I thought I was alone!" I gasped. "Please take your hand off mine," said the man. "I've been considering setting up an alt. country-ish type of night; something really miserable and hilarious at the same time; something with a subtle, political underbelly and punk rock attitude to turn the most undeniably unfashionable, changing the course of popular music forever. I was told you might be interested. Are you?" Calm now, I replied that I was. "Good. I'll be the guvnor and MC, and you can play the sad records". I believe, at this point, that there was drool coursing down my jowls, and that there was a curious stirring in my briefs. "Yes, but when I say.." – I moved my mouth right next to his ear, speaking as quietly as the insane shrieking poet on stage would allow – "…when I say 'country' to anyone, they just run away!". "I understand. We'll just have to change that, won't we? Brighton needs this," he assured me with a wink I have grown to adore. So, upon the exchange of Grant Lee Buffalo bootleg CD's and a secret handshake still only we know, the deal was done.

David is now back on the medication, so it only remains for me to add that Gilded Palace of Sin put on some extraordinary shows, are not afraid of providing seats and candles (nice touch), and Mr Morrison is known to shout 'Yee-ha, drinks are on me!' at the end of most gigs. And they say Country music is bad for the soul…

Integrated Circuits / Ian Helliwell

ianhelliwell@yahoo.co.uk

Easily recognisable round town with his trademark static hair, black-framed glasses and cravat, Ian Helliwell is a man of many passions, including electronic music, experimental film and car boot sales. His flat in the town centre is an Aladdin's Cave of records, projectors and assorted, esoteric equipment. Much of this arcane apparatus he has customised with new circuitry to make his electronic music. A film-maker himself, in between making regular appearances at European film festivals, Ian organises themed events at the Cinematheque ranging from experimental music nights (with live performances of pieces by the likes of Terry Riley and Stockhausen) to cinematic programmes such as Expo Worlds and Soundtracks for the City. For lovers of experimental film and readers of The Wire, Ian's events always prove stimulating, exciting and unique.

LOCAL RADIO STATIONS

F.I.P. *90.5FM/ 91FM*

www.fipradio.com

While not strictly local (in fact not even British), this cool, Parisian radio station has been broadcasting from a secret location in Brighton now for some time. Advert-free, and genuinely eclectic, FIP knocks the spots off all English music radio stations, by offering everything from Classical to Jazz, to Underground Pop and Dub Reggae, all interspersed with the occasional lilting tones of a spaced-out Frenchman. F.I.P. are also prone to playing whole albums at times (not just singles) and have eight favourites each month they like to promote. In the evenings, the

French Jazz does tend to take over, but, trust me, that's no bad thing.

The acronym, incidentally, stands for France Inter Paris.

Radio 4A *101.4FM*

Second weekend of every month
www.radio4a.com www.piratetv.net

Set up in 1999, this speech based community radio has since spread its wings to incorporate local DJs and plays some mean Techno, Reggae and Disco on Friday and Saturday nights. Sundays are, however, still given over to documentaries, poetry, news, drama, reviews, and comedy, and this is where the station's singular strengths lie. Previous highlights have included documentaries on toxic waste dumping in the South Pacific, spoofs of Gardeners' Question time, Desert Island Discs and the Archers (though strictly speaking, Hancock got there first with 'The Bowmans' back in the fifties). They've even coaxed special performance from Mark Thomas and the Dalí Lama. This is local radio in the truest sense – honest, questioning, playful, and with its ear to the ground.

BBC Southern Counties FM *104-104.8FM*

Local news for local people, Southern Counties is that tried and tested formula of traffic reports, bland music, intrusive adverts and Alan Partridge style presenters. At its best, however, it does probe into and discuss local issues and serves the community (well, the Brighton middle classes, anyway).

Juice FM *107.2FM*

Braindead, soulless and irrelevant.

Totallyradio

www.totallyradio.com www.totallywired.co.uk

This Brighton based internet station, set up by hairy, benevolent entrepreneur and retired ferret-breeder, Daniel Nathan, showcases non-mainstream specialist music and local bands (via Peel-style sessions at the Levellers Metway Studio), and utilises the cream of Brighton DJs to broadcast a truly varied, modern and exciting range of musical styles - the kind you won't hear on your FM radio.

The on-demand shows are all around one hour long and feature such local heroes as Boogaloo Stu (Dynamite Boogaloo), Russ Dewbury (Jazz Rooms), Dave Morrison (Gilded Palace of Sin) and Everett True (Careless Talk Costs Lives).'Totally Wired', the station's homage to new Brighton music, has its own website (www.totallywired.co.uk), can be heard on Juice 107.2 on Sunday nights, and also offers resource facilities to local bands - printing, duplicating and mastering CDs. Totally Radio plans to launch on digital radio in 2004, which means you will be able to listen to it everywhere in Brighton (if you have a digital radio or a metal plate in your head).

HOW TO FIND OUT WHO'S PLAYING

All the local magazines and websites will give you a run-down on who's playing and where. Some of the best places to pick up information are the record shops themselves, which have posters for last minute and low-key gigs. Rounder Records should be your first port of call for information on gigs, club nights and other music events, while Edgeworld Records is likely to have fliers for any lo-fi events that might otherwise get overlooked.

WHERE TO GET TICKETS

Rounder Records

(01273) 325440

The place for tickets and general info on who's playing, and when.

Dance 2 Records

129 Western Road (01273) 220023 /329459

Tickets for everything related to Dance, DJ and Club culture, including big festivals and the likes of Cream and Ministry of Sound.

Dome Box Office

New Road (01273) 709709

THE POP CELEBRITY
(HALL OF FAME)

It is a well-established fact that, apart from Chris Eubank, everyone in Brighton is a musician of some sort. And with current interest in the music scene here at an all-time-high (in 2003 Brighton was Radio One's 'Sound City', and six local bands were the subject of a TV documentary TV series), it seems that the time is right to celebrate the town's euphonious achievements.

Below is a helpful guide to the pop-stars of past and present who at some time have graced our city. I must admit, though, some of it could be based on hearsay and an over-active imagination.

FAMOUS FOR 15 MINUTES

The Piranhas
Frazier Chorus
(anyone remember 'Dream Kitchen'?)
Sharkboy
These Animal Men *(NME darlings who lived entirely off speed and hair dye)*
Peter and the Test Tube Babies
(still going, and still not very famous)
Tampasm
(noisy all-girl band with attitude who appeared once on the Girlie Show)
Kirk Brandon *(Spear of Destiny)*
Genesis P. Orridge *(Psychic TV)*
Kevin Rowland
(Dexy's Midnight Runners)
Leo Sayer *(sorry Leo, I just don't see that career revival happening)*
David Van Day
(erm, same as Leo I'm afraid)

Blur your eyes and the second guy along in Clearlake looks like he's got huge hands

STILL THROWING TELLIES OUT OF WINDOWS

Gaz *(Supergrass)*
David Thomas *(Pere Ubu)*
Nick Cave
The Levellers
Norman Cook
Simon Johns
(Stereolab / Imitation Electric Piano)
Paul McCartney
Lo-fidelity All-Stars
Space Raiders
Gary Moore *(ex-Thin Lizzy guitarist turned noodly Blues fart)*

THE NEW KIDS ON THE BLOCK

Hardkandy
Clearlake
The Eighties Matchbox B-Line Disaster
British Sea Power
Electrelane
Pilote
Electric Soft Parade
Oddfellows Casino

Simon Johns

Hardkandy

LEGENDS
in their own lunchtime
By the heavily hung-over Marcus O'Dair

In the eyes (or ears) of non-residents, the Brighton music scene is frequently reduced to the twin pillars of Big Beat / Skint Records / Fatboy Slim and Electric Soft Parade / Eighties Matchbox / British Sea Power. But whatever you make of these better-known elements (good luck to 'em, I say) they represent only a tiny fraction of the whole scene, which – supported by the fifty or so Brighton-based record labels – covers everything from psychedelic trance to trad jazz.

There are however, four long-running local bands who have been playing in and around Brighton for so many years that, like the Rutles, they have become 'legends in their own lunchtime'. As well as checking out their gigs, I spent an evening in the pub with each band, plying them with alcohol in the hope that they'd reveal their lewdest and crudest rock 'n' roll tales…

Peter and the Test Tube Babies

Formed: 1978
Band members: Peter Bywaters (vocals), Derek Greening (guitar), Paul 'H' Henrickson (bass), Christophe Saunière (drums)
Music: old skool punk
Career highlight: being flown to LA to play at the private party of pro skater Tony Hawk, whose film, The End, had featured their track Blown Out Again.
Career lowlight: When Peter, dressed only in shorts and T-shirt, was accidentally abandoned outside a German service station in the middle of winter for NINE HOURS.
Classic tunes: Banned From The Pubs, The Jinx, Elvis Is Dead, Leader Of The Gang.
Cheeky fact: drummer Christophe leads a schizoid life, being perhaps the only punk to also play the harp in several professional classical orchestras.

Undisputed founding fathers of the Brighton punk scene, these guys have been there, done it, and got an array of PTTB T-shirts to prove it. Despite the fact that they were initially "not the most proficient of musicians", they both played a gig and recorded a track within a week of the band's formation… now that's what you call Punk. Legend has it that at one prestigious, MTV-televised gig, Peter awoke from a drunken stupor to ask what time they were due on, only to be told that he'd already played – an event of which he has no recollection to this day.

Too Many Crooks

Formed: 1992

Band members: Dave Cook (guitar / vocals), Marlon Johnson (bass / vocals), Alan Perry (sax / vocals), Simon Taylor (drums), Brad Tullett (keyboards), Tony Fish (trumpet).

Music: mainly Ska – but don't mention Madness or The Specials!

Career highlight: Supported Desmond Dekker, The Levellers, Geno Washington, The Mighty Mighty Bosstones, and Bad Manners (in which band several Crooks used to play). Soundtrack for forthcoming Nick Moran gangster flick "Baby Juice Express".

Career lowlight: The original keyboard player falling off the stage, never to return.

Classic tunes: Baby Lotion, Spanish Fly, Crazy, Happy Song, Scream Like A Baby, and Too Many Crooks.

Cheeky fact: TMC tours are frequently hindered by their driver's obsession with bridges. He has a particular soft spot for London Bridge and attempts to incorporate it into every journey, however illogical.

Initially the Crooks would tell me only that keyboard player Brad is the son of Sixties celebrity clairvoyant Eva Petulengro – anything bawdier, they pleaded, and "my missus will kill me". Seven pints of Stella later, however, the band were laughing hysterically about the two sex-crazed  groupies known as Fat Bird and Thin Bird, who follow them everywhere and are "trying to collect the whole set" of Crooks. They told me of the time in Belgium when the lifting of the guitarist's kilt sparked a widespread display of genitalia that appeared in the local press under the headline: "Too Many Cocks". Finally, Dave recalled swapping T-shirts with a girl – "I just wanted to see her tits" – only to awaken next morning, back in his girlfriend's bed, wearing a tight black halterneck and with a phone number scrawled across his back. (They split up "shortly afterwards.") All of us slightly tipsy, my meeting with the Crooks drew to a close. I later heard that Dave had somehow managed to fall out of the car on his way home, but it didn't matter since he "didn't feel a thing."

The Fish Brothers

Formed: 1993

Band members: Martin Fish (vocals), Chesty Charnsworth (guitar), Chuffa Charnsworth (bass), "Mass Murderer" McGhee (drums)

Music: Music hall punk ("The Clash meets The Wurzels")

Career highlight: appearing in a German movie, playing... The Fish Brothers. Supported The Levellers, Bad Manners, The Damned, and The Blockheads.

Career lowlight: being booed off stage at a six-year-old's birthday party.

Classic tunes: 24 Hour Drinking, I Am The President (aka You Fat Bastard), I Wonder What You Look Like With No Clothes On and, of course, Brighton Breezy.

Cheeky fact: Of their 2,000 gigs, Martin has been sober (*"well, only a couple of pints"*) for a grand total of ONE.

Whereas, for most groups, the consumption of a wide range of toxins is merely an enjoyable sideline, for the Fish Brothers it is the entire point of the band (their initiation ceremony, for instance, involves drinking each other's urine). All Fish Brothers pride

themselves on drinking, well, like fish – they got fired from their first regular gig for drinking too much free booze (they were averaging 15 pints each) and once drank three tour busses dry in one session. On another occasion the band were locked in a bar all night, drinking heavily and pissing in the coffee pot – leading to riotous laughter the next day every time someone ordered a coffee. Then there was the time in Prague when The Levellers "helpfully" translated Martin's intro speech into Czech for him; he couldn't understand the stunned silence when he read it out... until they later told him the script actually translated: *"Hello, we're the Fish Brothers and we like having sex with little boys."* Their live show, which usually includes a down-in-one competition, the crowd chanting "You Fat Bastard" at Martin, and general drunken fun and games, has seen them banned from "about three hundred and fifty" pubs in Brighton. You'd be a fool to miss it.

Anal Beard

Formed: 1995
Band members: Grebn (vocals), MC Sofa (vocals), Heave Spillage (guitar), Rogar The Pedestrian (guitar), Bemble (bass), Ingnn (drums), Nathan Phenomenous (keyboards)
Music: "Pantomime punk."
Career highlight: Once played a gig at the Prince Albert with no less a support band than Travis (admittedly, a while ago).
Career lowlight: Apparently dubbed "the worst punk band ever" by Kerrang magazine.
Classic tunes: Fanzine Nerd, Bus Pass, Cheesy Mattress, Drugs Are Clever, No Escape From The Anal Beard, and the infamous Bird On The Blob.
Cheeky fact: In a typical example of rock 'n' roll excess, the group were banned from Brighton's Core Club for, er, wearing the chef's trousers on stage.

The thing that strikes you first about Anal Beard is, quite simply, the fact that they're called Anal Beard *(as my mum exclaimed, "it's such a peculiar name!")*. The band themselves admit the moniker has done little for their artistic credibility, but it has ensured that many Brightonians are at least

vaguely aware of "some band called Anal Beard", even if they have not yet memorised the entire lyrics to Bird On The Blob. Yet the group's success is also due to their ability to write lyrics of such heart-wrenching poignancy: "Anal Beard are back again / Eat your biscuits, drink your phlegm", for instance, surely ranks alongside anything Dylan ever penned, while "Drugs are clever / My mate Trevor / Says so" is a thoroughly convincing argument for the legalisation of narcotics. On live dates, the Beard (as they are affectionately known) have been known to play Fisher Price xylophones through giant Marshall stacks, run naked through the audience, and generally behave like crazy loons. Resistance to this band is utterly futile; after all, as the song title says, there's No Escape From The Anal Beard.

The wheel of life of a Brighton musician

1. You answer an ad in the Guitar and Amp Shop and spend the evening with an unhinged alcoholic in his bedsit, listening to demo tapes of his old group.

2. After another year of this you decide to form your own band and bring some purity back to pop music.

3. You audition hundreds of guitarists until you find someone who owns an original 70s Telecaster. Even though he can't play it, you know a cool guitar when you see one and this is way more important.

4. You wait another 3 years for a bassist and drummer to come along. The bassist is a frustrated guitarist, while the drummer is merely a psychopath who doesn't particularly like music but enjoys hitting things. They'll do for now.

5. At your first gig at the Free Butt the drummer punches the singer in the other band, your guitarist fails to notice that he is playing the wrong set and then gets in a strop about it, and you have a sneaking feeling that the bassist played slap bass on one of the tracks. Your friends tell you that you sound a bit like the Stereophonics, which is ironic because you hate them.

6. You record a demo, have 40,000 made, spend a week arguing over the track listing, send one copy to John Peel and put the rest under your bed where they still remain.

7. After 6 months the bassist announces that although still committed to the band, he has formed his own band called 'Funkypanda' playing Jazz-Funk covers. You are alarmed to notice that he is starting to wear corduroy and grow a goatée.

8. Your demo returns from John Peel with the message – 'sounds too much like the Stereophonics.'

9. The drummer by now has taken a preference to hitting the bass player rather than his drums and the only way to calm him down is by regular heavy doses of ketamine.

10. You discover the existence of a Swedish synth-pop band with the same name as you.

11. The bassist announces that he is leaving to concentrate on his Jazz-Funk career, so you hide the drummer's stash of ketamine and unchain him.

12. You read in the paper that yet another Brighton band have just done a Peel session.

13. The drummer phones from prison to say that he can't make the next 400 rehearsals.

14. The guitarist comes round to your house, you smoke a joint together, reminisce about the good old days and moan about all the bands you know who have sold out. You jam through a couple of Turin Brakes numbers, and then turn in.

15. A month later you turn on the telly and see the guitarist on 'Stars in Their Eyes'. The words *'tonight I'm going to be JK from Jamiroquai'* are like daggers through your heart.

16. You move into a bedsit, start drinking heavily and put an advert in the Guitar and Amp shop.

17. The cycle is now complete.

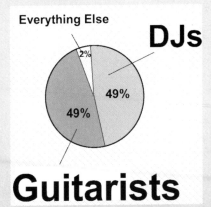

Everything Else

DJs

2%

49%

49%

Guitarists

BRIGHTON MUSICIAN'S PIE CHART'

LOCAL HEROES

This chapter pays homage to just some of the local artists who have bravely dragged their absinthe-raddled bodies out of (or into) the gutter to become champions of the unique, beautiful and bizarre.

Rob Ramsden
www.catchhenderson.com

An avid collector of cartoons, old children's books and comics, local illustrator, Rob Ramsden, is the man behind some of the most original and haunting illustrations since Maurice Sendak's award-winning children's book, 'Where the Wild Things Are'. Against hypnagogic landscapes of soft, creamy colours, Rob's pictures invariably depict gentle Tellytubby-like creatures, trapped within the strange dreams of a child who overdid it on the cheese just before bedtime. As well as contributing illustrations for the music magazine 'Careless Talk Costs Lives', Rob provided the artwork for the album cover of

local Pickled Egg band '100 Pets', which features his most renowned character, Catch Henderson. To see more of Rob's paintings and stories visit his website above. You can even buy t-shirts featuring Catch Henderson at the Hemp shop in North Laine.

Chris Macdonald

93 Gloucester Road (01273) 601639
www.acmeart.biz

Chris Macdonald has spent the last few years in
Brighton constructing beautiful and strange
sculptures out of wood and found metal
objects in his studio/ gallery on Gloucester
Road. There is something very Daliesque about
the way he juxtaposes curious metal gadgets
(such as old camera parts or giant cogs) with
beautifully carved wooden items, but the
finished pieces themselves are wholly original,
the work of a man who fell down Alice's rabbit
hole and never returned.

Chris's sculptures can be viewed and
purchased from his website or gallery at the
address below. If you want to visit the gallery, it's
best to phone beforehand, otherwise he'll most
likely be dancing around his studio to Talking
Heads, dreaming up another work of art.

Greg Daville

www.site-to-be-destroyed.co.uk (latest exhibits)
www.gallery-daville.co.uk
(Archive of complete visual and written work)

Beautiful and surreal, the images and words
of local artist Greg Daville touch something
deep in the unconscious, where the monsters
under the bed still lurk. His website,
www.gallery-daville.co.uk, covers a whole host
of art, past and present, although, for me, the
'Fourth Door Images' are the most stunning.
In Greg's world, strange creatures inhabit
centre stage in dream-like landscapes, with
motifs ranging from fetishism to mythical
buildings. If you like unusual, yet striking
images, pay this site a visit. All artwork is
modestly priced and can be mail-ordered
from 'gallery-daville'.

To see his very latest work, visit *www.site-
to-be-destroyed.co.uk*, a site that uses Flash
animation and photo-manipulated collage on
the theme of collapsing buildings, but still with
Greg's trademark haunting, hypnotic imagery.
But watch out for those rotating eyes…

Neel

Mostly found loitering around the photo booth in St James's Street post office, dressed as a Prozac tablet, a Cluedo character or in his floral gimp outfit, Neel has devoted his life to pushing the boundaries of photo-booth possibilities. He will invariably spend days preparing costumes, backdrops and make-up for each new project, then saunters down to Kemptown (sometimes with a bevy of monsters, film-stars and models) and get to work.

A typical day's work for Neel was the time he kitted out the photo booth in Brighton Station (his former haunt before it went digital) for a re-enactment of the shower scene from 'Psycho'. His friend Gwen, playing the rather distressed Marion Crane, cowered behind a shower curtain, covered in water and blood, while Neel thrust the knife in at the crucial moment just before the flash. Naturally this attracted the attention of the police, who thought he was making a porn film.

Apart from getting a full-grown Dalmatian dog in the booth with him, Neel's most ambitious project was when he arranged his own funeral at Brighton Station. His reason being –

I've always wanted a funeral party, and thought it a shame that I wouldn't be there to enjoy it with my friends.

The invitation read – *'everyone has to die one day...I'm just organised.'*

Having made himself a coffin, Neel then sent invitations to his 24 closest friends, asking each of them to come dressed as one of the many different characters required at a funeral. Vicars, undertakers, grieving widows, the Sally Army, a choir and even an Elvis impersonator all happily turned up and, after a bit of dutiful mourning and a speech by the deceased, one by one they all filed into the photo booth for their picture, ending with Neel, dressed as the corpse.

Nothing short of genius.

  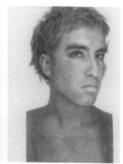

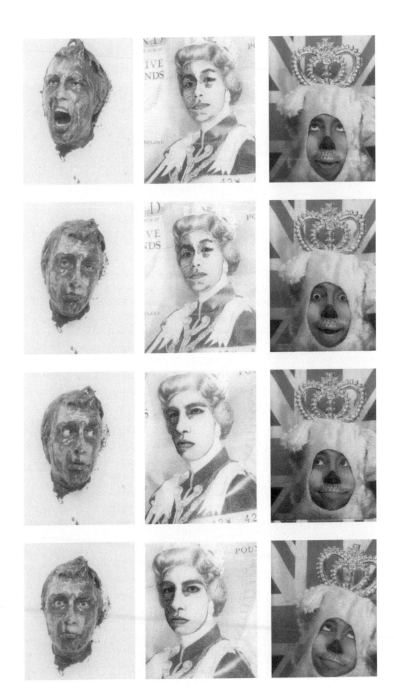

A SALUTE TO DEAN
(THE CHRISTO OF GRAFFITI)

A copycat 'Dean' shows how not to do it…

If you have ever travelled to or from Brighton by train, and bothered glancing up from your newspaper or paperback, chances are you will be familiar with the work of an artist who signs himself 'Dean.' In fact, that is all he does - sign his name, obsessively, in giant block letters, on every surface lining the track from here to Gatwick Airport. Maybe, when you saw it, it brought a smile to your lips, but you thought no more about it. Or perhaps you dismissed it as vandalism of the lowest order. Either response is entirely pardonable, as Dean's work is of a stature that cannot be properly assessed in one viewing

For years, now, graffiti art has been stuck in a Malcolm-McClaren-'Buffalo-Girls'-video rut - lazy shorthand for the Post-Modern, 'melting pot' city. But Dean's charmingly naïve tag recalls an era when the only adults who wielded spray cans were mechanics - the Seventies. Even the name is perfect. It conjures images of Raleigh Choppers, Sherbert Dabs and Latch-Key Children. The urban pretensions of all subsequent graffiti seem silly by comparison. Other tags celebrate only the artist - Dean's, somehow, speaks for the teenage miscreant in us all.

Moreover, it is the sheer scale and daring of his project that command respect. He has defaced the top of New England House, the side of the bridge on Dyke Road Drive, the cattle trough by the Burgess Hill viaduct, the old BR tankers at Gatwick -his tag has even been spotted at Nottingham station.

It is for this reason that I sometimes imagine it the work of a secret brotherhood of graffitists, all conspiring, Zorro-like, to one subversive aim. (Is Dean even his real name, or a nom-de-spray-can?) One thing is certain; I am not alone in my admiration. There are many pretenders to Dean's crown - Zulu, for one, and the cocky young upstart, Sen - but have you heard them mentioned with the same enthusiasm or affection?

So, the next time you're going up to London, look around. Someone has risked life and limb for no financial gain to make your journey a little more magical. He is worth your attention and to be saluted for his efforts.

Many thanks to Brian Mitchell for supplying this article

LEGENDS AND ECCENTRICS

Brighton has always had more than its fair share of outlandish individuals and below is a guide to some of the town's fruitiest and most loveable characters. Does anyone remember the bread man, who used to wander the streets of North Laine between six and seven in the morning with two French loaves strapped to his head like helicopter blades? Now he was a loony...

Mad Jack

This loveable, toothless old-timer frequents several cafés around North Laine, usually charming a cup of tea and a cake out of the owners on a daily basis. Full of life, but two buttons short of a cardigan, Jack will generally declare it to be his birthday most days of the week, claim to be building a brick and will usually call you Martin. My favourite story about Jack is when he was spotted in a café one day unscrewing the lid off the charity box by the till. Carefully he took all of the coins out the box, counting them as he went along until they were all out on the counter. With equal gravity he started to replace them, again counting as they were returned. As the last coin went in he announced 'It's one pound short!!' and began eyeing the other customers accusingly. After no-one owned up to the crime he turned back to face the person serving, and said, quietly, *'Cup of tea please'* and placed a pound coin on the counter.

Drako Zarhazar

Undoubtedly Brighton's greatest eccentric, Drako Zarhazar's life-story reads like some improbable work of fiction; he has danced at the Moulin Rouge and London Palladium, modelled for Salvador Dalì, starred in films by Andy Warhol and Derek Jarman and survived two serious road accidents and comas.

Decorated with exotic tattoos and piercings, Drako is a character you simply couldn't mistake, even in Brighton; his head sports a tattooed triangle and his face is adorned with bright blue eyebrows, facial piercings and an impressive Dalìesque wax moustache. A visit to his flat is somewhat like stepping into the pages of a psychedelic porn mag; all the walls, ceiling, cupboards, and even the bathroom, are adorned with phallic images. From flaccid to fully erect, there are thousands of them everywhere, some stuck casually onto the wall, some hanging from the ceiling, others accompanied by humorous comments.

Ask him about his movie career and Drako usually seems fairly nonchalant about it all, preferring instead to describe his favourite moment as 'one night in Rome when someone filmed me putting a candle up someone's arse, which I lit and then, with a big whip, whipped out the flame.'

> ## Drako recalls meeting Salvador Dalì for the first time.
>
> 'I remember being invited one day to a house on the outskirts of Paris. I walked down the stairs to a pool in the basement, and swimming naked in the pool were two beautiful girls. I remember coming and sitting on a big couch next to Salvador Dalì. He was just wearing a bathrobe and didn't say anything to me but kept watching these two naked girls swimming, when I suddenly noticed Dalì's hand moving up and down next to me. He was looking at these beautiful girls… and he was wanking.
>
> And I thought to myself 'here I am on the outskirts of Paris, sat next to the famous painter Salvador Dalì, with him wanking over these beautiful girls. Isn't life incredible?'

Sir Ralph Harvey

A well-dressed and genteel man, sporting the fading moustache of a brigadier, Ralph travels the world battling the likes of Vikings and Saxons with military re-enactment societies and makes regular appearances around the country with his own outfit dressed as the cast of Dad's Army with himself, of course, as Captain Manwaring.

More surprisingly, perhaps, Ralph is one of the country's leading authorities on the Occult, heading his own local coven (who follow the Wiccan faith) and is responsible for sorting out much of the poltergeist activity around the Shoreham area.

Having also regularly worked as an actor, at the height of his fame Ralph played Hercule Poirot on Belgium TV, where he became a household name, until the Agatha Christie estate stopped the TV Company from using the famous detective's name. From then on, even though he dressed the same and played the same role, Ralph had to be known as 'Inspector Sprout', but, somehow, it was never the same.

Look for him as Captain Manwaring, parading down the seafront during the May festival, or in town giving lectures on the Occult.

Adrian Shephard

To long-term Brightonians, the hooded figure of Adrian Shephard may be a familiar one, for, as well as being one of the co-founders of the Cinematheque, he can be spotted doing the occasional art performance (he once lay naked in a coffin for 6 hours at the Gardner Arts Centre) or carrying his trademark, silver-sprayed shop-dummy around the Lanes. But it is his interest in the spirit world that earn him a place in this chapter as, for several years now, He has been investigating EVP (Electronic Voice Phenomenon), which involves listening through silent audio recordings for

disembodied voices. This can be done using blank audiocassette or – in Adrian's case – scanning outdoor recordings for extraneous sounds.

Having taken himself off to Paris a couple of years back, Adrian spent two weeks in Père Lachaise, recording the silence of this vast graveyard and then searching through the recordings on the computer for unexplained voices. Back at his flat I have heard these strange spooky messages, rising out of a sea of white noise, proclaiming, 'I have a voice now,' 'I fell down,' and 'Brother announce me.'

'It's fear that keeps us from speaking with the dead. If you're receptive you'll find a way,' Adrian explains. In fact he's even built a 'brain machine' to help others tune their brains into frequencies more 'sympathetic' with the spirit world, and has showcased it around the world. To find out more go to his website, or seek him out at the Cinematheque. For more info, visit *www.testcard.org*

Dr Dolittle

Regularly seen whizzing along the seafront on an old butcher's bike, Dr Dolittle is – I can only deduce – attempting to beat the World Records for how many animals one can carry on a bicycle. From dogs, rabbits and parrots to rats, this white-haired, old pirate has the lot, and in abundance, sticking out of his pockets, perched on his shoulder, clinging to his shirt, and a good ten of them squashed into his basket, all hanging on for dear life.

Roy Skelton

When Kemptown resident Roy Skelton auditioned for a children's show in the early Seventies, he didn't figure that it would keep him in gainful employment for 16 years, and turn him and his characters into cult heroes. But having provided the voice for Rainbow's Zippy and George for all these years, that's exactly what happened (the bumbling duo are still the number one poster choice for today's retro and kitsch obsessed students).

On the subject of fan-mail, Roy will tell you that the most common questions he gets asked about the show are: 'What is Zippy?', and 'Is George gay?'.
He always replies that 'Zippy is unique', and writes back on George's behalf, saying, 'What is gay, I don't understand…'

The most priceless Rainbow footage is, by all accounts, a smutty version of the show, scripted by Roy. It starts with Zippy peeling a banana, mumbling:
'One skin, two skin, three skin, four….'
Where's Bungle?' buts in George. There ensues fifteen minutes of priceless innuendoes and jokes about Jane's maracas, but, alas, it has yet to be shown on TV.

On top of this, Roy, has provided the original voice for the Daleks, for over thirty years trying to exterminate everyone from William Hartnell to Sylvester McCoy (as well as taking other occasional pot-shots playing such universal miscreants as a Cyberman, Monoid and Kroton).

Though now in his Seventies, Roy is still sprightly and youthful, with more than a hint of Zippy in his smooth round head and bullfrog voice (though whether his alter-ego is placidly camp is another matter). Rumoured sightings of him recently loitering around a blue portaloo on Western Road clutching a sink plunger were yet to be validated at time of going to print.

Stephen Drennan

Enter the singular world of Mr Stephen Drennan - an obsessive collector of pop ephemera and Brighton's undisputed 'King of Charity Shopping'. He has even self-published two volumes of 'Stephen's little Book of Charity Shopping' on his passion, which include anecdotes and histories of some of his favourite purchases. Nowadays he claims to be 'cutting back' on his collecting, but, visit his bedroom, and it's still a mountain of boxes containing thousands of albums, toys, postcards and paperbacks.

When accused of merely being a collector of all things kitsch, Stephen is quick to disagree -

"Kenny Everett once released an album entitled 'The World's Worst Records'. I own several of the originals on seven inch and actually think they're very good. I don't consider them kitsch. I also love the graphic design on small things that most people don't notice - fruit and chewing gum wrappers for example. And I've just started collecting matchbox labels again. People think it odd that I'll research the designers of sweet wrappers but I see it as no different to hearing a record and wanting to know more about the band. Nobody knows this stuff; I feel that it's my responsibility to write about it."

Stephen can be found (in his regulation black roll-neck, black jeans and badge of the day) in Brighton Books in Kensington Gardens, where you can pick his brains on everything from Ivor Cutler to Pez sweets, buy his comics, or get engrossed in a conversation about his latest purchase (invariably some bizarre 1960s Bird's Custard novelty record he's just picked up). You even can read his live journal on: *www.livejournal.com/users/steviecat/*
God bless him.

Seb and Dunc

Brighton's most celebrated nerds, Duncan Games and Sebastian Briere-Edney are the proud publishers of 'Colin Cuts', the UK's premiere Colin Baker* fanzine, now approaching its 200th edition.

To Dunc and Seb, Colin Baker is the *only* important thing in the world; they eat, sleep and breath 'Colin', and even encourage their readers to send in Colin related dreams to the magazine.

A couple of year ago, inspired by finally meeting the 'great man', Seb and Dunc staged, for the Brighton Festival, an exhibition of over 200 different paintings, sketches and screen prints of their favourite Doctor, simply called '207 Colins.'

According to Seb, a typical day for the two of them involves: *"Getting up, making a brew, watching a bit of Colin for about three hours, petitioning the 'Bring Back Dr Who website', and continuing work on the next magazine. We also try and imagine what Colin would be eating that day. We'll consult our Doctor Who cookbook and sometimes invent recipes that we think Colin would like. We started eating a lot more puddings when we discovered he had a fondness for them."*

On the subject of girlfriends however, the pair are much more reticent and withdrawn.

"Women give you a wide berth when they find out what you're into," explained Dunc, *'but they don't know what they're missing. We can be sensitive. I cry sometimes. I mean, have you* **seen** *Dr Who and the Green Death?"*

As Seb and Dunc would say, 'Keep it Colin.'

*For anyone unfamiliar with Doctor Who trivia, Colin Baker played the sixth incarnation of 'the Doctor', but was so unpopular with viewers that he became the first, and only, actor in this role to be sacked.

Adventures with **Brighton's** most **Eccentric** Shopkeeper

These genuinely bizarre tales come from my own, and others', experiences of Brighton's mysterious Mr. R, a sort of unhinged version of the shopkeeper from Mr. Ben. I heard recently of one customer who, when discovered by Mr. R to only have 5p to his name, was offered a teaspoon of dried milk powder in exchange for his meagre bounty. Another acquaintance was refused entry to his shop on account that he was 'wearing the wrong buttons on his shirt', although Mr. R did kindly offer to sew on the correct ones, if he didn't mind waiting. And finally, one visitor to the shop was deeply perplexed when Mr. R started explaining to him how elephant skin waistcoats can be kept clean with white bread. Then, mid-sentence, he paused and said-

'But you know Sir, I just don't understand how elephants stay clean in Africa though, as there's no white bread out there.'

SOME VELVET MORNING

Hello, can I help you Sir?
Well I'm looking for a…
Certainly Sir.
And he leads me around the labyrinth, offering here a tweed overcoat, there cavalry pantaloons. Eventually I put my foot down and force the issue-
Actually I'm looking for a double-breasted velvet suit.
The world falls from around us and a heavy feeling hangs in the air.
Velvet?
Yes that's right – I say somewhat cautiously – Black and double breasted. *But……..velvet?* – Again the question comes.
Yes, but if you don't stock velvet I'll……
Am I right in assuming Sir wants a suit? A man's suit? Made from…what was it…..'velvet'?
Yes.
And suddenly noticing the very thing not a step away I pronounce –
Like that one.
But it's too late.
In all my years in the business, I've never heard of anything like it, he says incredulously.
A suit.
A man's suit!
MADE OF VELVET!!!
I decide to cut my losses and ask for any suit, just to end the spiral of recriminations against velvet. The storm breaks.
Of course Sir! I've just the thing.
And with that he brandishes forth the crumbling apparel of Napoleon. The thing has epaulets, gold braid and jodhpurs!
As I'm hurriedly leaving I hear him say-
Of course it is a little generous in the waist, but we could pad it out with citrus fruit no doubt……

Brighton in Books & the Movies

BRIGHTON IN THE MOVIES

Brighton Rock
1947 Dir. John Boulting

Discover a Brighton of Bovril adverts and Bryl-Cream. This classic Graham Greene story, set in the Thirties, has plenty of scenes from the Old Lanes, Queen's Road , Grand Hotel and the Palace Pier. Richard Attenborough plays Pinkie Brown, an evil, small-time gangster who tries to cover up a murder by marrying a young girl who could give evidence against him. The ending is better in the book (aren't they always?), but it's a genuinely chilling account of the gangster scene that once flourished here. If you're a Doctor Who fan keep their eyes peeled for a young William Hartnell.

Classic line from the film: *'People don't change; look at me. I'm like one of those sticks of rock. Bite all the way down and you still read Brighton.'*

Oh, What A Lovely War!
1969 Dir. Dickie Attenborough

Attenborough's first movie is an over-ambitious and heavy-handed affair, telling the story of the First World War through allegory, mild satire and *way* too much singing. The West Pier is the platform for describing the events leading up to the war, and the film also includes many fine shots of the seafront, the Downs and Devil's Dyke.

Despite its flaws, it's an interesting piece of British movie history, with some occasionally stunning moments. The scene in the trenches on Christmas day, when the Germans and English soldiers nervously meet in No Man's Land and share a drink, is genuinely moving. The film also boasts an incredible cast, ranging from the thespian gods of Laurence Olivier and John Mills, right the way down to the Fairy Liquid Queen herself, Nanette Newman.

Marina and Holly from 'Me, Without You'

Me Without You

2001 Dir. Sandra Goldbacher

Following childhood friends Marina and Holly through their teenage years and beyond, this rather lacklustre tale of jealousy and heartache suffers a bit from 'I love the Seventies/ Eighties' syndrome, with so much emphasis on perfectly placed songs, band posters and kitsch furniture, that the plot is almost inconsequential. The film's strength comes mid-way when the girls move to Brighton to study at Sussex University and, amidst lectures on Barthes, Baudrillard and other usual suspects, they both start to have a fling with their tutor (Kyle Mclachlan) who plays the sleazy lecturer down to tee, complete with V neck sweater, mane of hair, a coke habit, and the classic chat-up line 'let's discuss this over tea at my place.' From hereon, however, the film gets increasingly tedious over the theme of Holly's unrequited love for Marina's brother Nad, and by the end you may well be chomping at the bit for it to finish.

Quadrophenia

1979 Dir. Franc Roddam

Jimmy, a troubled young Mod, visits Brighton for a wild weekend but gets carried away, takes too many pills, loses his job and is so disillusioned with Sting's bad acting and lousy solo albums that he drives his scooter off Beachy Head. Or does he?

The shots of Seventies Brighton (masquerading as Sixties Brighton) are wonderful – it's all smoky cafes, Triumph Heralds and Wimpy bars. The fight scenes take place on the beach and down East Street, but if you want to find the famous alleyway where Jimmy and Steph cop off, go down East Street towards the sea. Near the end look for the shop LTS and above it is a sign for an alleyway that reads 'to little East Street'. It's down there. This was once a graffitied Mod shrine, but with the next Mod revival not due for another ten years, it doesn't attract so many visitors any more. Yes, the doorway is still there (now black), but it's locked, so no, you can't pop in and have a shag, though countless have tried…

Classic line from the film:

'I don't want to be like everyone else, that's why I'm a Mod see.'

Shadow of Fear*

1963 Dir. Ernest Morris

This bargain basement quickie made by Butchers Film Services at Brighton Studios, is an unlikely international espionage 'thriller' set in Hove, Seaford and Baghdad. An inept MI5 operation culminates in a tepid boat chase off Shoreham Harbour near the 2 old power stations. Reginald Marsh (who crops up in Reginald Perrin) is the only even remotely familiar face.

Smokescreen*

1964 Dir. Jim O'Connolly

Shot on location in Sussex, and at the forgotten Brighton Film Studios, this low-key thriller stars Peter 'Genial Harry Grout' Vaughn as a dogged and niggardly insurance assessor on the trial of a suspected fraudulent claim. Peppered with British bit part players, including Sam Kydd, Glyn Edwards and Derek Gulyer, this nifty 'B' movie features Brighton Station, the Grand hotel and the West Pier.

Villain

1971 Dir. Michael Tuchner

This Seventies movie is a tough, bruising thriller, with Richard Burton playing a vicious gay criminal. Though set in London, the story does, however, move to Brighton when Burton decides to visit his dear old mother. But the game is eventually up when he gets nabbed by the fuzz on the West Pier.

Thanks to Ian Helliwell for these two reviews

Others to look out for

Genevieve
1953 Dir. Henry Cornelius
Jigsaw
1962 Dir. Val Guest
Tommy
1975 Dir. Ken Russell
Mona Lisa
1986 Dir. Neil Jordan
Under Suspicion
1992 Dir. Simon Moore
The Fruit Machine
1988 Dir. Philip Saville

Ones to avoid like the plague

Dirty Weekend
1993 Dir. Michael Winner
Circus
2000 Dir. Rob Walker

The Brighton Movie Buff's Quiz

'Give her a hat with an ostrich's feather in it and there's no girl in Brighton on a bank holiday could hold a candle to her'
Who said it, and what was the film?

? ? ? ?

The first person to send in the correct answer (via email or snail-mail) wins a night out with Chris Eubank or a 50p book token.

CARRY ON BRIGHTON

Carry On Girls
(1973) Directed by Gerald Thomas

The Plot:

Sid James is on the make as usual, this time as the buttock-slapping Councillor Fiddler, who organises a beauty competition, only to be foiled by the sour-faced women's-libber June Whitfield.

Where in Brighton?

It all takes place in the pretend seaside town of Fircombe (oooerrr!!) which is, in fact, Brighton. The film features shots of the seafront, the West Pier and a fleeting glimpse of Regency Square.

My favourite bit of the film is near the end, when the contest goes awry and Sid James —being chased by a crowd of angry men — escapes down the West Pier in a go-kart.

Look out for the outrageous gay stereotypes in the movie – there's the camp film director with the flowery shirt and mincing walk, and June Whitfield's sidekick, a humourless, man-hating lesbian who dresses like Hitler. They just don't make them like they used to.

Trivia:

This was the first Carry On film that had to go after the 9pm BBC watershed, as it was considered too saucy.

Carry On At Your Convenience
(1971) Directed by Gerald Thomas

The Plot:

Hailed as a Carry-On masterpiece, this tale of industrial strife and romance at WC Boggs toilet factory meant that the lavatorial gags could really let rip (ahem). And, of course, no Carry-On movies would be complete without Brighton's own Patsy Rowland (as sex-crazy secretary Miss Withering) trying to get into Kenneth Williams trousers as usual. I just don't think you were his type dear.

Starring Kenneth Williams as WC Boggs and Sid James as…Sid. Well, why make life difficult?

Where In Brighton?

The gang take a bus trip down here for their annual work's outing and head for the rides on the Palace Pier.

Trivia:

Alternative title for the film was 'Carry On Ladies Please Be Seated'.

Beatniks
Toby Litt
This is the tale of three modern day hippies who move to Brighton to start a magazine called 'Café Bohemia' but all end up in bed together instead. The book tries hard to be hip but fails, and the descriptions of Brighton are woefully clichéd. Strangely enough, a Café Bohemia opened in Kemptown just as the book was released.

Breakfast in Brighton
Nigel Richardson
Having almost made a legend out of one of the least likely pubs in Brighton (the Grosvenor), Nigel Richardson has, with this book, weaved a meandering but insightful account of his time spent with the town's motley collection of old hammy actors, fishermen and improbable landladies. Opinions about the book seem quite divided amongst Brightonians; some love it, others find it all a bit dull. True, the plot is rather scant, but I rather enjoyed reading about a side of Brighton that is still quite unknown to me.

Brighton Ghosts, Hove Hauntings (true ghost stories)
John Rackham
The result of five years investigations and over 400 interviews with people who claim to have had supernatural experiences in the local area, the book is divided into locations (Pavilion, churches, pubs, theatres) and subjects (smugglers, Ouija boards) and even includes an

BRIGHTON GHOSTS, HOVE HAUNTINGS
TRUE GHOST STORIES
from Brighton, Hove and
neighbouring villages

John Rackham

account by Adrian Shephard (featured in the eccentrics section of this book), who, it seems, 'opened up a gateway to another world' after performing a live exorcism on local radio.

The book starts well with the introductory chapter 'What are ghosts', showing Rackham's open-minded enthusiasm and investigative approach to the subject, but, at over 300 pages, you may prefer this as something to dip into now and again, rather than read from cover to cover.

Brighton Rock
Graham Greene
(See film guide)

Hangover Square
Patrick Hamilton
Companion to 'Brighton Rock', detailing the sleaze and vitality of London and Brighton in the late Thirties.

The Illustrated Mum
Jacqueline Wilson

Though the Ray Bradbury reference may be lost on the majority of its readers, Jacqueline Wilson's widely acclaimed children/ early teenagers novel takes an insightful look into some of the problems surrounding an unconventional modern family and provides humour and compassion when dealing with 'difficult' issues such as the mother's manic depression.

And, with the family in question being Marigold (a single mum with a penchant for wacky clothes and tattoos) and her two daughters, Star and Dolphin, Brighton was, of course, the natural choice of setting for this novel.

The Neat and Nippy Guide to Brighton
Christopher Horlock

Rather than being *another* competitor (as I first assumed when I saw it), this concise and inexpensive little paperback covers Brighton's history at breakneck pace. Horlock takes a conventional, but playful approach to the town's chequered past and he clearly relishes a good tale. Most of the highlights come in the first half of the book, when Horlock details the lives of Martha Gunn, Mrs Fitzherbert and the Prince Regent, and the ensuing *'drunkeness, gambling and hanky-panky'* that took place in the Pavilion. And the stories about 'Prinnies' wayward pals the Barrymore Brothers are hilarious, though, afterwards, even Horlock concedes, *'The rest of this guide is going to seem a bit dull after that lot!'* The second half details the history of some of the town's oldest roads and twittens and, again, the reader is

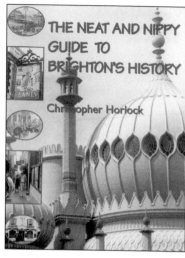

treated to ghost stories, architectural blunders and anecdotes of such fruity eccentrics as the 'Green Man'. A thoroughly digestible book that can be read from cover to cover in just a couple of hours. Recommended.

The Vending Machine of Justice & As Good As It Gets
Simon Nolan

Simon Nolan seems to like writing comedies set around Brighton, as these two novels demonstrate. 'As Good as it Gets' is a trendy novel about a bunch of Twenty-Somethings who find five kilos of coke and decide that they could find a better use for it than the police, while the Vending Machine of Justice revolves around a bizarre case at Hove crown court and a few local zombies. While Nolan's books include some good descriptions of the pub and club culture in Brighton and have some genuinely funny moments, it's all fairly lightweight stuff and may disappoint those with a penchant for quality literature.

Palace Pier
Keith Waterhouse
Actually set during the Brighton Festival, this new comic novel by the acclaimed author of Billy Liar promises to be a lot of fun, though as it only came out a few days before going to print I'm sure you'll forgive me for not having had the chance yet to read it.

The Snowman
Raymond Briggs
Christmas wouldn't be the same without this children's tale, brought alive every year through the magic of television and the lilting tones of a Welsh eunuch. Written and set locally, next time it's on the telly look out for the flying scene and you'll see the Snowman and the boy sail over Brighton Pavilion and the Palace Pier as they head south to the errrr…North Pole.

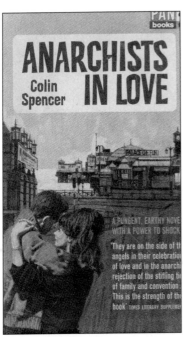

PAN books

ANARCHISTS IN LOVE
Colin Spencer

PALACE OF FUN

A PUNGENT, EARTHY NOVEL WITH A POWER TO SHOCK

'They are on the side of the angels in their celebration of love and in the anarchic rejection of the stifling ties of family and convention. This is the strength of the book' TIMES LITERARY SUPPLEMENT

Literary Events
In recent years it's Borders who seem to have taken up the mantel of organising book-readings and other literary events in Brighton. Look out for their monthly fliers in the shop for details of what's on. During the May Festival there's also a whole plethora of book readings and interviews from big names like Salman Rushdie and Hanif Kureshi, in different venues around the town.

QueenSpark Books
(01273) 571710
www.queensparkbooks.org.uk
www.mybrightonandhove.org.uk
QueenSpark Books began life over thirty years ago as a local campaign to save the Royal Spa building in Queens Park being turned into a casino by developers. The campaigners produced a regular newspaper, QueenSpark, which was sold at the princely sum of 1p (this was the Seventies after all!). Then, in 1974, Brightonian, Albert Paul, sent his life story, 'Poverty, Hardwork but Happiness', to the group and this became the first ever QueenSpark book, with Albert selling over 1000 copies door to door around Brighton. Since then, QueenSpark – set up as a voluntary non-profit making community publishing company – have produced over 80 titles, including individual life stories by local people, community oral histories and the occasional poetry anthology. Such gems include 'Moulsecomb Memoirs' and 'Tales from the Fishing Community'.

OCCULT BRIGHTON

With Brighton as the chosen resting place of Aleister Crowley; home to the famous witch, Doreen Valiente; birthplace of the notorious 'Temple of Psychic Youth', and current host to the world's largest annual occult festival, it seems fairly clear that there's something a bit 'Sunnydale' about the place.

No less remarkable is the fact that the two greatest UK occultists, Dion Fortune and Aleister Crowley, have both **written** about Brighton in their novels. In Fortune's occult thriller 'The Demon Lover', the two heroes, Lucas and Veronica, have a 'Brighton experience' as their trip to the town makes them 'profoundly aware of their own karmic links and the magical task set before them'.

Finally it may come as no surprise to learn that Sussex was the last county to convert to Christianity. In 666A.D. no less!

BRIGHTON OCCULTISTS PAST AND PRESENT

Aleister Crowley

Being the author of the 'Book of the Law', a drug fiend, a poet, and dubbed 'the Wickedest Man In The World', Crowley naturally had a connection with Brighton and, though he died in Hastings in 1947, chose to be cremated at Woodvale Cemetery down the Lewes Road.

At his funeral, selections of his work were read, along with the recitation of the 'Hymn to Pan', which thoroughly shocked the locals and caused the town council to hold an emergency meeting to see that such a ceremony would never take place again in their town. Don't go looking for him though; he's all blown away by now.

Paul Hughes-Barlow

www.supertarot.co.uk

Said to be the world's leading expert on Thoth Tarot, Paul lectures around the world and is the author of 'The Magus - Opening the Key of Tarot and Magic', a book which presents new methods of invoking spirits using divination techniques. Paul can also be found under the Palace Pier. No, it's not where he lives, but where he operates as a Tarot consultant.

Doreen Valiente

Described as the 'Mother of Modern Witchcraft' this remarkable lady first encountered the Craft back in the early 1950's, under the tutelage of influential Witch, Gerald Gardner. Later, Doreen breathed life into rather fragmented rites and rituals contained in the *Book of Shadows (the Bible of Gardnarian Wicca)* using her poetic skills. Today, nearly every Witch in every coven in the world repeats the sacred invocation, 'Charge of the Goddess' penned by Doreen. She is credited for inspiring the current popular interest in Witchcraft (along with Joss Whedon), and has left several important works on the subject.

Doreen lived in in Kemptown. Upon her death, in 1999, she bequeathed the most important collection of Wiccan memorabilia to the Centre For Pagan Studies, including the carefully guarded Book of Shadows, whose contents are forbidden to non-Witches!

Genesis P. Orridge

This notorious former Brighton resident first made a name for himself in the Seventies through his group Throbbing Gristle and live 'art' performances known as the Coum Transmissions. Owing to the rather explicit and esoteric nature of the performances, Orridge began to incur the wrath of the press and government, being described by one Tory MP (in response to an art performance at the I.C.A.), as a 'Wrecker of Civilisation'. But the worse was yet to come.

In the early Eighties Genesis set up in Brighton the Temple of Psychic Youth (TOPY), a 'Cyberian Anti-Cult', whose collective of like-minded 'searchers' aimed to explore altered states through scarification, piercing, sado-masochism and sex magick. While tattoos, piercings and S&M are pretty much de-rigueur in Brighton nowadays, back then the group's singular activities were enough to cause a witch-hunt in the media and, in 1991, a Channel Four documentary 'exposed' TOPY as a 'sick Satanic Cult'. Witnesses spoke of being drugged, raped and forced to eat babies in the basement of Orridge's house in Roundhill Crescent. The police raided the house and Orridge (who was then in Thailand) was strongly advised not to return home.

He never did, preferring instead to settle in the US, where he still lives today, despite the fact that subsequent enquiries into the documentary showed it to be a malicious stitch up (Orridge's house didn't even have a basement!).

What makes Orridge such a fascinating character is his ability to constantly re-invent himself and, true to form, he is still courting controversy, having spent the last few years exploring transexuality with his partner 'Miss Jackie Superstar'. The two have been 'breaking the boundaries of male and female polarity' through plastic surgery, adopting each other's mannerisms and dressing identically.

And, seeing as though Orridge helped spearhead Brighton as the tattoo and piercings capital of the UK, is he, I wonder, once again spearheading the dissolution of another great taboo? Can we eventually expect to see hoards of transsexual clones alighting the train from Hassocks and Croydon every Friday night?

We live in hope.

Hexagon Archive

www.occulture.tv

The Hexagon Archive is an independent resource that collects rare and unusual material related to the occult. It has an extensive photographic library featuring relics such as ritual swords, magic wands, genuine witches curses and Shamanic rites. Run by the rather eccentric duo of Jonathan and Justin, they are among only a handful of people allowed access to Stonehenge for historical and research purposes. The archive houses a vast array of CD Roms, documents, books and research, all connected to the art magical. Hexagon welcome submissions of all esoteric material bar UFO's, declaring-

" We'll talk to anyone except crazies!"

Did the Man from Atlantis really exist ? Colin Wilson reveals all at the Occulture festival...

Occulture

www.occulture.tv Every July
See programme on above website for
venue and price details

Set up in 2000 by Justin Hankinson and former Bollywood stunt double, the Reverend Jonathan Tapsell (another story in itself), this incredible event has grown to become the largest occult festival in the world. Though initially set up as a weeklong event, Occulture is now all neatly squeezed into a long one-dayer, offering lectures, demonstrations, films, stalls and more besides.

Previous highlights have included talks from cult author Colin Wilson, a visit from the Tibetan government in exile, the Church of Satan, Jon Ronson, comedian Ken Campbell and lectures on subjects ranging from Gurdjieff, Chaos Magic and Wicca to fetishism. Notable antics include a near-riot in 2002 (as things got ugly between Aleister Crowley devotees and Armado Crowley's followers) and, in 2001, host John Belham-Payne taking great pleasure in reading to the audience an irate letter in the Leader complaining that 'ritualistic animal sacrifices were taking place at the Hanbury Arms in Kemptown!' Well, I've been to every event and, from what *I've* seen, the guests and audiences that attend are an intelligent and open-minded lot and animal and human sacrifices are kept to a bare minimum.

Occulture perfectly sums up the diverse, creative and esoteric spirit of the town; to miss it would be criminal.

221

GROUPS

Brighton Moot

A monthly gathering of like-minded people with interests in paganism, wicca, druidry and other spiritual paths. Described by one of their organisers, Allan, as a group who are *'into celebration, not sulking'*, Brighton Moot meet monthly at the Hobgoblin pub (naturally) and have a full roster of events for the year, including talks, walks, open rituals, camps and the Broomstick Rally (!) at end of August .

First Thursday of the month, upstairs at the Hobgoblin, London Road

Contact: Allan (01323) 645573

eucalyptus.tree@btinternet.com

Order of Artemis

The Order of Artemis was founded in 1959 by local legend Sir Ralph Harvey (see Brighton Eccentrics chapter). Following the old 'hereditary' ways of Wicca, Ralph has been instrumental in bringing renewed interest to the Craft and he now has Covens flourishing throughout Britain, most of Europe, Australia and the USA. In March 2002, Ralph initiated his 100th Priestess, so furthering the expansion of the Craft and Artemis. At the age of 74 he is one of the last of the old school, hence the moustache.

contact: *order-of-artemis@ntlworld.com*

True Occultism

Contact Graham on 07944 788857

"We are Brighton-based students of Amado Crowley 777. We meet weekly to travel together the ancient sacred path to self-knowledge and Truth. Ours is an oral tradition, delivered in plain speech and modern style. It is a shamanic religion that dates from pre-history. We seek to recover our rightful place in nature, and to become what we were meant to be. The way is not easy, but there is strength in fellowship. If you feel that life is not what it's meant to be, then we may be able to help."

OCCULT AWAY-DAYS

Chanctonbury Ring

5 Miles North of Worthing

This small Iron-Age hill fort, noted for its ring of Beech trees* is a beguiling place steeped in folklore. According to legend, if you walk or run seven times around the Ring at midnight, the devil appears, offering a bowl of milk, soup or porridge (!?). If you accept these comestibles, he either takes your soul or offers you your heart's desire (which is obviously a bit of a gamble for anyone daft enough to risk it).

Long associated with witchcraft, Chanctonbury Ring was once described by Crowley as a 'place of power', while local witch, Doreen Valiente, revealed it to be 'the meeting place of an ancient coven'. That the place has, in the past, been used for occult practises is indisputable, as evidence of makeshift altars have been found there on several occasions, not to mention other known occult symbols and artefacts. Whether the Ring is a spot favoured by black or white witches is unknown, but, as the Sussex archaeology and folklore website put it; *'Being Chanctonbury Ring, it is probably black.'*

Chanctonbury Ring is also associated with sighting of UFOs and 'fairies'; there have been countless reports over the years of strange coloured objects and dancing lights seen there.

If you're planning a visit, it's best not to come alone. And certainly not at night.

*Though, sadly, most were lost during the '87 hurricane

The Gay Scene

Ever since the 1900s, Brighton has been home to an ever-expanding gay scene. Secretive at first, but now very much integrated into the town, it has grown to become the UK's most celebrated gay community. The town's theatrical history is deemed to be one of the main factors that helped kick-start the scene, as, earlier in the century big gay icons like Ivor Novello and Noel Coward lived here for some time, helping make Brighton a magnet for drama queens and men with handlebar moustaches. And, with the town already established as a fashionable pleasure capital and with place names such as Dyke Close, the Queen's Arms and even Tidy Street, it seemed the obvious choice for the gay scene's headquarters.

From the Sixties onwards the gay community has developed around Kemptown and the Old Steine. This is still where the majority of Brighton's gay population live and socialise. You will find most of its bars, clubs and shops here, especially around St. James's Street. Many of the gay haunts in Kemptown were originally developed for cruising, but, as it's so easy to be 'out' in Brighton now, the new clubs and bars seem less about a quick fumble in the loos and more about just hanging out, posing and socialising (though, believe me, plenty of naughtiness still goes on).

The latest statistics show that now an incredible 19% of adult males in Brighton are gay, with the number still rising. As a consequence, Brighton now has a gay 'everything' – gay shops, gay clubs, gay saunas, gay coffee bars, gay B&Bs, gay carnivals, gay plumbers, gay estate agents, gay comedians...... and Simon Fanshawe.

LOCAL GAY BARS

The Aquarium
6 Steine Street (01273) 605525
Back-street bar for the old-school crowd. Very cruisy and populated with 'mature' gentlemen, many of whom seem to prefer staring to speaking. A good place to get sucked off by a German tourist.

Bedford Tavern
30 Western Street, Hove (01273) 739495
(See review in Watering Holes)

Regency Tavern
32-34 Russell Square (01273) 325652
Indisputably the campest pub in town, but not wanting to shout about it. Worth a visit at weekends, just to see the décor, eat the food, choke on the clouds of cigarette smoke and marvel at the barman's shirt.

224

(See review in Watering Holes)

The Bulldog
31 St. James's Street (01273) 684097
In the heart of Kemptown, The Bulldog is one of the town's most established gay bars with more Happy Hours than any other pub in Brighton, and about as far removed from the John Inman school of 'whoops, ooh, hark at you' as it gets. Ever-popular with the clones and moustachioed brigade, it still carries that lecherous old-school vibe, and is best experienced at weekends when the crowd is a little more diverse.

FASHIONABLE BARS

Amsterdam

11-12 Marine Parade (01273) 688825

This European-style bar on the seafront attracts a large, mixed crowd in summer. It could be argued that when the Amsterdam first appeared a few years ago it heralded an important change; making Brighton's gay social scene more up-front and not just about cruising. The huge patio overlooking the sea is a prime spot for sitting in your thong with a mug of Horlicks to shock the fifteen-year olds from Hassocks, queuing up for the Escape next door.

Charles Street

8-9 Marine Parade (01273) 624091

This new bar (modelled on Bass's London version, Rupert Street) attracts the trendy, twenties/thirties crowd and out-of-towners looking for where the action is. Quite a bit of cash has been spent here on making the place look like some vast airport departure lounge, but if you don't go for that minimalist look, when it's warm you can always go and grab a seat on the sundeck and have a good bitch about what an eyesore the Aquarium Terrace is. For the posers amongst you, Charles Street should be your first port of call.

Dr Brighton's

16 Kings Road (01273) 328765

(See Watering holes for full review)

CABARET AND KARAOKE HEAVEN !!

Legends Bar

31-32 Marine Parade (01273) 624462
www.legendsbar.co.uk

Attached to the New Europe Hotel, this place attracts a mature crowd for its regular cabaret and entertainment. During the week there are karaoke strippers, quiz and bingo nights, while, at weekends, Legends arranges pre-club get-togethers for events at Revenge. Downstairs here at weekends you'll also find the leather-only Schwartz Bar, home to a gaggle of flabby men in tight leather trousers and caps. What's it like? As one frequent regular explained, 'Expect to go home with a bad back and dirty knees.'

Queen's Arms

7 George Street (01273) 696873

Traditional gay pub with more or less constant entertainment. From cabaret and quizzes to karaoke and piano playing, no matter *when* you arrive, there is always something lively about to happen. For many the highlight of the week is still the Sunday cabaret. And well done guys for finally getting round to a 'showbiz refit'.

TRANSVESTITE BARS

Harlequin

(Formerly Ruby's, Marilyn's, Charlotte's, Catherine's, Tina's, and Tony's Discount Toolshop)
43 Providence Place (01273) 620630
Late license until 2am, closed Sundays

Hidden behind Woolworths off the London Road, this is *the* hangout for transvestites and pre & post transsexuals (if not the only one), though still welcoming to all and sundry. Started by the king of camp, Danny La Rue, the whole place is a real flashback to the Eighties and, during the week, there is cabaret in the large, glittery bar area upstairs, which can include some pretty wild drag acts and karaoke. Worth a visit, whatever your mode of dress.

CLUBS & CLUB NIGHTS

Envy

(Upstairs from Charles St)
8-9 Marine Parade (01273) 624091

Envy lies upon the hallowed ground that was once the Heavy Metal Valhalla, the Hungry Years. For ages I joked about the place being appropriated by the gay scene and then, suddenly, it was, bringing new meaning to the phrase 'having studs on your back'. Its first incarnation was as the Pool Club, but under new manager Chris, it transformed into Envy and, under his guidance, appears to have found a better formula for success, offering a schedule packed with busy club nights, including several nights a month just for the girls.

Kruze

7 Marine Parade, Brighton
(01273) 608133

More a bar really, but with a terrific sea view, great cocktails, and not so poncy a crowd as Charles Street.

Club Revenge

32-43 Old Steine (01273) 606064

The biggest gay club on the South coast, open six nights a week with special events, drinks promotions strippers and cheesy pop nights. A little on the expensive side, but still ranking as one of the best gay clubs in the UK. Sure, newcomers *will* find the inevitable cliques, but don't be put off; it really isn't difficult to meet new people here. With all those bodies beautiful sweating it out on the upstairs dance-floor, you shouldn't find it hard to be caught up in the contagious party atmosphere.

Top tip – Be nice to the sexy and flirty bar-staff; they are your best port of call to find out everything about the hottest bars and parties. Recommended.

Wild Fruit

(See 'special club nights' in Discotheques)

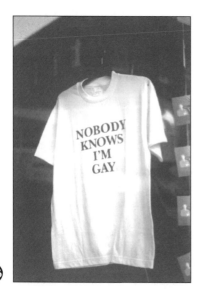

CAFES / FOOD

Scene 22

St. James's Street (01273) 626682

Scene 22 is a popular first stop for gays and lesbians coming to Brighton, and its owner, Freddie, is a real charmer, who seems to have endless time for anyone who drops in. It's amusing just to listen to the banter between him and the regular customers, as the saucy double-entendres flow thick and fast. There, you see? – I'm at it now.

Scene 22 is also a good place to find information on health matters and free maps and magazines. You can even make hotel bookings, collect tickets for shows, and leave messages on the notice board for anything (or anyone) you fancy.

Don't forget to have a nose around the shop in the back; it sells the usual toys, lubes, vibrators etc, and don't be surprised if Freddie talks you into buying a kit to make your cock ten times bigger. It's his way of saying he likes you.

Wai Kika Moo Kau

42 Meeting House Lane
(01273) 323824

This veggie café in the Old Lanes is by no means exclusively gay, but popular with those who don't always need to be in an exclusive gay bar.

The food is great, the staff lovely and they sometimes do music on Saturday nights.

CRUISING AREAS

Hove Lawns / Behind the King Alfred

Increasingly popular cruising area for gay men, especially on Sunday evenings. There is a lot less cover here than at Duke's Mound, but it's a more convivial place to (ahem) hang out.

Starbucks Coffee

201 Western Road and corner of Market Street in the Old Lanes (01273) 709709

Popular with a young, gay frothy-lipped crowd, and quite cruisy at times.

BRIGHTONS ONLY GAY SHOP & COFFEE BAR
129 ST James Street, Brighton.   Telephone: 01273 626682

Nudist Beach

Located 10 min east of the Palace Pier

Brighton's nudist beach is primarily a gay haunt. Straights are welcome but in most cases will feel slightly uncomfortable, especially if confronted by the old bloke who does windmill impressions with his erection. In summer there is a lot of parading, plenty of stiffies, a whole host of voyeurs and way, way too many flabby bottoms.

Duke's Mound

Located 10 min walk east of the pier, overlooking the nudist beach

This small hillside of bushes on the seafront has been an integral part of the older cruising scene in Brighton for countless years. It affords enough privacy for those who require it, yet is risqué enough for naughty exhibitionists. While it isn't that commonly reported, there are occasional stories of people getting mugged and robbed after being picked up and taken to Dukes Mound, so take care.

For years there have been rumours of this area being redeveloped, but nothing ever seems to happen. Last I heard there were plans for a hotel, a coffee shop, a café-bar and Disneyland. But seeing how long it's taken this council just to build a bloody library, I wouldn't worry, *just yet.*

SAUNAS

Used as social clubs in Brighton by the gay community, these saunas attract a wide age group and all come with rest room facilities.

Brighton Oasis

75-76 Grand Parade (01273) 689966
Weekend pass Fri 12pm-Sunday 12am £20.

Opposite the Pavilion, and done out in a glorious Egyptian theme, Brighton Oasis has a whirlpool, a steam room, sun beds, coffee shops and qualified masseurs.

Amsterdam Hotel

11-12 Marine Parade
(01273) 688825

The hotel sauna is open to the public and has a steam room, showers and many darkrooms. Half price for Hotel guests. Open until 6am.

Bright 'n' Beautiful

St Margaret's Place
(01273) 328330

Denmark Sauna

86 Denmark Villas, Hove
(01273) 723733

Pride

early August, Preston Park

Attended by just 100 people when it first started, 'Pride' quickly expanded to become one of the biggest highlights in Brighton's gay (and even straight) calendar. Nowadays, it's a huge carnival parade with dancers, drag queens, fabulous costumes and floats pumping out a vast spectrum of music ranging from the camp disco classics of the Seventies right through to the Eighties. The march usually starts at 1pm from the Peace Statue and dances, shouts and camps it up all the way to the park, stopping only for a sandwich and glass of fizzy pop at the Woolworths café on the way. It's simply fantastic; don't miss it.

www.brightonpride.co.uk

THE LESBIAN SCENE

For years the lesbian scene in Brighton had been almost non-existent, which is strange considering the large numbers of gay women living here. Although, in principle, most of the gay bars welcome lesbians, few take up the offer. Recently however, a social scene for gay women has been growing in Brighton. The first lesbian-run pub, The Marlborough, has been established for many years now and, with the arrival of the Candy Bar and several women-only club-nights, things seem at last to be changing.

Candy Bar

33 St James's Street (01273) 622424
Mon-Sat 11am-11pm, Sun 12-10.30pm
www.thecandybar.co.uk

Continuing in the footsteps of their Soho bar, the Candy Bar is a modern, stylish, lesbian hangout with a bright and airy ambience, table-service, sofas in the corner, a basement room open at weekends and plenty of entertainment to keep everyone happy. Weekly events here range from arm-wrestling competitions (Disarm a Dyke) and Karaoke to Jazz and quiz nights, while at weekends the DJs take over.

While the Candy Bar seems to appeal more to couples and a slighter older, less boisterous crowd than the Marlborough, when I said to Vicki, who works there, 'So not a cruisy kind of place?' she replied; 'Ooh, I wouldn't say that. The crowd do pretty well. As do the staff!'

Marlborough

4 Princes Street (01273) 570028

Tucked away behind the Old Steine, Brighton's long-established lesbian pub attracts quite a young crowd of gay women, ranging from the civilised to the downright lairy. There are two bar areas, a lively one – usually occupied by feisty dykes monopolizing the pool table – and one next door, that's a *little* quieter, and has nice big armchairs to sink into. Well-known for its little theatre upstairs, the Marlborough still puts on plays, comedy nights and other events, especially during the festival, and is a good place to pick up gay magazines and information. This pub is also reputed to be one of Brighton's most haunted; the ghost of Lucy Packham occasionally pops her head round for a quick game of pool, but cheats by dropping her eyes down the corner pockets.

Club Nights

These seem to change around quite a lot, but at time of press the favourites were 'Wet Pussy', running the first and third Friday of every month at Envy and offering DJs, Go-go dancers, House, Disco and R 'n' B tunes. Also popular is Bootylicious, the first Sunday each month at Envy. For more details, check local mags or chat up the staff at the Candy Bar. They're pretty clued up on what's going on.

Understanding the Lingo

The old gay dialect, Polari, was first developed back in the 1930s when homosexuality was still illegal (unless you were involved in theatre, where it was compulsory). This secret language enabled gay folk to get on with matters at hand without fear of persecution. It was later popularised by Julian and Sandy on the radio show 'Round The Horne' and by the 1970s had evolved into such an esoteric and bizarre tongue, that Oliver Postgate used it in the Clangers to send secret messages to many of his lovers around the UK.

Bona palone / homi

Dictionary definition – Good looking woman/man.
Eg. That bloke from the Cheeky Guide, what a bona homi!

Chicken

Dictionary definition – Waif-like young men.
Eg. Check out the chicken outside the Young Conservatives Club.

Trade

Dictionary definition – *Your pick-up for the evening.*
Eg. Take your trade home and give him something to remember you by.

Varda

Dictionary definition – To check out.
Eg. Varda the legs on him/ her/ that lovely Regency sofa.

Cruising

Dictionary definition – Sail to and fro for protection of shipping, making for no particular place or calling at a series of places.
Hmmm, that just doesn't seem to be what's going on in the bushes.

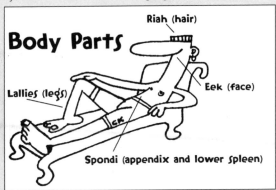

Body Parts

Riah (hair)

Eek (face)

Lallies (legs)

Spondi (appendix and lower spleen)

SHOPS

Cardome

47A St James Street, (01273) 692916
Open 10am-6pm Mon-Sat

A wonderful cross between a local craft market, WH Smith's and a sex shop, Cardome even lays claim to being Brighton's oldest established gay shop (close to 20 years in the business!). This is a good place to come for greeting cards (gay and straight), local hand-made art, jungle juice, and T-shirts with slogans such as 'some mornings I wake up miserable, other mornings I let him sleep'. In the over-18s basement is a wide range of pornographic magazines for straights, gays and pervs. It's friendly owner Mike will answer any discreet questions you may have about all aspects of the sex scene in Brighton (if he hasn't died of joss-stick poisoning, that is).

Can't find what You're **looking** for?

ARE YOU ASLEEP DOWN THERE?

10 % off
when you spend over £5
WITH THIS ADVERT

Then why not try

CardOME
the card specialist

Special art - Adult and everything in between
47a St James Street (Up from Tin Drum)

est. 18 years

CloneZone

St James's Street   (01273) 626442
Open Mon-Thurs 11am-7pm, Fri-Sat, 11am-9pm, Sun 12pm-6pm

Selling a range of toys, videos, fashion, cards and rubber-wear, this is definitely a good place to get stocked up for a weekend of unashamed wickedness. They also have a modest selection of music CDs from the likes of Hazel Dean, and a particularly wide range of magazines, including Latin Inches and Euroboy. If only there were a 'Pale Northerner Monthly' I might earn myself some extra pocket money. Never mind.

The Pink Pamper

1 St James's Street   (01273) 608060

Recently moved further down St James's Street, the Pink Pamper sets out to live up to its name, and pamper the Pink. There are now four floors of treats for your delectation; two for beauty, two for hairdressing. Therapies include; massage, eyelash tinting, aromatherapy, reflexology and Indian head massage. Facial anyone??

LOCAL MAGAZINES

The following magazines can be found in most shops, bars and clubs around Brighton, especially Kemptown.

G-Scene Magazine

Free, monthly

The gay and lesbian bible for your time in Brighton (along with the Cheeky Guide, of course), with previews of all the special club nights, up-to-date information, health and community issues, and personal ads.

3sixty

Free, monthly

Done by the same group who put together The Source, 3sixty covers news, interviews, travel, gossip and reviews, in their inimitably glossy and stylish format.

Safe Sex?

Condoms are given free almost everywhere, but after all these years, they still don't appear to be used. Syphilis, HIV and AIDS numbers are staggering, yet 'it won't happen to me' seems to prevail over common sense. Thankfully, most gay prostitutes in Brighton do enforce the condom rule. Just remember, sex is as safe as you're prepared to make it, so wrap up your peckers, guys.

Violence towards the Gay Community

Despite the fact that the Gay Scene is a big part of the town's life, and that most people in Brighton are totally cool and supportive of the gay community, there are still plenty of attacks. Although it's sad to have to say it, be careful when you are out at night. Just try and avoid snogging in the middle of West Street at 2 in the morning, and you should be OK.

Hanky Panky

*Developed in the days when secrecy was necessary, the coloured hankie in the back pocket is still used in **some** bars for gay men to express their sexual preferences.*

Yellow Hankie

Into water-sports

Red Hankie

Into fist fucking*

Green Hankie

Into the washing machine it goes for a good clean

KEY CHAINS

Worn on the Left – Active

Worn on the Right – Passive

Hundreds of keys on one key-chain – Geek

*In the left back pocket means you like taking, right back pocket means you like giving. Or is it the other way around? Oh well you'll find out, one way or another.

GAY ORGANISATIONS AND SUPPORT GROUPS

Madison Travel World Choice
118 Western Road, Hove (01273) 202532
www.madisontravel.co.uk
Gay-friendly travel agency. Fully
bonded and highly recommended.

Brighton's Women's Centre
Lettice House, 10 St. George's Mews, off
Trafalgar Street
(01273) 600526
Offering supportive help and
information in a friendly atmosphere.
Their services range from
accommodation boards, use of
photocopier and computer, to free
pregnancy tests, crèche, counselling
and legal advice.

Brighton Lesbian / Gay Community Centre
(01273) 234005
Information centre and informal
support on lesbian and gay issues.
Mon-Fri 10am-12noon.
Drop in Thursday 12noon-4pm,
women only on Friday 12noon-4pm

Brighton Relate
(01273) 697997
Specialist advice for lesbian and gay
relationships.

HIV Related Support Open Door
(01273) 605706
Support, referrals, advice, meals,
therapies for HIV.
Mon-Fri 10am-4pm.

Gay Men's Health Matters
(01273) 625222
Information about HIV and sexual
health, free condoms given.

Brighton Body Positive
(01273) 693266
Complementary therapies, information,
support, and counselling for HIV/AIDS.

Street Outreach Service (SOS)
(01273) 625577
Mobile AIDS prevention unit, lots of
advice, free condoms and lube.

Claude Nicol Centre
(01273) 664721
Testing and treatment for HIV (Same
day results on Mon-Tues). Free and
confidential service.

Wilde Clinic
(01273) 664722
Gay and Bisexual men's health clinic
offering HIV testing, STI testing and
treatment, hepatitis A & B vaccinations.

Gay Hotels

Amsterdam Hotel
Marine Parade (01273) 688825

Avalon
Upper Rock Gardens (01273) 692344

Bannings
(Women) Upper Rock Gardens
(01273) 681403

Boydens
St James's Street (01273) 601914

Catnaps
Atlingworth Street (01273) 685193

Cowards
Upper Rock Gardens
(01273) 692677

Four Seasons
(Women) Upper Rock Gardens
(01273) 673574

Hudsons
Devonshire Place (01273) 683642

New Europe
Marine Parade (01273) 624462

Sex, Fetish

AND BODY MODIFICATION

Traditionally, Brighton has always been the place where fat London bosses with hairy bums bring their secretaries for more than just a Tele-sales conference. And, being a fashionable resort and the perfect short break from the Big Smoke, it's easy to see why Brighton has earned a reputation for 'dirty weekends' and countless indiscretions. Even the Prince Regent was at it, having secretly married Mrs Fitzherbert here. (The passageways connecting the Pavilion bedroom to her place were a means of assuring their midnight rendezvous were kept a secret.)

There are also rumours that Brighton has its own 'Dogging Scene' up at Devil's Dyke, which, if you're unfamiliar with such antics, involves randy couples, cars, and the odd voyeur. (I'm sure you can piece the rest of the jigsaw together for yourself.)

Brighton's saucy nature today comes more from the liberal nature of its citizens than anything else. It's a good place to live for anyone who wants to come out of the closet and feel relaxed with his or her sexuality. And with this town being home to everyone from fetishists to drag queens, you can feel secure here in the knowledge that, in your very neighbourhood, there'll always be someone kinkier than you.

Kinky boots from Spanki

SHOPPING

Ann Summers
75/76 North Street, opposite the
Clock Tower (01273) 205744
Open Mon-Sat 9.30am-6pm, Sun 11am-5pm
www.annsummers.com

Banana dick lip, after-dinner nipples,
beginners SM kits, maids' outfits, sexy
lingerie, cheap rubber and PVC, dildos,
bondage tape and naughty books. It's
sex with a smile and the perfect
starting point if you're here for a saucy
weekend. Most of the clothes are
aimed at those dipping their toes for
the first time into the wonderful world
of sexy glamour-wear, and are not
always great quality, but then you won't
necessarily be wearing them out, will you?

Private Shop
11 Surrey Street Adults only
Open Mon-Sat 9am-5.30pm

The usual collection of dildos, magazines,
videos, blow-up dolls and mild fetish
toys and clothes. They do, however,

seem to have a good selection of foot
fetish magazines and did I really once
see a whole collection of mud-
wrestling videos in here?

Cardome
(See shopping section in Gay Chapter)

Kentucky Woman
www.kentuckywoman.co.uk
Alas Kentucky Woman closed quite a
few years ago, along with its fully
equipped dungeon, but all is not lost.
Their website contains everything
from corsets, leatherwear, petticoats
and bondage gear, to clothing for
transvestites. What's more, they offer a
specialist fantasy service for men
wishing to spend the weekend as
French maids, Victorian maids or Sissy
Boys, in a Regency apartment in
Brighton. The two-day stay is with Sir
Richard and Lady Elizabeth and costs
£300, including accommodation at a
nearby hotel.

Spanki
33 Sydney Street (01273) 697475
Open 10am-6pm Mon-Sat

Having flitted around Sydney Street
and Trafalgar Street for many years
(and in various guises), owner Martin
finally parked his pipe and slippers in
the North Laine with Spanki. Selling
fetish-wear, bondage trousers, kilts and
customised Punk shirts, this is the kind
of shop that separates Brighton from
just about every other town in
England. Spanki also stock a modest
range of rubber and PVC clothes
(nurses dress and hat – a snip at £45),
corsets, hair extensions, handcuffs and
just about anything else you'd need for
a pervy night out (or in, for that
matter). Staff will also fill you in with
information on fetish nights and other
related events.

And they called it Puppy love...

She said (Erotic Boutique)

13 Ship Street Gardens (between Ship
Street and Middle Street) (01273) 777822
Open 11am-7pm Mon-Sat, 12pm-5.30pm Sun

She Said is the creation of Nic
Ramsey, who, having only rolled into
town a couple of year ago, has already
made a big impression with her shop,
wild parties and candid appearances
on Channel Four's 'Sex Tips for Girls',
when she and her partner became
the first heterosexual couple to
openly discuss anal sex on a British
television programme. But I digress.
Nic's shop has been the talk of the
town ever since it opened, and offers
alluring and exotic lingerie, superior
quality sex toys and a modest
collection of kinky club-wear. Upstairs
you'll find sexy knickers, stockings,
Audrey Hepburn-style silk dresses and
a large range of corsets. To not try
anything on in their alluring red velvet
changing room up here would be a
crying shame.

Downstairs is where the 'naughty
stuff' can be found; rubber clothes, a

good range of dildos, handcuffs, whips
and even a sling suspension for the
serious bondage lovers. When I asked
Elaine (who works there) what had
been selling well recently, she pointed
outside to the spring sunshine and
said, 'Everyone's got the horn at the
minute, so naturally, it's toys and
lubes.'

It is the elegant touches though
that make She Said the 'Marylyn
Monroe' to Ann Summers 'Jordan'; the
décor is beautiful and stylish and the
staff too, dress to impress. Some
Saturdays they even pick a theme of
the day (fetish, cowboy, Heidi etc),
and get glammed up for it.

A kinky and mischievous version of
the shop that Mr Ben used for his
psychedelic travels, (though where
he'd have ended up dressed in exotic
underwear and a corset is anybody's
guess), with its sassy staff, sexy lingerie
and elegant layout, She Said must
surely lay claim to being one of the
most glamorous shops in England.

Tickled

15 Gardner Street (01273) 628725
Open 11am-6pm Mon-Fri, 10.30am-6pm
Sat, 12pm-5pm Sun
www.tickledonline.com

After witnessing an argument about why women couldn't buy dildos outside of male-orientated sex shops, Estate Agents, Helen and Alison, threw away their pin-stripe suits and mobiles and set up 'Tickled'. Exclusively for women, this shop offers a range of sex-toys, videos and 'novelty' gifts, combined with friendly and discreet advice.

On the ground floor, the stock leans more towards the novelty end of the sex/gifts market (such as good love-making guides and T-shirts) while, downstairs, things get more 'serious'.

For ladies only (men must be accompanied), the basement offers a small selection of lesbian softcore videos and exclusive leather products such as harnesses. But it is Tickled's range of dildos and sex toys that are their real strength, particularly as they can be tried out discreetly (something not always possible in Anne Summers). But, I hasten to add, it's *not* a changing room down there. So don't get stripped off naked as one customer did, they've got cameras down there and will have a good laugh watching you if you try. Instead, you can try the products out on your nose instead (which is apparently the closest test to how sensual a vibrator will feel on a lady's naughty bits).

Tickled also sell a range of silicon dildos, which are said to be long-lasting, durable and (according to Helen) 'can even be cleaned in the dishwasher'.

Sexy shoes for kinky midgets, courtesy of She Said

Worrying for men is the fact that their 'Brighton Babe' T-shirt, satin sheets and 'Rampant Rabbit' dildos are still the best sellers, which to me sounds like the ladies are having a fine time on their own these days. Boys, if you're not careful, you'll soon be relegated to simply washing the sheets and keeping the ladies in fresh supplies of batteries for the rabbit...

FETISH EVENTS

Torture Garden

www.torturegarden.com
This established, grand-scale London fetish club has been holidaying in Brighton for some time now, but at time of going to print, there was still some debate as to whether they were staying put at the Honeyclub. Best check their website for up-to-date information.

Vinylla

Every other month at the Hanbury
Ballroom *www.vinylla.co.uk*
A 'softcore' fetish night aimed at *'those who want to 'dabble', get dressed up, and dance without being too extreme'.* The club features erotic projections and live performances.

TATTOOISTS AND PIERCERS

In the last few years, Brighton has seen a real boom in tattoo parlours and body piercing studios. The following are only a small selection of what's on offer, but are recommended because they take the art of body modification seriously.

While tattooing is a widespread skill, bear in mind that design and style are very individual. So if you're tempted, I'd recommend you make an appointment first with the artists below. Go in person to see if you feel comfortable with them and what you think of their work. All good tattooists should carry a portfolio.

One last thing – if you're having something written, make sure your tattooist is clear on the spelling. One local tattoo parlour, which shall remain nameless, used to have a big sign outside that read –

***'Come inside, we have 1000's of desings.'** Enough said.*

Penetration

29 Sydney Street (01273) 623839
Open Mon-Sat 10am-6pm, Sun 12pm5pm
'Vatican Approved since 1995'
Downstairs for tattooing, by appointment only

Friendly and approachable, Penetration's resident piercers, Danny and Nick, extend such care to their 'patients' that, if you're a fainter, they mollify you with sweeties. For the more hard-core body-modifications addict, they do PA's and ampallangs (for which you need a consultation to be…ahem…measured), surgical steel implants and cosmetic dentistry. While he pierces your tongue, Nick will tell you all about when he got his willy pierced for the benefit of an Italian TV fashion programme (at which the Pope didn't bat an eyelid), while Danny politely asks that you 'please wash your privates' before coming for a piercing down below.

Prices start at around £10, lip with ring £17, ampallang £30.

In the basement, Mickey specialises in custom-designed tattoos, with a lot of influence drawn from Maori, Celtic, Haida and Art Nouveau traditions, while Woody Clarke leans more towards Nu-School, portrait and colourful graffiti-style designs. They also do grey shading and cover-up. In short, anything beautiful.

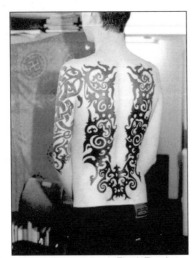

Temple Tatu design

Perforations

21 Preston Street (01273) 743723
www.perforations.com

A popular and friendly state-of-the-art studio, where piercings are more than just skin-deep. Check their website, it's really informative.

Temple Tatu

9 Boyces Street (01273) 208844
Open 12pm-6pm Tues-Sat
www.templetatu.com

This impressive studio is located just off West Street. Although they do walk-ins, appointments are encouraged, in order to give people the chance to really examine their motives for getting a tattoo. The five resident artists have a deep knowledge and understanding of the history of tattooing, and make each design unique. One of its artists, Pier, even specialises in 'traditional' tattooing by hand.

Newcomers are made to feel at ease by discussions over a cup of tea of all the process involves. In fact, the reception room at Temple Tatu probably contributes a lot to instilling you with confidence in these guys' creative skills. From hand-made sequin tiaras to Hindu tiles and stickers, this place has been decorated to welcome you and make you feel at home.

While here, look out for the kitsch-looking alchemical shrine, built by some mad-genius New Zealander, with plastic dolls, driftwood, electric bulbs and old soapboxes inside. You can activate it by inserting a coin and pressing your palms on the designated space. Loads of weird things happen, including stuff whizzing around and the machine talking to you and playing strange music. The shrine is designed to release positive energy and, frankly, with the effort and esoteric detail that has gone into these things, I'd happily have one in my lounge if I could afford it.

I can't really tell you what they specialise in, since their portfolio is so varied (black, tribal, colour, cover up), but they're quite particular about researching every design, so you can find out what the tattoo you're about to get really means.

Wildcats

6 Gardner Street (01273) 606489
Open Mon-Sat 10am-6pm
www.wildcat.co.uk

Quite simply the largest suppliers of body jewellery in the world. They also stock tattoo books and, downstairs, clothes, mags and sex toys for the more adventurous (including steel butt-plugs).

Look for the shrunken heads on the window, the incredible photos of the 'Sundance Ritual' on the walls and the fliers for all fetish-related events around town. But someone, please, try and get the buggers to turn off that bloody scary music and play some Herb Alpert instead.

The Adonis Cabaret Show

Babylon Lounge Kingsway, Hove
(01273) 778407 *www.adoniscabaret.co.uk*
Admission: £29.00 (for 2-hour show, 1 free cocktail, Buffet Dinner, VIP pass to a Top Brighton nightclub, and a free photo with the boys) Every Saturday throughout the year, 7pm-10pm, club finishes 2am

With enough screaming to kill a cat, hoards of lary women and Chippendale-style performers, the Adonis Cabaret is packaged very much for the Hen Parties and gangs of girls who descend on Brighton every weekend and is a no-holds-barred male strip-show, designed to get the ladies wet with excitement and ready for a full night out in Brighton.

Hosted by drag queen, Davina, the show's highlights include the boys in the shower, some silliness with a giant piano keyboard, the boys dressed as firemen, and the boys dressed….well, in nothing at all. As well as the cabaret, the night includes a free drink, buffet, raffle, and tickets to another club of your choice for the night (though you can also stay on, if you choose, as, afterwards, it turns into a nightclub spinning tunes from the Eighties and Nineties).

For those who enjoy suave, sophisticated, crooner-style entertainment, it's best to keep away. But for those after a raunchy night out with the girls, as our reviewers Michelle and Sarah put it:
"They promise the Full Monty and that is exactly what you get. The show is on for two hours, and worth every penny. The music is brilliant and we danced till the end. We loved it."

Top Tips – if you're a wine-drinker it pays to buy by the bottle, try to arrive early for the best seats, and don't forget your camera!

LAPDANCING CLUBS

The Pussycat Club

The Basement, 176 Church Road, Hove
(01273) 735574/ 709100
Open 5pm-1.30am Mon-Sat
Admission ranges from £5-£25, depending on time of day, and whether you're a guest or member. £10 for each lap dance
www.pussycat-club.co.uk

If your idea of fun is having a beautiful girl rubbing her voluptuous breasts in front of you, then you may want to pay this place a visit.* The club attracts stag nights, rugby teams and visiting businessmen, there's a friendly feel to the place and everyone seems genuinely eager to please.

Shy voyeurs, be warned – it's quite small down there and not the sort of place you can hide yourself away. Jeremy (from Cheeky) had to go down once to chat to the owner about advertising, but auditions were going on all afternoon, so he ended up as the judge. When one of the women said she'd been quite nervous in front of him, Jeremy unwittingly blurted out – *"It was just as hard for me."'*

*if you don't know the law, you can pay for a personalised topless dance, but no physical contact is allowed

PROSTITUTION

You'll find a variety of cards and phone numbers in the phone boxes around the Old Steine and Western Road areas. £40 for 30 minutes is a typical price to pay, but, if you shop around you might get a student discount. Typically, new laws have been pushed through to stamp out the card system here, which has pushed prostitution back onto the street a bit more. There are also numerous brothels around town but we couldn't possibly tell you where they are, sorry. Here, instead, are a couple of saunas where you can have a nice massage.

Above photos taken from pimple.tv'

SAUNAS

Ambassador's Sauna & Massage

(As featured on Radio 4's 'the News Quiz!')*
Portland Road, Hove 0870 7409439
Open 12noon-10pm Basic cost £20

This highly rated five-star sauna, with a Jacuzzi, offers a full range of services, including more unusual massages and photographic portfolios of all the members of staff in various costumes (such as Tarzan's Jane and Miss Santa). Private parties can be catered for, and in summer there's even an outdoor massage facility.

Like Sainsbury's, they have a reward card system, save enough points and you can have a free two-girl Swedish massage or a digital watch.

Top to Toe

Lower Market Street 0870 740 9442
Open 10am-10pm Basic cost £30

Another five-star establishment boasting a sauna, a Jacuzzi, uniforms and videos. An international range of lovely ladies await to tickle your fancy with a sensuous massage.

*Jeremy Hardy read out the review

Swallows

Massage and Escort service

Mind Body Spirit

From Yoga and Tai Chi classes to Buddhist centres and homoeopaths, Brighton has the lot, and in abundance. Look in the corner of every park and you'll find someone practicing Qi Gong, meditating, doing yoga or, at least (and more typically for Brighton), reading about it. If you're curious about what day courses are on offer, or need somewhere to meditate or practice headstands, your best starting point is to pick up a copy of The Insight or Wave Magazine from the shops in the Lanes.

Since living in Brighton I have developed many new interests, and probably wouldn't have discovered things like Ayurveda without being in the town where anything goes and where so many different lifestyles co-exist together. Sure, there's the usual mystical crap, like places where your cat can have its aura cleansed, but if people believe in it, what's the harm? I love the fact that Brighton people are, on the whole, tolerant and open-minded. After all, why shouldn't you enjoy meditating and chanting as well as, say, clubbing, carpentry and fisting?

The Jeremy Hardy Sketch

From the Radio 4 Series, 'Jeremy Hardy Speaks to the Nation'

-Hello, is this where I register for a course?

-Yes love, have you filled in an application form?

-No, not yet.

-Well what area of study are you interested in?

-I want to know more about myself.

-Well, I'm not sure we have a course in **you** specifically. How about biology?

-No, I just don't believe I can be reduced to bones and atoms.

-Oh, I don't know dear, give me a hammer.

-But don't you think there has to be something more?

-Well let's see.....there's physics, art, literature, archaeology, languages... medicine?

-Alternative?

-No, dear, **effective**....

But there's nothing about **me**. I mean the answers I'm looking for must be inside myself.

Well dear why don't you have a look for them since you've already got your head up there? Tell you what, I'll put you down for gymnastics shall I?

(The quote is by kind permission of Jeremy Hardy and Positive Television)

MIND, BODY, SPIRIT

Culpeper

12D Meeting House Lane
(01273) 327939
Open Mon-Sat 9.15am-5.45pm,
Sun 11am-5pm
www.culpeper.co.uk

Named after the 17th Century
herbalist and philosopher Nicholas
Culpeper, this company has been
around since the 1920s as an
advocate for herbal remedies and
the healing powers of food.
Unfortunately, because it's stuck in
the Old Lanes, everyone thinks it's a
poncy tourist shop selling pot pourri
and strange marmalades. On closer
examination, you will find a universe
of medicinal herbs, essential oils and
organic food. All the products here
are 'as natural as possible'; everything
is guaranteed not to have been
tested on animals, even the
marmalade. And their sandalwood
eau de cologne comes highly
recommended. I have it on good
authority that it has the power to
turn the heads of men *and* women.

The Green Buddha Bookshop

15 Bond Street (01273) 324488
Open Mon-Sat 10am-6pm, Sun 12pm-5pm

This is a spiritually orientated
bookshop marked by its eye-
catching window displays and
attention to quality reads from
across the holistic spectrum. From
ecology to the Occult via religion,
health and shamanism, the friendly
and helpful staff manage to lay on
some mind-boggling gear, and play a
mean cosmic CD or three from
their stash of global
beats/trance/mood music. They also
do a tasty line in greeting cards and,
of course, the obligatory incense.

Greenwich Village

Bond Street (01273) 695451
Open Mon-Fri 10am-5.30pm,
Sat 10am-6pm, Sun 12pm-5pm

Think of Camden Market circa 1992,
and you're not too far off the mark.
These two thin passageways in Bond
Street actually open up into a wealth
of different stalls which, against the
odds, seem to have survived the
backlash against all things tie-dye. If
you're the kind of person who likes
Native American dream catchers,
handicrafts from Thailand, sparkly flip-
flops, wind chimes, Batik cards or
clothes for that classic 'Stevie Nicks'
look, welcome home.

Infinity Foods

(See review in Food Chapter)

Neal's Yard

2A Kensington Gardens (01273) 601464
Open Mon-Sat 9.30am-5.30pm,
Sun 11am-4pm
www.nealsyardremedies.com

A franchise of one of London's
original herbal emporiums, this place
has become Brighton's *de facto*
alternative doctor's surgery. With a
veritable armoury of (mainly organic)
herbs, oils, tinctures, vitamins and
homeopathic remedies, Neal's Yard
also has, at its disposal, some very
clued-up staff (all naturopaths,
homeopaths and herbalists) who can
help you make informed choices
about what you might need. Self-help
books are also on hand, as are all the
obligatory pampering products should
you be suffering from nothing more
than a prolonged bout of self-
indulgent whinnying. The most usual
complaints they deal with are still
colds and hay fever, but recently some
guy came in for herbal hormone
replacements for his dog.
Typical Brighton.

Practical Books

14 Western Road, Hove
(01273) 734602
Open Mon-Sat 9.30am-6pm
www.practicalbooks.co.uk

Granted, this cute little corner shop does an impressive sweep of language/education study books, but its heart lies in the mind-body-spirit arena. As if to prove the point, it has now started hanging an elf's grotto's worth of crystals in one of its windows, meaning sunglasses are now required, day and night, to walk from Norfolk to Brunswick Square. The friendliest bookshop in town, Practical Books is positively chock-a-block with highly obscure literary offerings of the mystical/self-help variety.

Spiritual Matters

21A Prince Albert Street (01273) 206593
Open 11am-5pm Mon-Sat, 2pm-5pm Sun
www.spiritualmatters.co.uk

In the heart of the old Lanes this mini-temple, run by celibate Krishna monk, Dharani, sells books and gifts on a Hindu theme. There's a good range of Vedic literature, statuettes of old favourites Ganesh and Buddha, music, clothing, Hare Krishna related material and, according to Dharani, the best incense in town.

Winfalcon Healing Centre

28 Ship Street (01273) 728997
Open Mon-Sat 10(ish)-5.30pm,
Sun 12noon-4pm

Brighton's no-holds-barred New Age shop, Winfalcon stocks every crystal, stone and karmaceutical known throughout the cosmos and, upstairs, runs workshops in things like 'Psychic Development' and 'Know your Inner Butterfly'. Here is the place to score stuff even the most green-eared hippies might think twice about – unicorn posters, books called 'Full Esteem Ahead' and stickers saying, 'It's A Druid Thing'. But, for a shop of this nature it seems all the more bizarre (and unintentionally funny) that the bloke who runs it is one of the most miserable and unfriendly shopkeepers I've ever had the misfortune to come across. Now here's a guy in need of a taste of his own medicine...

MIND, BODY, SPIRIT

Bodhi Garden Dharma Centre

7A Ship Street Gardens (01903) 218963

Tucked away in a skylit and quiet ex-art gallery in Brighton's oldest lane is this sacred space, dedicated to Buddhist meditation and study. Described as a 'non-sectarian Dharma centre' and operating as an umbrella space for numerous Buddhist groups (Theravadan, Tibetan, Zen, Gaia House etc), the Bodhi Garden organises drop-in evening meditations, talks, quality courses and weekend day retreats for Brighton's burgeoning Dharma bum scene. There is also an extensive library. As a charitable concern, it walks the Buddha's walk by not charging for teachings – almost everything is by donation. Monthly programme details are available at the centre.

Bubble

Above The Mad Hatter Café,
Montpelier Road (01273) 722279

Erring on the hippydippy side of New Age, this place probably **would** be home from home for their Ab Fab namesake. Located above the Mad Hatters café, Bubble manage to squeeze 'transformational healing' classes, 'celestial touch' workshops, 'know your archangels' sessions and a spot of Kundalini yoga* into something the size of your living room. It's a lovely space, though, and has the added advantage that, after a class, you can pop downstairs to the café, stuff your face with cake, buns, tea and smoke lots of fags.

*A friend who has been studying yoga for the past ten years visited this class and couldn't believe how flaky the teacher was. Not recommended for beginners or those who take yoga seriously. Highly recommended for the comedy factor.

The Buddhist Centre

14 Tichborne St (01273) 772090
Open 12-3pm weekdays for visitors

This group is part of 'The Friends of the Western Buddhist Order' and their centre is situated just off the beaten track in North Laine. It has two stunning meditation and yoga rooms and a library where you can drop in to study, or borrow books and tapes for a nominal fee. The Order members wear strange little white collars around their necks, are very friendly and make a decent cup of tea. Look out for more unusual stuff going on here too, like theatre and lectures. I went to a great talk during the May Festival one year where a Buddhist theatre director talked about the genius of Tommy Cooper and Frankie Howerd. Sunday school was never like this.

one roof – one a charity-based children's clinic (the first of its kind in Europe), the other an adult's natural health clinic offering osteopathy, homeopathy, acupuncture, reflexology, medical herbalism and totally legal full-body massage. Being next to the Theatre Royal means there is the added interest of possibly bumping into a celebrity actor who either twisted an ankle treading the boards the night before or who simply can't find the other sort of massage parlour.

Natural Bodies
28/29 Bond Street (just by Toucan)
(01273) 711414

Set up by Gary Carter (known to make the ladies swoon), this is definitely one of Brighton's more capable yoga centres, which runs around 20 sessions a week, from beginner's level to the very advanced. Classes are mostly drop-in, cost around £5 and run throughout the day, with workshops at weekends. Follow the screams and you'll find them on the first floor. All the teachers are friendly, clean and sober and come from the Vanda Scaravelli (an expert Italian yogini) school, which emphasises gentle movement and breath work to undo tension and reinvigorate the body. Tying yourself in muscle-bending knots and shouting *"Look at me!"* is definitely not what is encouraged in here. I can thoroughly recommend theses classes as I've been coming (sporadically) for about five years now, and my mum doesn't tell me off for slouching any more. Be warned; they **never** answer the phone, so get a programme and find out when to come.

The Clinic Upstairs
Above Hocus Pocus 38 Gardner Street
(01273) 572204/572101
www.hocuspocus.co.uk
£25/£30 for 60/90 minutes

Follow the shop's spiralling incense upstairs to discover this little known world of shift-working tarot readers and two cosy therapy rooms regularly used for massage, reiki, spiritual healing, psychotherapy and N.L.P. But the real gem here is the Floatation Tank (the only one in Brighton), offering that unique opportunity to switch off your mind, relax and float, gravity-free. Ideal, in fact, for accelerated learning (play a language tape and you'll be fluent in no time), hypnosis (available upon request), creative thinking, meditation, relaxation and planning the perfect bank job. Please don't start playing with yourself though; you'll get the water all messy.

Dolphin House Clinic
14 New Road
(01273) 324790

This started as an acupuncture clinic 20 years ago and has since blossomed into two multi-skilled clinics housed under

Planet Janet

86 Church Road, Hove (01273) 738389
www.planet-janet.com

This co-operatively run project in Hove comprises a healthy options-type café and Osho-orientated shop on the ground floor, plus five consulting rooms and a group room divided between upstairs and the basement. Depending on who is renting which you will generally find an entertaining cocktail of Chinese kick-boxing, 'oneness' meditations, 'chakra dancing' classes, tai chi and astrological counselling. Each room is named after a planet, apart from the colonic hydrotherapy room, which is appropriately called 'The Moon Room'. Some drop-in yoga/meditation classes also occur. See website for details.

Evolution Arts and Health Centre

2 Sillwood Terrace (off Western Road)
(01273) 729803

One of Brighton's longest running centres for all things arty and alternative, Evolution offers everything under one roof – aikido, didgeridoo playing, pottery, African drumming, stained glass making, flamenco guitar courses, nutrition workshops, bear-baiting etc. Look for their brochures around town, but be warned the courses here can be a tad expensive.

Unit 4

20-26 Roundhill Street
For info contact *peteblackaby@aol.com*
www.aiyp.co.uk

Perched serenely on the summit of Roundhill, above The Level, is this centre of yogic excellence. Started up by Brighton's legendary yoga guru and Kinks fanatic Pete Blackaby, it is almost entirely devoted to yoga of the Scaravelli style, with classes for all

levels guided by Pete, his protégés and other excellent yoga teachers. More specialist stuff, such as yoga for pregnancy, teacher-training courses, Feldenkrais treatment and one-to-one classes is also available. The centre houses two treatment rooms as well, one for bodywork, the other for acupuncture. There is no phone so drop by to find out more info or use the web / email details listed above.

A Cautionary Message For Yoga Novices

While Brighton has some truly excellent yoga teachers in its midst (including the iconic Peter Blackaby), there are a small minority of practitioners in this town who, quite frankly, are clueless, and still seem to be operating on that ludicrous Eighties principle of 'no pain, no gain'. Should you find yourself at a beginners' yoga class where the teacher launches straight into difficult and demanding poses (and without even bothering to check if anyone in the group suffers from high blood pressure, back problems or is pregnant) you are well within your rights to advocate that he/she be tarred, feathered and torn apart by wild dogs for their negligence. And don't be afraid to ask how your teacher was trained. Most training of any repute lasts a minimum of two years, while you'd expect a teacher to have done at least six years of Yoga practice themselves before even considering taking a class.

Finally, if you're interested in giving yoga a try, but feel confused by all the different styles out there (Hatha, Astanga, Iyengar, Jenga, Menga, Mango etc), the drop-in classes at Natural Bodies make a perfect starting point.

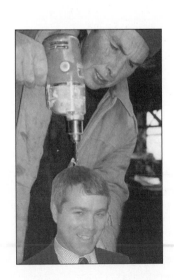

THERAPISTS

There are literally hundreds of therapists working in Brighton and to list them all would be bonkers. For a full list of what's available, seek out the Alternative Practitioners Handbook from Neal's Yard, or simply drink a bottle of scotch and watch your problems miraculously disappear.

These fellows below get a special mention because through friends, or from personal experience, they come highly recommended.

Acupuncture with Keith Simpson Lic.Ac. MBAcC

(01273) 622294
£30 Initial Consultation £24 Subsequent treatments Some concessions available

It is comforting to know there are practitioners out there who don't conform to the stereotype of being either a flaky New Age hippy or a sombre, bearded, pipe-smoker with a German accent. True, Keith does have a beard but is a surprisingly charming, personable and down-to earth sort who treats his subject with care and passion. Combining Five Element and TCM styles of acupuncture, Keith can help in the treatment of a wide variety of named complaints such as back pain, piles, IBS, insomnia and depression. For anyone new to acupuncture, this is also an excellent way for *keeping* in good health and helping you feel better in a more general way (i.e. increased energy and vitality, better sleep, a more normal appetite and an increased sense of well being). Keith will make you feel completely at ease, give excellent advice on lifestyle/ health issues and even wash your car for an extra fiver.

Ged Peck – Bioenergetic Analyst

(01273) 324057
Fees are £37.50 per hour, but negotiable

Brighton is full of all kinds of alternative medical practitioners and counsellors, working on body and mind. Bioenergetic Analysis (which has its roots in the work of psychoanalyst Wilhelm Reich) aims to do both of these and, consequently, can have profound effects, even where other therapies have failed

Ged Peck is one of the few accredited Bioenergetic Therapists in Britain. He has been practicing in Brighton for nearly 20 years and also does regular group work in Germany. Ged's therapy sessions can last from a few weeks to a number of years, and have been effective with a wide range of problems.

ASTROLOGICAL CHARTS

Tim Burness

(01273) 271469
www.timburness.com

All-round good egg, Tim Burness is an experienced and professional astrologer with 15 years extensive experience. During this time he has worked with thousands of people from all walks of life (including Chesney Hawkes!) and appeared in local and national media. He charges £75 for a 1-hour basic taped and written birth chart interpretation, including 4 hours preparation time. This can be either as a consultation in Brighton or by post.

All readings are taped, with a personal interpretation. For a sitting you will just be required to know the exact time and place of your birth. (Ask your mum if you can't remember).

KIDS' BRIGHTON

Brighton has always been a great place for kids. With scary rides on the pier, special theatre and cinema events, paddling pools and the seafront, there's always plenty of mischief for them to get up to. (OK, we don't have a beach suitable for buckets and spades, but at least dads can be spared the time-honoured fate of being buried up to their necks in sand.) And when it is chucking it down in the middle of August, there are innumerable family-friendly cafés, bars and restaurants where ankle-biters are free to run around, scream and be sick. Fact is, nearly everything in Brighton – apart from the nightlife – is child-friendly. Saying that, there's always the Event2…

ABC Magazine

If you are a parent, or have someone else's kids to cater for, then you really, really need a copy of ABC Magazine, affectionately known to Brighton parents as their 'bible'.

It's a chunky glossy mag, full to the brim with every snippet of useful local information you might possibly require when manhandling a sprog or two. The purpose of ABC is to make life easier for parents, carers and their kids - so they can all have a bit more fun!

ABC is free, which is nice, and can be picked up all over the city, in libraries and tourist info centres, as well as the many child-friendly shops and services in Brighton. You can also contact ABC on 01273 542257, visit the website at www.abcmag.co.uk, or email info@abcmag.co.uk.

This Chapter of the Cheeky Guide to Brighton was compiled by ABC, and is their selection of some of the places you can safely frequent, happy in the knowledge that the kids are well catered for.

Information provided by Melanie Hickford, ABC Magazine

WEIRD AND WONDERFUL THINGS TO DO

Beacon Arts

Knoyle Road, Brighton (01273) 557124

Offers classes in everything from music to messy arts and crafts play.

Lifecycle

The Tile House, Preston Park
(01273) 542425

Hire bikes (of every imaginable kind) to cycle around Preston Park.

Paint Pots & Painting Café

39 Trafalgar Street, Brighton (01273) 696682
31, North Road, Brighton (01273) 628952

Let the kids go crazy painting psychedelic patterns on pottery while you nip outside for a fag.

Middle Farm

A27 between Lewes and Eastbourne
(01323) 811411

Great tearooms, food shop, animals to fondle and the English Cider Centre, where, after sampling a few brews, mums and dads are overcome with the urge to sing old Wurzels songs.

Junior Dukes

Kids' cinema session at the Duke of York's cinema (01273) 602503 (children over 8 can stay without parents' supervision)

With its own hard-core cult following of diminutive movie-buffs, Junior Dukes is, if nothing else, the cheapest baby-sitting facility in town. As well as showing new and old children's movies every Saturday, its organisers host a raffle for the kids, hand out sweets and, if it's someone's birthday, they'll let him/her press the button to 'start' the film. (OK, it's a con, but it makes them happy.)

And at the end of the movie there's even time for the children to draw pictures inspired by the film. According to Tara, who works there, 'some are quite disturbing' and, recently, one kid drew a microwave that turned 'packets' into 'proper food like McDonalds'. Have a look behind the bar next time you're there – that's where they stick the best ones. Highly recommended.

Sunrise Cycle Hire

Beside the West Pier (01273) 748881

Family bikes available for hire, for pedalling along the seafront.

Typical Brighton mum

Museums Trips

(01273) 296977

Brighton & Hove Council run lots of activities at the museums and libraries throughout the year, especially in school holidays. For full details call the number above and check museum reviews in 'Weird and Wonderful Things to Do', which I've just realised is confusing as this section is also called 'Weird and Wonderful Things to Do'. I was trying to be clever by doing a mini-version of the book within this chapter but it's all backfired. Bugger.

Kids' Komedia

Gardner Street (01273) 647100 £4.50/£4

Running every Sunday during term times, Komedia presents the best in children's national and international touring theatre for 3-7 year olds. A big favourite, of course, are Brighton celebrities Bodger & Badger who, to the great delight of small people (and not their mums and dads) splash their mash into the audience with a wild frenzy. The venue opens one hour before the show for drawing, cappuccinos and sticky treats.

Stonywish Farm

Spatham Lane (off B2116) Ditchling
(01273) 843498

Animals, children's play area, tearooms, and walks in the countryside. Look out for local resident, Jamie Theakston, walking around his back yard in his pants.

Story time

Free story-telling sessions for kids at Borders Bookshop (Saturdays 11am) and Hove Library (Wednesdays 10am). Hosted by Irvine Welsh, Will Self and Kathy Lette.

Toddler Gym Sessions

Portslade Sports Centre, Chalky Road,
Portslade (01273) 411100

Under-fives supervised play-area with trampolines, bouncy castles and gym equipment. And, no, you can't have a go; it's strictly for the kids.

Volks Electric Railway

Brighton Pier to Marina, every 15 mins

Ride along the seafront in Victorian style, at top speeds of up to 5mph!!

www.brightonboarders.co.uk

Why not hire a mobile dry ski slope for the kids to try out their snowboarding, tubing, and skiing stunts! (Hospital bill not included in price.)

SHOPS

Baby Bazaar (0-8yrs)

58, Church Road, Hove
(01273) 719739

Traditional European toys, ranging from classic wooden items to the downright quirky (and that includes the staff).

Baby Stuff

116, Portland Road, Hove
(01273) 703134

Changing bags, biodegradable nappies, organic toiletries, wooden toys, mobiles (not the phone variety) and swimwear for ages up to five. Very popular are their Kaloo Bears, which, unlike the usual soft toys, won't turn into porridge after a machine wash and tumble dry.

Cupcake (0-14yrs)

98 St George's Rd, Kemptown
(01273) 624134

Set up by Kate and randy Frenchmen, Lionel (pronounced Yurnell), this beautiful, family-run shop, in the heart of Kemptown village, offers an unusual and unique collection of gifts for children (age range 'two pounds to fourteen years'). Poles apart from the tacky and predictable world of Argus, Mothercare et al and their plastic and battery-powered toys, Cupcakes instead, offers such original and beautiful items as nostalgic wooden toys, retro fabrics, old Victorian playthings, French and Dutch clothes, mushroom lamps and pirate lunch boxes. If Lionel is around, make sure to say 'Trois bananes'. It's a private joke, but anyone can join in.

Great Expectations (0-3yrs)

42 Lewes Road, Brighton
(01273) 622993

Cotton nappies, organic clothes, Fairtrade, washable nappies and other environmentally friendly products. 'Very Brighton!' (as the owner put it).

Daisy Daisy (0-6yrs)

33 North Road, Brighton
(01273) 689108
www.daisydaisy.me.uk

Specialising in top-quality wooden toys, ranging from mobiles to their best-selling dolls houses and castles. Also stocking nursery goods, slippers, some clothes and cards. Kids love this place as its owner Hilary is more than happy for them to come and play with everything on display (though she might draw the line if they start chewing on a train set).

Wigwam/ Wigwam Baby

267a/ 93 Preston Drove, Brighton
(01273) 505504

While their 'Baby' shop specialises in groovy nursery goods and developmental toys, their (elder) sister sells clothes, wooden toys, and a fruity selection of slogan T-shirts including 'Enjoy Milk', 'Future DJ', and 'Made in Brighton'.

WHERE NOT TO TAKE THE KIDS

The Bulldog
The Pussy Cat Club
Spanki
Downstairs at Tickled
Kemptown Bushes
Torture Garden
Hastings
Hove

CHILD-FRIENDLY RESTAURANTS

While the following places don't offer crappy plastic toys, disease-riddled burgers and aren't staffed by spotty teenagers who spend the day picking scabs off their faces and dropping them in the coffee machine, they do offer quality food, are welcoming to families, and don't mind the odd bit of projectile vomiting (even if it is due to dad having overdone it the night before). Sorry – didn't mean to put you off your dinner.

```
* = Child-friendly
+ = Take away service
v = Vegetarian only
```

Bardsley's (Fish & Chips)*+
22-23a Baker Street (01273) 681256

Cactus Canteen (Mexican)*
5 Brighton Square (01273) 725700

Donatello's (Italian)*+
3 Brighton Place (01273) 775477

Dorset Street Bar*
28 North Road (01273) 605423

Dig in the Ribs (Tex/Mex)*
47 Preston Street (01273) 325275

Waikikamookau v
11a Kensington Gardens (01273) 671117

Food for Friends v *+
18 Prince Albert Street (01273) 202310

The Tin Drum (Café/bar)*
95 Dyke Road (01273) 777575

Lee Cottage (Chinese)*+
6b Queen's Road (01273) 327643

Piccolo's (Italian)*+
56 Ship Street (01273) 203701

Pizza Express*+
107 Church Road, Hove (01273) 770093

Quod Restaurant, Bar and Gallery*
160 North Street (01273) 202070

Seven Dials Restaurant*
1 Buckingham Place (01273) 885555

Tootsies*
15 Meeting House Lane
(01273) 726777

Terre À Terre v *
71 East Street (01273) 72905

Battle of Trafalgar
Guildford Road
(01273) 327997

Lunchtime menu. Kids welcome in beer garden and family room.

Casa
North Street (01273) 738763

Family-friendly bar/restaurant

The Constant Service
Islingword Road (01273) 607058

No menu. Kids welcome in beer garden.

Fiddlers Elbow
Boyces Street (01273) 325850

Lunchtime menu. Kids welcome in family room.

The George
Trafalgar street (01273) 681055

All day vegetarian-only menu. Kids welcome until 8.30pm.

Hanrahan's
Brighton Marina (01273) 819800

Children's licence, restaurant and beer garden. Family friendly no-smoking area.

Horatio's Bar and Victoria Bar
Palace Pier

All day menu. Kids welcome until 8pm.

Lion and Lobster
Sillwood Street (01273) 776961

All-day menu. Kids welcome in family room.

Open House
Springfield Road (01273) 880102

Kids welcome in garden and lounge until 6pm.

Park Crescent Inn
Park Crescent Terrace (01273) 604993

All-day Mexican-themed menu. Children welcome in pub and beer garden.

The Pub With No Name
Clarence Gardens (01273) 328263

All-day bar food. Children welcome in pub and, and beer garden until 9pm.

The Greenhouse Effect
Church Road (01273) 204783

No menu. Kids welcome in family room.

Hove Place
First Avenue (01273) 738266

Lunchtime menu. Kids welcome in the beer-garden in summer.

St Aubyns
Victoria Terrace (01273) 733983

All-day bar food. Kids welcome in beer garden and family room.

OUTDOOR PLAY AREAS

The Level
Bottom of Southover Street

This 'inner city' park has two big skateboarding pipes, play equipment and a paddling pool. In summer it's a haven for slouching teenagers in Offspring T-shirts doing themselves a mischief with poorly executed skateboarding stunts.

Hove Park
Old Shoreham Road

One of the two parks worth a visit in Hove. It's a large, open area loved by squirrels and77 offering bowls, a cycle track, a playground, a miniature railway and café.

Blakers Park
Southdown Road

A quiet park with good play equipment, sandpit, tennis courts, and a café that seems to open at odd times.

Pirates' Playground
Brighton seafront, near the West Pier

Brilliant play area, right on the seafront, with lots of fun equipment. Always rammed in summer with thousands of parents sitting around, sharing gossip. Refreshments and loos are nearby.

For all other Brighton Parks see 'Here, There and Everywhere'

KIDS' BRIGHTON

INDOOR PLAY AREAS

Candy Castle Enterprise Point
Melbourne St. (01273) 276060

Megazone King Alfred Leisure Centre
Kingsway (01273) 779789

Deep Sea Den Saltdean Tavern
(next to Saltdean Lido)
(01273) 304614

Tumble Tots Gym
(needs pre-booking)
Brighton and Hove (01273) 723511

Westows School Road
Hove (01273) 711944

Charlie Chalk's
Tongdean Lane (01273) 330055

SWIMMING AND LEISURE CENTRES

Awash with activities for kids and/or with useful crèche facilities.

King Alfred
Kingsway, Hove (01273) 290290
Moulsecoomb (01273) 622266

Prince Regent
North Road, Brighton (01273) 685692

Saltdean Lido
Saltdean Park Road (outdoor, summer only)
(01273) 880616

Stanley Deason
(01273) 694281

Sussex Uni Sports Centre
(01273) 678228

Withdean
(01273) 542100

WEBSITES

abcmag.co.uk
The ABC Magazine portal, dedicated to giving you absolutely everything you need to know as a parent in Brighton and Hove. Links to loads of useful local sites.

brighton-hove.gov.uk
The city council website - very informative In particular look at the 'life' section, or search under 'parenting'

thisisbrighton.co.uk
A comprehensive site. Again, best to search under 'kids' or 'parents'

BRIGHTON & HOVE COUNCIL SERVICES

Playschemes
(01273) 292733
Childcare / Crèches.

Children's Information Service
(01273) 293545
For information on all types of local registered childcare provision, nurseries, holiday and after-school clubs, call this number above. Every summer they also organise outdoor events for families all over the city.

DROP-IN & HOLIDAY CHILDCARE

The Pheonix Brewery Drop-in Crèche
2 Pheonix Place (07788) 848 455

Class of Their Own (Holiday Club)
(01273) 424324

Action Station (Holiday Club)
(01273) 501919

What's On

Isn't it only right that the town that likes to party should be host to the biggest arts festival in England? Not only that, but every month there are always special events going on here, from car rallies and bike rides, to Gay Pride, the Burning of the Clocks, the Children's Parade, and a fireworks' display every two weeks or so. And with the numerous party conferences that take place here, where else could you combine a lovely seafront environment with the pleasures of egg-throwing?

The Fair at the Level

End of April, into May

Two weeks of flashing lights and projectile vomiting, signifying that the Festival has begun and summer is just around the corner.

Arts Festival

May

www.brighton-festival.org.uk
www.brightonfringefestival.co.uk

In May Brighton goes bananas. For three weeks the whole town is packed with comedians, circuses, street performers, musicians and thousands of blokes on stilts. It's the largest arts and entertainment festival in England and, if you want to see this town at its most vibrant and colourful, this is the time to visit.

Alongside the main festival runs the Brighton Fringe Festival, offering more homespun and contemporary performances from DJs, bands, comedians and theatre groups in numerous smaller venues, theatres, pubs and cafes in town. Also – and rather confusingly – there is the Brighton *Festival Fringe*, formerly the Umbrella Festival (not to be confused with the Brighton Festival of Umbrellas) which features comedy, theatre and

'Open Houses'. The latter, when Brighton artists open their homes to the public in an attempt to flog their work, has become a festival staple. (It is, of course, as much an excuse to have a nose around people's houses, as an exhibition of art.)

During the festival you can expect everything from guided tours of the gay scene to special club nights, experimental theatre, street parties and parades. Look out also for the Dieppe Market, the Mackerel Fair and the Blessing of the Nets, which usually takes place on the third weekend of the festival.

Three festivals all rolled into one, with the inevitable free fireworks party. And, if you do nothing else during this time, go see the hugely talented and very funny local comedienne, Joanna Neary.

FRINGE POLITICS

For the past eight years, the Arts Festival in May has been organised by two separate groups – The Brighton Fringe Festival and Brighton Festival. The Brighton Festival – council funded and host to the more highbrow arts events such as dance, opera, book readings and big comedy names – was contrasted perfectly by the independent organisation the Brighton Fringe Festival, who made an effort to support the more contemporary aspect of the Brighton art scene, by organising DJ events, experimental film nights, underground bands and plenty of home-spun local talent in small venues around town (and, on the whole, at prices much more affordable than most of the events in the mainstream festival).

All that changed in 2003, when the Brighton Festival organisers appeared to do the dirty and publicise its events in two magazines – one called the Brighton Festival and the other called….The Brighton *Festival* Fringe, causing untold confusion to visitors, and anger amongst Brightonians (not to mention, of course, those who run the real Fringe).

Whether this will be sorted out by 2004 remains to be seen. To show your support for the original Brighton Fringe Festival visit:

www.Brightonfringe.info
www.brightonfringefestival.co.uk

London to Brighton Bike Race

Middle of June

Occulture Festival

One Saturday in July

Annual one-day festival of all things esoteric. (See Occult Chapter for more details.)

Gay Pride

Middle of the second week in August at Preston Park

(See Gay Chapter)

Comedy Festival

Beginning of October

Set up in 2002, this is principally a chance to see lots of the big names in comedy at the Brighton Dome for a few weeks.

Lewes Fireworks

5th November

Still upset about a bunch of Protestant martyrs who were burned here centuries ago by the wicked Catholics, the people of Lewes remember the occasion by hosting the biggest and most phenomenal bonfire night celebration in the UK.

Along with the procession of carnival style floats, you'll get the chance to see the townsfolk dressed up in Freddie Kruger jumpers and marching down the streets holding big torches and throwing bangers around. Around 8pm, the crowds head off to bonfires in different corners of the town, where some loonies, dressed as cardinals, stand on scaffolding and encourage the audience to hurl abuse (and fireworks) at them. A few effigies of the Pope and political figures are then ceremoniously blown up for good measure, followed by huge firework displays.

The whole thing has a very dark, anarchic feel to it and there are definite hints of the Wicker Man in there too. It's only a short train ride from Brighton but I recommend getting there no later than 6pm if you want a good view of it all. Best not to bring any pets. Highly recommended.

Veteran car Rally

First Sunday in November

Not being one who gets particularly excited by vehicles in general I never take much notice of this. They all seem to congregate down at Madeira Drive, share notes on the pros and cons of tungsten drive-cam-shafts and then disappear back to their stately mansions. It's some kind of existence I suppose.

But as my one friend said, *"surely the sight of a lot of lovely old cars putt-putting away stirs the little boy in you?"*

Burning of the Clocks

Winter Solstice (22nd December)

While most seaside towns go into hibernation for the winter, Brighton celebrates the shortest day with this pagan procession along the seafront, culminating in a fireworks display. Expect hundreds of strange and beautiful designs around the theme of time, and lots and lots of candles. It all has that perfect, dark wintery spirit to it, mixed with the excitement of knowing that Christmas is just around the corner. One of my favourite events in the Brighton calendar.

Poseidon's Day

December 28th

Once a year, 23 Brighton councillors gather on the nudist beach to offer blessings and sacrifices to this venerable sea-god. Hosted by Simon Fanshawe the dancing, nudity and orgies normally go on until the small hours, weather permitting.

LOCAL PRESS

In this town people will sell their own grandmothers just to get good wall space in a café for their poster. The problem in Brighton is not so much finding information, as how to avoid spending the weekend sifting through thousands of fliers, posters and magazines trying to find a club that plays Def Leppard. In our continuing efforts to cull all forms of freethinking, listed below are some of the best papers and magazines for finding out what's on. The following publications can be found in most newsagents, cafés and bars around town.

The Brighton Source
Free monthly magazine

Colourful, glossy local magazine, with a saucy, hedonistic slant. Covering everything you'd want on the local club scene from what's hot and what's not, to reviews of pubs and restaurants, and articles on such topics as pirate radio and body modification.

The Insight
Free monthly magazine *www.theinsight.co.uk*

Set up initially as an antithesis to the stylised club/pub magazines, The Insight leaned heavily towards features on alternative lifestyles and the New Age scene. Over the years, however, it has branched out and now covers all local events, including comedy, theatre, music and the gay scene, and features well-written articles, probing features on local issues and even organises its own 'Eligible Balls'. The best bit is still the 'Eccentrics Column' though. Whoever pens it should be given some kind of award – a knighthood say, or Legion of Honour.

The Latest Homes
Combining the winning formula of adverts for houses you can't afford with celebrity gossip.

This is Brighton
Free fortnightly magazine

Arguably the most up-to date local magazine for news as it comes out every two weeks. Since its arrival, 'This is Brighton' has filled the gap left by the dissolution of previous, but similar, local magazines such as the Punter, Latest and Impact. With comprehensive coverage of music, theatre, art, film, dating and pretty much any kind of local event you could think of, combined with a clear, attractive layout.

What's On
Free monthly pocket-guide
www.whatsonguide.co.uk

Comprehensive listings on live music, bars, clubs, cinema and more.

WEBSITES

www.brighton.co.uk

They own just about every domain name that even comes close to the word Brighton, so you are going to find them even if you don't want to. There are listings for everything, from clubs and pubs, to hotels, cinemas and local weather, but there are better sites if you want more specific information and something less corporate and busy looking.

www.brightonfriends.co.uk

A Friends-reunited for Brighton. Free to register and simple to use. Not sure how many people use it though.

www.brightonlife.com

Last time I checked it, it hadn't been updated for 8 months. I suspect they've done a runner, died, or accepted a place on a PGCE.

www.brightononline.co.uk

A directory for shops and businesses.

www.thisisbrighton.co.uk

Associated with the Argus newspaper, this website includes local news with classifieds, sports, leisure and up-to-date information on local events.

www.seelife.brighton.co.uk

Fast-loading colourful site with lots of Brighton news and up-to-the minute information on clubs, gigs, theatre, and community events. Definitely worth exploring.

www.whatsonguide.co.uk

This site is excellent, easy to use, fairly fast loading, and offers up-to-date and extremely comprehensive listings for clubs, live music, food, cinema and theatre.

www.mybrightonandhove.org.uk

This community website contains quirky and little known aspects of local history, together with people's memories and photographs. Regularly updated by volunteers, the site publishes local knowledge and answers enquiries about Brighton and Hove, both past and present. The group is affiliated to QueenSpark Books and supports its aims of enabling local people to have a voice.

www.hedweb.com/brighton

50 bizarre Brighton deaths catalogued by local munchkin Dick Witts, ranging from poisoned chocolates to the trunk murders and the tale behind the death in the Green Dragon (now the Office). While the presentation is a bit dull, the tales themselves merit a read for anyone with a love of Brighton and a sense of the macabre.

pimple.tv

Though nothing to do with Brighton, this hilarious website was put together by local maverick filmmaker Tom Hickmore and comedy writer Paul Sinclair, and features over 50 short films (no longer than 10 seconds each), ranging from Fifties sex education spoofs, to Brighton's own Stella Starr doing a spot of nipple-tassel swinging. Look for the sperm-drinking lady. Marvellous. And at time of writing it was getting over 5,000 hits each day!

See images in Sex & Fetish chapter

CHEEKY NEWSPAPER OF THE YEAR

NIGHT FINAL

Evening Anus

www.cheekyguides.com

Our infamous daily rag features everything from local news to the usual Nazi rants in the letters page. And while being indispensable for keeping up with local issues, every now and again the Argus likes to surprise its readers in a Richard Madeley does Ali G sort-of-way, with bizarre and funny stories.

Personal highlights in recent years have included:

OVER AND SPROUT

A Beano-style tale about a policeman who slipped on a sprout while chasing a flasher outside the fruit and veg market. 'The detective, who enjoys flying, came crashing to the ground like a sack of spuds.....he said he was in a lot of pain but the accident has not put him off sprouts.'

LIMPETS MUCHING AWAY AT COASTLINE

I can only deduce that this was a four-in-the-morning job after the full effects of the hash cakes had kicked in.

I FOUND CHRIS EUBANK IN MOULD STAIN

Many years back the Argus did this now-legendary feature about a model who discovered Eubank's apparition on a mould stain on her living room wall. Freddie Star, eat your heart out!

I FOUND JESUS IN MY PANCAKE

Following on the success of mouldy Chris came this similar theme.

'The 29-year old couldn't believe his eyes when the outline of a beard, nose, eyes and hair appeared among the burn marks in the batter... *"I suppose if it is a sign, there's no reason why it shouldn't be on a pancake"* he exclaimed.' (But how did he know it was Jesus and not any old beardy bloke?)

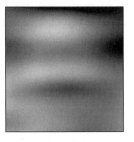

I FOUND A SCORPION IN MY SUITCASE...

CREATURE COMFORT: Gemma Cox with the case in which the scorpion stayed for two days in her bedroom

I found a scorpion in my suitcase

HOLIDAYMAKER Gemma
...ught an unusual
...n her
...dowaway
...its tail.
...ator,

She had dumped her suitcase on her floor after a two-week break on the Greek island with friends. She then went to sit down near the unpacked case to watch the England v Brazil World Cup match.

...ma, 19, from Ironstone said: "I caught a
... of the corner
...ing ran
...t 30cm

ARCHNID: The scorpion scuttled away and hid

...And even –

JULIE BURCHILL FOUND IN TRIFLE

Though this later proved to be a typing error and should have read – 'Julie Burchill fond of trifle.'

Places

to Sleep

Brighton has hundreds of places to sleep, from hotels, B&Bs, guesthouses, hostel and hotels to that old Mod favourite – under the pier in a sleeping bag. And with the recent appearance of such places as Hotel Du Vin, the Pelirocco and Blanch House, some visitors can even expect to find their room decorated by Lenny Beige, themed as some Moroccan harem, containing DVD players, Play Stations and even the odd vibrator. With the growth of all these new stylish places, however, the price of a good room in town has increased considerably. So, in our efforts to bring you an intriguing slice of what's out there, we've tried to cover a range from the priciest to the cheapest, the friendliest to the rudest, and the simplest to the most outrageous.

The Grand

Kings Road, Brighton seafront
(01273) 321188

The most famous hotel in Brighton and, at £1450 per night for the Presidential suite, by far and away the most expensive. This *may* seem a bit steep, but it's worth bearing in mind that Ronald Reagan and JF Kennedy have flossed their teeth in this very room. The over-the-top grandeur of this white palace is matched by its facilities, which include pool, health spa, hair salon and a full-sized, indoor, dry-ski slope track, which was said to be a favourite of Ronnie's.

Dress code - Armani, Hugo Boss etc. No jeans unless you're royalty.

Singles £165, doubles £240. Add £50 if you want a sea view (or save your cash and walk the 9.4 feet to the door and look from there).

270

Metropole (Hilton)

Kings Road, Brighton seafront
(01273) 775432

Another grand affair situated right on the seafront between the two piers and, again, catering for the more affluent ladies and gentlemen. There is a small, heated swimming pool (if you don't want to get greased up for swimming in the channel) three restaurants and a tacky nightclub.
Rooms with dinner/bed/breakfast from £90

Royal Albion Hotel

35 Old Steine (opposite the Palace Pier)
(01273) 329202

While priced in the same bracket as the other major chains on the seafront, the Royal Albion isn't **quite** as grand. Service is excellent, staff are friendly, but the rooms really are in need of renovation. That said, it offers great views of the Pier, and if you open your window, you can even catch the smell of fish and chips/ doughnuts/ the odd fire.
Singles from £90, Doubles from £145, Suites from £205

QUITE POSH WITH A HINT OF BOHEMIAN

Amsterdam Hotel

11-12 Marine Parade (01273) 688824
www.amsterdam.uk.com

Though catering primarily for a gay clientele, everyone is welcome here. The rooms have all been recently renovated and now include nice colour schemes and hardwood floors, and the patio out front is an excellent place to sit, relax and people-watch.
Midweek all rooms £55-£65, weekends range from £70-120 including breakfast Rooms 10 and 11 have good sea views, rooms 24 and 34 have couches

Blanch House

17 Atlingworth Street, Kemptown
(01273) 603504
www.blanchhouse.co.uk

Located just off the seafront in deepest Kemptown, Blanch House probably just pips it for being the best of the new breed of colourful, themed, Brighton hotels. All the rooms are imaginative, interesting and spotless (my favourite is the Moroccan), and each comes complete with CD player, TV, chocolates, and other special treats that I promised not to mention. Downstairs they have a fantastic bar serving loads of specialist cocktails. This is open to the public and, even if you are not spending the night here, it makes a great place for an evening tipple.

Rooms range from £125-250 inclusive of breakfast and all taxes. Special midweek rates are available.

Cavalaire House

34 Upper Rock Gardens, Kemptown
(01273) 696899

Still my favourite hotel on Upper Rock Gardens, the Cavalaire offers a rather unusual tropical breakfast with mango, kiwi fruit and a whole host of other goodies (though if you prefer, you can opt for the fry-up instead). The rooms are pleasant and bright, the bathrooms are clean, and they offer Internet access, fancy soaps, and four-poster beds. Make sure to bring a camera, as late night sightings of naked women walking the halls are not unheard of. I am always made to feel welcome here; it's the perfect example of how to run a small hotel. Quote 'luvvies' for a special deal.

Single £30-49, double £49-80, triple £80

Hotel Du Vin

Ship Street, Brighton (01273) 718588
www.hotelduvin.com

Stunning design, beautiful rooms, friendly staff…the Hotel Du Vin just oozes with style. The rooms are all named after famous wine houses (hence the name) and include dual pedestal baths where you and your lover can get up to all sorts of adventures. The restaurant and the adjoining bar come highly recommended, but try and avoid getting a table near Julie Burchill (she loves this place) or you'll be subjected to her jabbering nonsense all night. During the summer, try to book well in advance, as there seems to be about a three-month waiting list for some of the suites.

Doubles from £115, Suites from £185

VERY BOHEMIAN

The Granville Hotel

124 Kings Road, (01273) 722525

Since the last edition, the Granville has undergone major renovation. Rooms that were once lifeless now shine brightly with various themes and colours. While the renovation and upgrading of rooms continues, the Granville has done more than enough to now be considered a good quality and entertaining place to stay in Brighton. *Doubles from £85, Singles from £65 and the grand double (4-poster and Jacuzzi) from £145.*

The Oriental Hotel

9 Oriental Place, Brighton (01273) 205050

Leave behind the world of floral carpets and gaudy wallpaper and enter the stylish surroundings of the Oriental. Done out in lively colours with themed rooms spattered with art, pine furniture and loads of plants, this place shines a light for all visitors to Brighton who want somewhere 'fab and groovy' to stay. And the odd famous novel has been scribbled here, too. *Doubles £80-100, balcony suite (sleeps 4) £115 per night during the week, and £140 per night on the weekend. All rooms come with healthy organic breakfast. Extra people charged at £20 per person.*

Hotel Pelirocco

10 Regency Square (01273) 327055

Located just off the seafront in Regency Square, the Pelirocco is the antithesis of just about every other hotel in Brighton. Here, artistic heroes have transformed each room into individual pockets of creativity. With rooms named 'Sputnik', 'Bettie's Boudoir', 'Modrophenia', 'Pussy' and 'Lenny Beige's Love Palace', it is easy to see why the Pelirocco created such a media phenomenon when it first opened. Ever evolving, it seems that every time I arrive here there's a new room in the offing. This time around there was a fantastic suite downstairs called the o2 room with round beds, plasma screens built into the walls, Internet connections and a stunning bathroom. Also new is the Nookii room, which comes with a sex-toy catalog, vibrators and other 'goodies'.

The only downside to the place is that with sponsorship overload from the likes of Play Station, Smint and Absolut Vodka, you can't even take a shower without being reminded to get drunk and keep your breath fresh. That aside, this is the last word in chic and will especially appeal to hip, media types. There should even be a Cheeky room sometime in the near future which will include a Chris Eubank voodoo doll, a dartboard with the faces of the Cheeky Girls on and Horlicks on tap. *Singles £50, doubles £85-£125, 185-235 including breakfast, something for the weekend menu and vibrators. (Rates set to increase by 10-15% shortly). All rooms include Sony Playstations.*

Dylan

Abbey Lodge

19 Upper Rock Gardens, Kemptown
(01273) 605061

Recently opened by Bernie (from the Avalon), Abbey Lodge has four rooms, each with fridge, CD player and TV. Note: they only have four rooms, so book early!

Rooms from £55-80 weekends and £45-65 during the week.

Avalon

7 Upper Rock Gardens (01273) 692344

At time of going to press, Avalon was up for sale, but do not let this discourage you; it's still fantastic. Former owner Bernie has just opened the Abbey Lodge (10 doors up the street), as he wanted a change, but I'm sure the Avalon will survive just fine without him. Everything is spotless, the quality of the rooms is excellent, there are CD players in most, sweeties everywhere, and even a four-poster bed. They do target the gay community, but everyone is welcome.

Singles £30, doubles £50-75, family £90

Bannings Guest House

14 Upper Rock Gardens
(01273) 681403

After eleven and a half years of suffering, Steven, the owner, has decided that he wishes to attract a predominantly gay female clientele. Put simply, *"Women are less hassle than blokes".* Saying that, he did recently have to put up with one mad woman who asked him to call Buckingham Palace to complain that Princess Anne had broken into her room, stolen her purse, and left her with only £10.

No single rooms, doubles £25-30 per person (women only at weekends).

Colson House Hotel

17 Upper Rock Gardens (01273) 694922
www.colsonhouse.com info@colsonhouse.com

After a recent game of musical owners, the winners Mark and Eamon have kept up the quality, and Colson House seems to be as modern and clean as ever. The garden has had a touch up, and now includes a picnic table where you can sit and waste away the day…. Still gay friendly, women friendly and, as Mark put it, *'Everyone friendly.'*

Doubles £25 - £35pp, £30 pp for a triple/family room.

Grapevine

29-30 North Road (01273) 703985
www.grapevinewebsite.co.uk

If you're young and want to be right in the thick of things, then this makes an excellent choice of accommodation. The rooms – while not spectacular – are certainly pleasant enough for the young traveller types that frequent Brighton. The restaurant is no longer here, although breakfast is still served. Recommended for Hen Parties.

No en-suite rooms, rooms priced at flat rate of £25 per person.

Keehans Hotel

Regency Square, Brighton (01273) 327879

This family owned guesthouse is vehemently non-smoking; they would rather gnaw their own arms off than let you in with a fag. Owner John just had his 70th birthday when we went to press and still has plenty of tales to tell of his football hero grandsons. (The latest update is that he is now going for the record of having 4 grandsons playing in the football league.) They've also got indoor parking for bikes and a good sea view. Watch out for the floppy old dog who'll lick you to death if you let him.
Single room and breakfast £39, doubles from £60.

The Lanes Hotel

70 Marine Parade (01273) 674231

Located on the Brighton seafront, this typical hotel offers good views of the Palace Pier and the beach, and has eight rooms with four-poster beds. 'Room of the week' award goes to 118 for its fabulous waterbed. Not advisable if you get seasick.
Midweek double rooms start from £50, weekends from £90, and all include breakfast. The 4-poster room is £80 mid week and £125 on the weekend.

New Steine Hotel and Bistro

12a New Steine, Kemptown
(01273) 681546

Owned by the ever-smiley Herve, the New Steine reminded me of some of my trips to Paris. Rooms are attractive, clean and, with Herve, as your host, things couldn't be better. The restaurant downstairs offers some fantastic food and good wine. A nice improvement from the first time I visited.
Singles from £25, doubles from £49, weekends from £65-105.

PLACES TO SLEEP

THE CHEAPEST IN TOWN

Abbey Hotel

Norfolk Street, Brighton (01273) 778771

Not to be confused with the Abbey Lodge in Kemptown, The Abbey Hotel is probably the cheapest weekly rental hotel in Brighton. The cheap, self-catering rooms are on the first three floors and, on the whole, are cramped and pretty hairy and, if it's really all you can afford, I'd rather you came and slept on my floor. The rooms on the fourth floor, however, are pleasant, clean, and start at about £155 for the week.

Last year some American guy totally pissed off the manageress by plonking a pair of shoes on the counter and saying, in an arrogant voice, *"Have these cleaned by the morning."*

She's still angry about it, so, if you're afflicted with the accent, tell them you're Canadian.

Shortest stay is 3 nights. Singles for three nights start at £63, with shower £75. Doubles start at £135 for a three-night stay. Cheaper weekly rates are available.

Aquarium Hotel

13 Madeira Place (01273) 605761

In the heart of Kemptown and a stone's throw from the Palace Pier, this little B&B stands out as it has negotiable pricing based on what you can afford. They do a veggie breakfast on request and the rooms are clean, if a little compact.

Rooms from £20 per night.

George Hamilton V

(As featured on 'The UK's Worst')
27 Lower Rock Gardens

I incorrectly thought this place was named after the Scottish Country and Western singer and thought it might be interesting. When the door opened, a rather unshaven man emerged, smelling of booze…

Me: **Hello.**

Him: What do you want?

Me: **I am writing a guide book on Brighton and…**

Him: I'm not interested. (Shuts the door)

The end.

276

BED & BREAKFASTS AND GUESTHOUSES

If you don't have any luck with the ones listed, or fancy going it alone, you will find countless B&Bs and guesthouses in the places below. In the most traditional B&B areas, like Madeira Place, prices change daily and, sometimes, in accordance to what they think you'll pay, so be terribly polite and dress down for the occasion and you'll get a better offer.

Madeira Place, Lower Rock Gardens & New Steine

Located close to the seafront but without a proper sea view. Fairly cheap, plentiful and close to just about everything.

Grand Parade

Right in the town centre, ten minutes walk from the sea and close to North Laine.

Regency Square & Bedford Square

These squares are found just past the West Pier and the rooms overlook the sea (unless of course you get one at the back with a view of the gasworks).

A few others to try

Adelaide Hotel
51 Regency Square, Brighton
(01273) 205286

Aegean Hotel
5 New Steine
(01273) 686547

Ainsley House
28 New Steine
(01273) 605310

Alvia Hotel
36 Upper Rock Gardens
(01273) 682939

Ambassador Hotel
22 New Steine
(01273) 676869

Barringtons
76 Grand Parade
(01273) 604182

Brighton House Hotel
52 Regency Square, Brighton
(01273) 323282

Funchal
17 Madeira Place
(01273) 603975

Genevieve Hotel
18 Madeira Place, Kemptown
(01273) 681653

Leona House
74 middle Street, Brighton
(01273) 327309

HOSTELS

Baggies Backpackers

33 Oriental Place
(01273) 733740

Close to the West Pier, Baggies has two lounging-about rooms; the upstairs one has TVs and videos, while the other is for listening to music and general hanging about. Since we last visited, they have also added a quiet room, which makes for a great escape when you have to share a room with many others. All rooms have built-in sinks and are always clean and fresh, as are the showers and bathrooms. While still the best hostel in town, quality and tidiness are not as great as they used to be.

Dorm rooms are £12.50 pp and doubles are £25 (£12.50pp). Laundry machines are on site, free soap powder is provided and, if you ask nicely enough, Homeopathy and foot massages are provided too.

Brighton Backpackers

75-76 Middle Street
(01273) 777717
www.brightonbackpackers.com

Brighton Backpackers is the typical hostel that you find in most cities around the world; loads of fun, full of colourful people and with enough Reggae to keep even the most ardent Rasta happy.

The rooms aren't particularly tidy but I can't blame the staff for this as they do clean them, it just seems that everyone throws their junk, tapes, towels and general shit all over the floor. Come on guys, you might have travelled India by dingo but clear away those smelly socks!

The rooms are all painted different colours and most doors in the older building have Disney characters on them. You can get some discounts if you feel like a spot of painting.

Despite the odd mess, it's a lot of fun staying here and there's a good chance you'll meet some cool people who know how to party.

Dorm Rooms £12 pp and £30 for a double room

Walkabout Hostel

78-81 West Street
(01273) 770232
www.walkabout.eu.com

The hostel is part of a chain of Ozzie bars that cater mainly for the young traveller. While the Brighton branch is the only one with accommodation attached to it, they plan to open more in the future.

The hostel rooms are clean(ish) and, if you need some privacy for a little saucy fun, then rumour has it that the laundry room cupboard is getting some pretty heavy use, so you may well have to book in advance, or queue until it becomes available.

Important note, they do not accept individual bookings; group booking of no less than 6 people are required. Dorms £12-15 daily, £60-75 weekly, twins £30 daily, £150 weekly, triples £13 daily, £60 weekly.

CAMPING

Sheep Cote Valley

Behind the Marina off Wilson Ave
(01273) 626546

Non-member peak charges – caravan from £20 per night with electric hook-up, two people in a tent (with car parking) starts at £15.50 per night.

Beachy Head

Celebrated suicide spot, which featured in Quadrophenia and several Monty Python sketches. It can get pretty windy up there, so be careful near the edge, but, if you're feeling brave, look for the spooky old burned-out car half way down the cliffs, I think it's still there. It takes about forty-five minutes to reach Beachy Head from Brighton and while there's not much else around, it's definitely worth the trek, as its pretty wild up there and the views are spectacular. There is also a pub nearby if you get thirsty, though the Samaritans adverts in there might have a sobering effect on your spirits. *(45 minutes drive from Brighton, east along the coast)*

Devil's Dyke

So the story goes that the devil started to dig a deep chasm to let the sea in to drown all the pious villagers of the Weald. But an old lady, on hearing the noise, lit a candle in her window and tricked the devil into believing it to be the rising sun, causing him to scarper and leave behind his unfinished business – a 300ft valley in the heart of the Downs. Now I know there are several flaws in this local myth (like why didn't the devil come back the next night?), but we'll let it pass as, flaws aside, it's a good one.

The Dyke remains an unusual and striking Geographical feature that offers plenty of opportunity for long walks and great views across the Downs (there's a terrific one down the hill to the Shepherd and Dog in Fulkin, if you can face the journey back again). The Dyke is a twenty-minute drive out of Brighton and, in summer, you can usually catch an open-top bus there. Expect crowds at the weekend. *(Take the Dyke Road out of Brighton, cross the motorway and follow signs)*

Ditchling

Your typically 'quaint' country village, with an amazing cake shop to boot (huge treacle tarts for about a quid). Beyond the village pond there's a very

agreeable walk offering great views of the Downs. To find where it starts, look for the sign that says –
'Public right of way, except for 21st December when for legal reasons this is not open to the public'*. Go up the hill, take a picnic and enjoy the view. Expect to share your field with a few friendly cows.
(Take the Dyke Road out of Brighton, join the motorway going east, take the left turning for Ditchling Beacon and follow signs)

*Since the last edition I got an e-mail from law student Rob Linham, who explained why this was:
"If it's available to the public all year, there then becomes a legal right (an easement) meaning that it couldn't be closed again ever without nasty legal proceedings and lots of stress. By closing the path for one day of the year, they stop this happening, allowing them to turn all crabby and close it off if they ever feel like it."

Lewes

Generally speaking, this is a cosy little town, ideal for taking ones parents for the afternoon for a stroll round the castle and a nose through some old bookshops. It is most notorious, however, for being host to the largest fireworks event in the UK (see diary of events). Below the surface, the town has more than its share of occultists, witches and eccentrics, but whether you get any feel of this from an afternoon visit is another matter.

The best pub here, without a doubt, is the Lewes Arms, a wonderful little place tucked away down one of the many side streets. Host to a number of bizarre games, including an annual Pea Throwing Competition (the rules of which are very amusing), it's probably your best port of call for a real taste of Lewes and a chance to meet some of the town's fruitier characters.
(15 minutes drive from Brighton, east along the A27)

Stanmer Park

Head out of Brighton for Sussex University and you'll find this large park. There's ample room here for big footie games and Frisbee throwing, and a chance to take some long rambles in the woods. There's also an organic farm, a small church and a teashop, (although it's unfortunately located next to a stable full of cows, so if you sit outside be ready for some fruity odours and flies dive-bombing your baked potato). This is the closest place to Brighton where you can forget the crowds, especially if you take the walk past the village and continue up the hill. Look out for the tree trunk carved into animals behind Stanmer House.
(10 minutes drive from Brighton, on the A27 towards Lewes)

Eastbourne

To many people, Eastbourne is the world's largest open-plan hospice, home to a population of the walking dead, more hearing-aid shops than cafes and a neat line in Poodle Parlours. And while this isn't too far from the truth (OK – it is the truth), this sedentary coastal town still has enough tricks up its sleeve to merit a visit, even if you *are* under sixty.

For as well as the very pretty area known as the 'Old Town' (for obvious reasons), Eastbourne has a surprisingly attractive seafront. Lacking the naff commercialism of Brighton's seafront, Eastbourne's is, rather refreshingly, adorned in lush greenery. In summer* the promenade teems with palm trees, flower beds, bushes and trees, brass bands in full swing and old couples in cardies and blazers, strolling arm in arm. Add to this the facts that the beach is infinitely cleaner than Brighton's, the pebbles are smaller, and the pier isn't full of drunken Londoners and hen parties and the prospect of spending a genteel day here sloping around, lounging on the beach and swimming, can seem very appealing.

Of course, let's not get carried away, Eastbourne's town centre could rival that of Doncaster's for blandness but when the grime and chaos of Brighton get too much for you, a day out here *can* feel like a nice long soak in the bath. Just don't stay too long; you might end up all wrinkly.
(Take the eastern coastal road out of Brighton, or the A27 for a slightly quicker inland route)

** This is the **only** time to visit Eastbourne; for the rest of the year it goes into catatonic hibernation.*

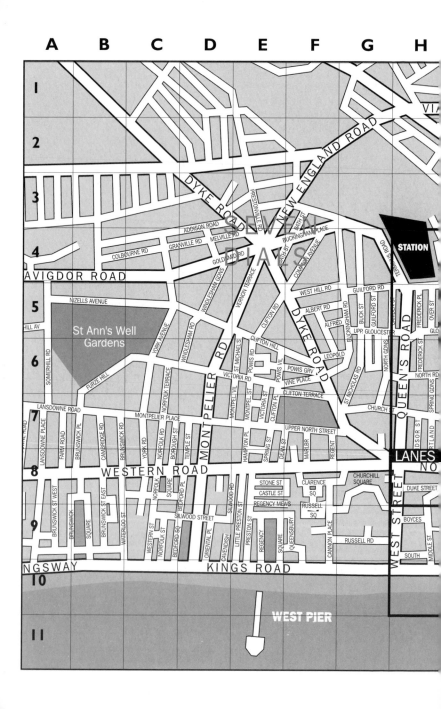

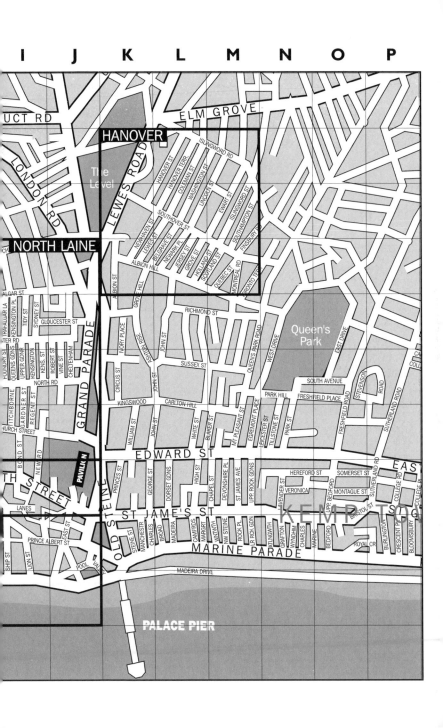

Also Available

The Cheeky Guide to Student Life is the essential item that no student can afford to be without. The book offers a tongue in cheek insight into all aspects of student life with useful tips, anecdotes, games and advice (most of which is legal). It is a humorous but highly informative whistle-stop tour of everything the modern-day student needs to know for squeezing the best out of their time at university.

Along with chapters on accommodation, food, housing, finance and politics, the book also includes some Cheeky trademarks including a photo-love story, the weirdest places to study in the UK, how to plagiarise essays, the best male-to-female ratios for each college, stories about infamous students and lecturers, advice on how to ditch your childhood sweetheart, and what to do at the end of it all should you find yourself with a 2:2 in Philosophy and completely unemployable.

The Cheeky Guide to Student Life - ISBN: 09536110 35 - 384 Pages

A wealth of useful information and sound advice - John Clare, Daily Telegraph

Part of the fabulous Cheeky Guide series, this is a hilarious read for past, present and future students. Prepare for 'laugh-out-loud' moments! - Kickstart life.co.uk

✶ ✶ ✶ ✶ ✶ ✶ ✶ ✶ ✶ ✶ ✶ ✶ ✶

The Cheeky Guide To Oxford
ISBN 0 9536110 51

✶ ✶ ✶

The Cheeky Guide To Love
ISBN 0 9536110 43

✶ ✶

www.cheekyguides.com